MY NAME IS PHILIPPA

My Name is Philippa

Philippa Ryder

MERCIER PRESS

DEDICATION

For Helen and Jenny. Of course.

MERCIER PRESS
Cork
www.mercierpress.ie

Cover design by Sarah O'Flaherty

© Philippa Ryder, 2021

ISBN: 978 1 78117 793 8

A CIP record for this title is available from the British Library.

Printed and bound in the EU.

Contents

ACKNOWLEDGEMENTS

(In no particular order)
Thank you to Helen Ryder; Jennifer Ryder; Thomas E.L.
Bayne; Isabelle Dempsey; Bernie and Grazyna Baldwin;
Theresa and Ian S. Lee; Angela and Bill Lewis; Peter
Baldwin; Shirley and Michael Cooke; Declan Brennan;
Caroline Kennedy; Margaret Moran; Noreen Monahan;
David and Nicola McConnell; John Kerr; Natalie Conroy;
Sara R. Phillips; Gloria Jameson; Victoria Mullen; Dermot
McCarthy; Gillian Fagan; Aileen McHugh; Jean Murray;
Tom Brosnahan; Collette McNulty; Enda Brennan, Emma
Brent; Orla Daly; Pauric Hopkins; Damien Gorman; Ian
O'Neill; Leagh West; Gerry Cleary, Mary Noonan, Aideen
Lyons; Caroline Barry; Lorraine Coghlan; Karen Gray;
Fiona McNeill; Audrey Dunne and all in the Property
Registration Authority; Louise Flynn; Aideen Collard;
Nicole Bork; Aidan Walsh; Roland Hempel; John McAree;
Karina Murray and all at Sporting Pride; Catalyst McIlroy;
Ulrika Westerlund; Richard Kohler; Julia Ehrt; Anna
Kristjánsdóttir; Leslie Hurd; John Kenny; Brynn Craffey;
Sthirabandhu, Colm Nicell and all the cast and crew at
Under the Clock; Deanna Alexandria; Fiona Armstrong
Astley; John Reeve; Penny Smith; Judith Finlay; Kate
Drinane; Adam Egan; Peter and Karen White; Dr Edel
McAteer; Phil Thomas; James Bellringer; Katherine
Zappone; Tara Flynn; Ryan Tubridy – and many, many
others including everyone in Transgender Equality
Network Ireland, Transgender Europe, BeLonGTo and
LGBT Ireland.

Over the past few years I have presented elements of this

story to the management and staff of many companies and government departments. Thank you all for your support and encouragement, it meant a lot to me.

Support Organisations

Transgender Equality Network Ireland www.teni.ie
BeLonGTo www.belongto.org
LGBT Ireland www.lgbt.ie
Under the Rainbow www.undertherainbow.ie
Other links may be found on the websites of the organisations listed above.

FOREWORD

Katherine E. Zappone[1]

My Name is Philippa offers every reader a story that will change their heart. So be prepared, even with a mind open enough to hear Philippa's story, to feel altered by the palpable love that fills these pages. As she herself proclaims in the opening line, 'This is primarily a love story'. Philippa's honesty, motivated by exceptional courage and commitment to truth, adds a very significant narrative to the construction of the ongoing unfolding of being human.

I feel very privileged to write some words that come *before* Philippa's. Over the past decade she, and her remarkable wife Helen and beautiful daughter Jenny, have helped me to understand more than most others what it means to be trans in our world today. For this, I will always be grateful. Especially – though not only – because they helped me to understand this as a public representative, as one who made law and policy, as one who held public power. Politicians need to know how people who are different from them experience the world and are impacted by cultural and social conditions, so that they are better equipped to make law and policy for everyone, not just the elite few.

It was 2012 – almost a decade ago.

The small meeting room in Leinster House 2000 Building was a bit stuffy. Or, maybe it just felt like that because I was preparing for my next meeting with an advocate from the trans community and I was nervous.

---

1 *(Former) Minister for Children and Youth Affairs, Government of Ireland.*

Ireland had no gender recognition law at the time, and as a senator I felt obliged to do something about that.

In walks Helen Ryder. She came to speak on behalf of herself, her partner Philippa and their daughter Jenny. Helen proceeded to tell me a little of their story – the fullness of which is now reflected in these magnificent pages. What struck me most about that encounter were three things. Firstly, that Helen loved Philippa – both as the man she married and as the trans woman Philippa became. Secondly, not only did she insist that the law must recognise her partner for who she is, but that it must also allow them to remain married. Thirdly, they were both committed to whatever it would take to raise their daughter Jenny with love, and the safety and security she would need to withstand the eyes and tongues of those who would not understand, nor accept.

Today, Ireland is a transformed culture because of Philippa, Helen and Jenny. The book you are about to read outlines much of why this is the case. It offers answers to many questions people ask, genuinely, to understand. It describes the physical as well as emotional process of transition. There is something, however, that is of equal if not greater significance and it is the following.

While every trans person's story is different (as is everyone's story about their gender or sexual identity) the life of Philippa as she tells it – the private thoughts she had over the early years – now public; the difficult and wrenching conversations she had with Helen – now so impressive in the way she bares these exchanges; and the endearing quality of honest and direct conversations with Jenny, especially as Philippa comes out to her daughter, *hold universal meaning and appeal.*

'Can I still call you daddy? asks Jenny. 'Of course, baby,' responds Philippa, 'as long as you want.'

A parent's love, a daughter's love never looked more beautiful.

I write from a land where its leader, after his first one hundred days in office, said the following to a joint session of Congress and the Senate:

> To all the transgender Americans watching at home—especially the young people who are so brave—I want you to know that your President has your back. (Joe Biden, 29 April 2021).

Philippa's life, in Dublin, Ireland ripples across the Atlantic, travels through time and, through this publication, joins the global march to freedom and empowerment for every gendered human being. She voices truth out of silence, courage through fear, and joy by following the horizon she sees.

We owe Philippa, Helen and Jenny a great debt. It is a privilege to add my voice in expression of gratitude to who they are individually and together.

I want to thank them for how they help us to become the new Ireland, and indeed the brave new world that we all so desperately need.

KATHERINE E. ZAPPONE

16 May 2021

International Day Against Homophobia, Transphobia and Biphobia

New York City

INTRODUCTION

This is primarily a love story. It would not have been possible without the support of so many people, foremost amongst them of course my wife Helen and daughter Jenny whose love and support sustained me through some very difficult and challenging periods in our lives. I quite literally owe them my life.

It is a story of privilege. My journey was made all the more possible by acceptance of me by key friends and work colleagues but also by the fact that, although I started questioning my gender at an early age, I was fortunate to have a loving family and some close friends in my teenage years, then a secure job and an ever-supportive wife. Many, many trans people do not have those advantages and I am in awe of those who manage to succeed despite the incredible challenges we as a community face.

It is also an extremely personal story. I don't live my life in black and white, I always seek colour, embracing difference and new experiences. We only get one go at life and I try to live it to the full. There are no holds barred within these pages, every incident is true and very little has been glossed over and then only because to include certain details might distress or embarrass others. It is not my intention in any way to hurt and I hope the reader can understand the choices I have made. Some names have been changed to protect identities, but the basic elements of the incidents remain true. I encourage you to approach this story with an open mind and not judge. We all face challenges in our lives, some more than others. Read these words and try to understand.

I hope that the authenticity in my memoir will show through and the reader will learn of the difficult choices those in the trans community may have to make as we find the path to our true selves. The journey of every trans person is different and mine is just one of many possible paths. None of these paths are the 'correct' path, each is appropriate to the individual and I hope you, the reader, will bear this in mind as you navigate the joy and sadness of my specific journey of discovery.

My close friend Declan suggested that I write this memoir. Despite my comment that 'apart from the obvious, what else has happened in my life?' he encouraged me to start putting words on a page and some 250,000 words later I agreed that, just possibly, I had enough to submit to a publisher. A lunch with a good friend, Tara Flynn, resulted in me submitting an early draft to Mercier Press and I was delighted to be formally accepted by them last year. The manuscript has been cut, trimmed and tweaked down to what you hold in your hands now. I am honoured to be able to publish this and my editors in Mercier have been wonderful, giving me extensions to deadlines when the writing became too emotional for me. It is a labour of love and many tears were shed in the writing. It was as cathartic as I had hoped and to some degree at least serves as closure for my journey.

Some terms used were appropriate to my knowledge at the time and I have kept that usage here to allow the reader to come with me on my journey of discovery. Terminology in any field changes over time and within the LGBTQ+ field, specifically the transgender (or trans as I have used it throughout) area.

There are sections within these pages that may trigger or

upset some readers. If you are affected by anything, please reach out to any of the support groups or organisations listed after the acknowledgments. There has been a lot of progress in the LGBTQ+ field in the past ten years since I began writing this book and some of the situations and challenges I faced are no longer an issue, though there are many new hurdles.

Read this book and learn of the overwhelming joy tinged with the sadness of my life as I attempted to find my true self. I hope you enjoy it.

Philippa Ryder

The Skirt

Age: 0–16

It was a lovely early summer's afternoon in 1977. I was planning a trip to my best friend later and had some school homework to finish. I was 16, a teenage boy whose mind was full of the usual teenage worries and concerns. But unknown to everyone, in the wardrobe in my room, carefully hidden, was a plastic bag containing two small skirts.

The first inkling I had of having any sort of feminine feelings happened at a family picnic when I was ten. My aunt, handing me a slice of chocolate cake, remarked on how it looked like I was wearing eye shadow. I was horrified, not knowing really at that point what eye shadow was and I blushed as everyone laughed. It stuck in my mind and may have been a portent of what was to come.

I found myself at home alone one afternoon and the incident that was to define my life from that point forward occurred: My mother and sister had gone to visit relations and my father was at work. We lived in a large semi-detached house in a newly developed estate in Dundrum in south Dublin.

I felt mischievous, wondering what I could do to annoy my sister while she was out. I skipped up the stairs, listening to John Lennon singing 'You, you may say I'm a dreamer, But I'm not the only one' on the kitchen radio, permanently tuned to RTÉ. The smells of summer wafted through the open windows and I wandered towards my sister's bedroom, grinning. There was a close bond between us, and I, the older brother, never felt that the five-year gap in age mattered. I liked being with her, playing and teasing, sometimes being too rough (I punched her playfully on the nose once, just to see her reaction, earning – justifiably – a furious reaction from my father who stopped my pocket money that week, something that was quietly rectified by my mother). Despite our regular arguments, I always wanted to be there for her.

My mind was wandering and flitting between many other teenage thoughts as I opened the door to her room. Looking into the small, tidy bedroom I saw something on the neatly made bed. A skirt. A normal, ordinary school skirt, slightly fraying around the hem. No doubt it would be thrown out at the end of the school year – there was no possibility of our mother allowing one of her children out looking less than perfect. The simple tartan pattern, signifying St Philomena's Catholic Girls School in south Dublin, was like most of the designs for local schools, usually the only noticeable difference was the colour. Or so it appeared to me, not the most observant at the best of times.

Something drew me to it. An urge rose within me. I felt my heart race. 'Boys don't wear skirts', I thought, embarrassed, and closed the door. But I couldn't move away. The desire wouldn't leave me. It was wrong. It was stupid. I was a boy and boys didn't wear skirts. My hand was still on the door handle and something was urging me to turn it. I pushed slightly and the door swung open. I walked over and picked up the skirt.

I slipped it over my slim hips. It was very tight, obviously not my size at all and I worried about splitting it. But it felt nice, natural, and I enjoyed the sensation of it on my bare legs as I walked around the room. Wrong. It felt wrong. Did it? I was confused and upset yet I just didn't want to take it off. My emotions swirled and spun like the skirt as I moved. I caught myself in the small silver mirror on the wardrobe and, just for a brief moment, replaced the reflected image of the teenage boy with that of a girl. I almost allowed myself imagine …

I picked the skirt up from the floor a few minutes later from where I had flung it in embarrassment and replaced it carefully on the bed. What had I been thinking of? Just a moment of madness I told myself, shaking my head before I went back downstairs.

Yet from that point on I would open the door to my younger sister's and mother's rooms and carefully look through their skirts and dresses. The act upset me, as every time I knew it was invading their privacy. It was a horrible thing to do, even if they didn't know. I was careful to replace everything perfectly. The pretty dresses and skirts drew me to them, the feminine shapes and colours were irresistible, they seemed to speak to the core of my being.

I wasn't outwardly effeminate during my school days. The long hair I had was typical of the time, even in the Christian Brothers secondary school I attended and otherwise my 'uniform' was jeans and a t-shirt. Although I had plenty of school friends who were boys, I never enjoyed being in a group with them, feeling that the pack mentality brought out the worst in them and I preferred the company of just one or two close friends. From an early age I was naturally attracted to the girls in my neighbourhood who seemed to accept me, to some degree at least, into their circle. Even at an early age perhaps others did sense a difference within me. The boys' changing rooms in school before the weekly physical education sessions had always been an uncomfortable place for me as I was very self-conscious of my developing adolescent male body, unwilling to strut and parade like others. On occasion, this was noticed and I would be made fun of. 'Ooohh what are you hiding?' one of the class jokers might say. I did my best to ignore them.

What was it that pushed me to slip on a skirt or blouse? As I matured, I found the feelings it brought out in me were confusing and upsetting to me. I became excited and happy, and for a few minutes my mind, usually racing ahead to think of girls, food, reading, school or any of a million other subjects, was at ease and calm. What did it mean?

Most nights I would slip a skirt over my hips and enjoy the feelings it engendered. Then, I would feel frustrated and get into bed below the posters of Farrah Fawcett and Kate Bush on the ceiling – my dream girls.

Falling into a fitful sleep I thought about the many times I agonised about my desire, the times I had hated myself for these feelings and for secretly trying on my sister's or mother's clothes. Yet I couldn't stop. It felt as if an important part of me was being expressed in those brief moments. Despite promising myself time and time again that I wouldn't dress again, I knew I would. Years later I discovered that one of my heroes, David Bowie, had also spent many evenings in his bedroom agonising over who he really was, developing a different persona almost every week. An agony I was experiencing myself.

Why couldn't I dress in what seemed right for me? If I wanted to show a feminine side who would it bother, really?

Me putting on a skirt or even a dress was hardly going to cause an international crisis. Yet if the sensationalist media was to be believed there could be nothing worse than cross-dressing or, even worse in their eyes, being gay.

I wasn't going to discuss any of these feelings or desires with my parents who would have disapproved. As issues arose at the dinner table I already realised the differences in our attitudes. It wasn't me rebelling, it was a different viewpoint – they were intolerant of diversity, of standing out. Even at the dinner table we were told to keep our voices low in case the neighbours overheard. The neighbours. Were people that curious about the goings-on in our household to be listening to every word? I doubted that and anyway, who cared? I was discovering that I enjoyed being with people who challenged my views. I was determined that in the unlikely event that I had children I would encourage them to be themselves. I felt if I let my little secret out, I would be out – of the house and probably their lives. No, difference and diversity were not accepted. So I hid my dressing very, very carefully from everybody.

2

To boldly go ...

Age: 17–21

I woke on a bright winter's afternoon, late as usual, after a night of reading and listening to music. I was being called for dinner on 1 January 1978. I was almost seventeen and I had tossed and turned through the small hours of the morning, thinking about what the New Year might bring. School was becoming increasingly challenging, but I wasn't too stressed. I had a nice 'new' electric typewriter (fished out of an office supply firm's skip by some friends for me) to feed my rapidly developing interest in writing.

My passion for science fiction was the only outward thing in my life that was in any way different to many other boys of my age. I had not been tempted into drink, drugs or even sexual encounters with girls (or boys). I either had no interest or I lacked the courage. My middle-class life was interesting enough – safe, happy and content. Mostly.

At the dinner table downstairs were my father, mother and sister. Dad was a stressed-out insurance broker who nonetheless always found time for me, bringing me to my first music concert, showing an interest in my hobbies (at that time science fiction, stamps and chess), girlfriends (I had none) and trying to get me interested in sport. He teased me regularly and knew exactly which buttons to press to get me annoyed, taking a great pleasure in it.

His family history was interesting – he came from a

line of gunsmiths and shoemakers, a mix of Protestants and Catholics from Shankill, Co. Dublin and Askeaton, Co. Limerick. But as we grew up there was little or no discussion of the Protestant side, our family at that stage being quite nationalist and Catholic.

My eleven-year old sister was developing into a very strong woman already and I sensed she would soon outgrow the need for me as the protective big brother I had been. It was a role I would miss. She played an important part in my life, introducing me to Radio Luxembourg and opening my eyes to a whole new world of music. I wondered how our relationship would change as we matured, and I hoped we would continue to be close.

As I opened the wardrobe to get a pair of jeans and t-shirt before descending to the kitchen I saw the small bag containing my secret skirts. I placed a school bag on top of it, away from my mother's prying eyes.

Mum's bedroom was a haven of femininity with small bottles of perfume and jars of night cream on the dressing table, a testament to the care she took in her appearance and movie star looks. The family rumour was that she had met James Dean and had even been asked out by him – or so the story went. As I looked through the array of beautiful ball gowns in the wardrobes and imagined her twirling in her heels with her style and grace at a dinner dance, I knew the story had to be true. My mother always looked perfect leaving the house on a Friday or Saturday evening for a dinner dance or a show, the scent of her perfume filling the hall and landing.

Her family descended from strong Catholic farming backgrounds – the McNamaras of Ardree in Kildare and the Greenes and Rafterys of Ballinlough in Roscommon.

Her father had been a city bus driver and as a young child I loved hearing his amusing stories of difficult and argumentative passengers.

There were the usual light-hearted arguments at dinner and I was glad to finish, escaping the inevitable grilling about *Star Trek* and 'that pointy-eared bloke' and I hopped on my bike for the quick cycle to my best friend's house. Cycling always energised me and even the steep hill by the police station in Dundrum along the road that I also took to school didn't bother me. Chess, science fiction and computers were the nerdy subjects that we talked about for the few hours we were together. I thought of my other classmates and what they probably thought of me and smiled. Did I care? No. I felt different, had always felt different, and had learned to cope with my feelings by staying positive and thinking of the future.

Declan and I met when he moved from a primary school in Kilmacud to my school, St Benildus, at the start of the first year of secondary school. I had just discovered chess and was delighted to find that the school had a chess club. The maths teacher encouraged me to join and the friendly rivalry between Declan and I began, he quickly claiming the number one board on the school team, a position I could only dream of. As the friendship developed, we discovered more common interests, in science and science fiction especially. He quickly became my closest friend, our relationship surpassing any of the friendships I had until that point. I enjoyed the challenges in our conversations, feeling I could discuss almost anything with him. *Almost* anything.

One of our common favourites was the science fiction author Isaac Asimov who talked about science fiction fans in his books. A few years later I discovered the Irish Science

Fiction Association and my involvement in science fiction fandom began.

Science fiction and music were the bedrock of my life then. My bedroom walls and ceiling were covered in posters. Farrah Fawcett's 'swimsuit' poster – look it up! – was my pride and joy and was the most visible sign to my mother that I was developing an interest in girls. A powerful hi-fi system nestled in amongst the book and record shelves ensured regular complaints emanated from downstairs: 'Turn the music down Brendan!'

The Irish Science Fiction Association had a major influence on me and following a couple of meetings I became involved in the organisation. This was a frustrating part of my nature as I got older as I don't seem able to just enjoy something, I have to be in the thick of organising.

***

I was busy with membership forms and sign in sheets when I glanced up to see a slightly built, attractive teenager walk through the door of the third floor room of the Parliament Inn on Parliament Street where we held the meetings. Despite his age (he was a few years younger than me), Colum was very wise to the world. He immediately made an impact in any crowd, exhibiting confidence, ease and humour, fitting in with a quirky, cheeky charm. All of which I was lacking.

We quickly became friends, discovering a mutual love of music. Well actually it was more that he discovered my love of music for me. We would go on regular trips around the second-hand record shops and he had endless recommendations – 'You'll love this group Bren', he would say and almost always be right. Before meeting Colum my musical knowledge was limited to the charts, Radio Luxembourg or whatever LPs my parents had.

But following my break-up with my first serious girl-friend a few weeks earlier, Colum saw my distress and asked me to meet him in Bewley's Oriental Café in Grafton Street, a Dublin institution. 'Just for something different,' he said. Our Saturday afternoons were usually a mixture of wandering around a few record shops and having a coffee to look at our purchases. Colum would also have made some tapes of albums he recommended for me and I almost always liked them. Colum carefully and painstakingly wrote the album name, artist and track titles on the tape sleeve. He was very careful in everything he did, and thoughtful too. A good friend if a little odd and I was beginning to think that odd was good. Never the most rebellious I felt it was almost my duty as a teenager to rebel or challenge in some way – I would let the side down otherwise.

'So why did you want to meet here Colum?' I asked looking around at the stained-glass windows and eyeing the pastries and cakes laid out on the little stands and the waitresses in their black and white uniforms.

'I liked it last time I was here. Anyway, I wanted to have a chat to you, to tell you something. And I thought you might like a break from thinking about that girl!'

I gave a wry smile and nodded. 'Damn, was it that obvious? I just can't stop thinking about her. I just don't understand why she broke up with me.'

'She was too young, and a bit full of herself, I think. But hey you had your first proper girlfriend. Anyway, I've just broken up with someone too …' I looked surprised.

'Really? I didn't know you were seeing someone. Is she someone I know?'

'Eh, no, *he's* not.'

'Oh,' I said awkwardly. Silence. 'Oh. So you're *gay*,' I whispered.

Colum laughed and said, 'Yes, did you not guess?'

'Well, no. I've never met anyone gay before, didn't know what to look for! Wow! this is a surprise.'

'No, I did have a girlfriend a while back, but it didn't last, I just wasn't interested. I do enjoy flirting with girls though! So how do you feel about it? And how do you know you haven't met anyone gay apart from me? It's not like we have a big pink badge saying *GAY* on us!'

'It doesn't bother me, as long as it's what you want Colum, I'm happy for you.'

As we chatted more, quietly in the noisy café, my mind was spinning. I felt an increasing urge to tell Colum my own secret, but what would I tell him? That I sometimes put on a skirt? No, I was genuinely happy for Colum. My brief interludes of slipping on a skirt were unimportant. After all, nothing was going to come of it unless I was discovered and my world disintegrated in embarrassment and shame.

We left the busy café to join the crowds on Grafton Street and as I glanced at the faces of people, most smiling, some harried, a few obviously upset I thought back to Colum's words and wondered: 'How many of you are gay? And how many of you have a secret like mine?'

Colum's revelation had surprised me and each time we went out together, for a party, to a concert or just to browse in record shops, I felt the urge to tell him about my occasional dressing. I needed to know what these feelings meant. Would Colum know? I didn't feel I could broach the subject with anyone else, being led to the conclusion, by the media and any comments from my parents, that men trying on women's clothes had to be gay. And freaks. Abnormal. I felt very uncomfortable every time a stereo-typically gay man appeared on television, avoiding any comment when my parents expressed their disgust. And if there was ever anything about cross-dressing in the newspapers I discreetly devoured the article, terrified of being caught reading the story. Of course, it was more *exposé* than informative. Typical headlines: *Shocked wife 'I caught my husband wearing my dress – is he gay?'* Always the link between cross-dressing and being gay. The 'expert' replying usually wrote how some men felt a need to cross-dress at some stage, that it was nothing to worry about and was just a phase. If that was true for me then the 'phase' was lasting a long time, as I had been dressing in my sister's uniforms or my mother's dresses since I was eleven or twelve. I couldn't accept that I might be gay, though in later years I would explore my sexuality a lot and eventually come to realise that I was bisexual, or that the gender of the person I might be attracted to was irrelevant. However at that time I had close male friends and never felt any attraction to them, my interest was always in my female friends who for some reason seemed to treat me as one of their own, talking about their boyfriends, their clothes or even make-up when I was around. I felt confused and increasingly distressed. As Colum and I walked down the busy Dublin streets I would sometimes gaze at the clothes displays in the shop windows, imagining myself in the latest women's fashions, hoping that Colum might see me looking, ask me why and that I might have the nerve to tell him. And if we sat in a coffee shop I would find myself staring at the women, attracted to them in different ways, longing for their figures, their style and their confidence.

Passing the female bathrooms I would hear laughter, see women emerging looking glamorous, amazing, full of energy and life. How my teenage self longed to experience the joys of that magical place. How different to the male bathrooms I imagined and I often considered the chasm between the two sexes as society saw it at that time – Man: hard, making money, fighting wars, drinking beer and telling lewd jokes. Woman: gentle, soothing, healing, glamour, charm and beauty. I knew on which side of the chasm I yearned to be.

Colum rang me one evening to invite me to see Hawkwind, an experimental heavy rock group, something different for us. He arrived in the latest jeans, a tight t-shirt and a stylish haircut. He looked great and was attracting quite a few admiring looks which he was clearly enjoying. I was basking in his reflected glory and not minding. Much. We teased each other as we made our way through the lines of people towards the stage, anxious to get the best view of one of the leading groups of the era.

A couple of hours later as the music died away and we left the arena I was convinced that my ears were bleeding from the volume, not really believing that I hadn't burst my eardrums. Colum was ahead of me and I could see how he was becoming more and more 'camp' as he became more comfortable and confident with his sexuality. As we walked through the venue, I was surprised at how blatantly he looked at some of the guys. I found it amusing to be with him.

We pushed our way through the crowds outside the venue, gasping for air in the smoky atmosphere. We reached a little haven by a pillar and Colum started to look around. 'Oh, he's cute', he said, looking at someone who must have been twenty-five, ancient to our eyes. But a very attractive girl joined the object of Colum's desire and they disappeared into the night.

'Don't look now but there's a guy looking you up and down,' said Colum. 'It's the long hair, it's very attractive and maybe they think you're a girl!'

Did he see me blush when he made the comment? Did he guess? I felt excited and curious, my mind raced at the thought. I was aching to turn and look. But no, I told myself I wasn't interested. I dismissed it, it was just a joke. Most of the guys at the concert had long hair like mine. Nobody could mistake me for a girl. Could they? And yet deep, deep in the back of my mind was a little curiosity about men. A little part of me enjoyed the attention. A little part of me changed.

***

Some weeks later I made my way to the bar above Dun Laoghaire shopping centre nervously, having convinced my parents I could be trusted. Brighton, the World Science Fiction Convention – indeed the whole planet itself, beckoned.

My friends from the ISFA were waiting, laughing and planning in the large, smoky room which overlooked Dun Laoghaire harbour. Some publications from the organisation lay spread on the table, being sorted for the world science fiction community. I had suggested to Declan and Colum that perhaps they might like to come too: it would have been an amazing trip for me to have my two best friends along but unfortunately neither could attend.

Some 3,100 fans from all over the world attended the convention, interacting with authors, artists and film-makers and discussing their latest projects. I felt that it was the beginning of my adult life as I discovered the differences and similarities of so many nationalities and I drew comparisons with Ireland and the Irish. I had always been attracted by the future, to the possibilities, and my discovery of science fiction was inevitable. Never the most confident, I found the science fiction community welcoming, a collection of intelligent people that didn't quite 'fit in' to 'normal' society, whatever that was. I felt comfortable, accepted and as a committee member of the ISFA I found I got a certain amount of respect and recognition.

The convention showed me so much of what could be achieved, both in my career and in life. My worldview, so narrow and restricted in Ireland, had been broadened hugely. I would never see life in quite the same way again.

The AGM of the ISFA was shortly after Worldcon and I stood for the committee again, this time becoming chairperson as some of the older committee members left after a few years of work. I had more responsibility and continued to edit the newsletter, updating the membership list and organising the meetings.

I had finished school a few months before with an acceptable Leaving Certificate, then took a temporary job while I considered my future, working in a local hardware shop carrying bales of briquettes and stacking shelves. That lasted until one of the bales broke, fell on my toe and in an instant I became convinced that perhaps heavy lifting and hardware stores weren't the profession for me.

I felt that most people by the time they left school seemed to know exactly what they wanted. I had no real desire to continue my formal education by going to university, not yet anyway, even if I could have obtained a place. I knew I had a passion for learning, thinking of what

Asimov had written: 'The day you stop learning is the day you start decaying', but I wanted to learn from life, at least for the moment.

Still in the background was my urge to dress. Now that I had a little money from odd jobs I was tempted to risk embarrassment or shame by going to one of the shops on Grafton Street, maybe at a quiet time to buy skirts, a dress or even lingerie, but the fear of discovery held me back. I might pick up something from a charity shop, hide my face as I approached the counter, blushing furiously and feeling like a criminal. Trying it on later in my room brought release, from the tension of daily life, of hiding even from myself. At times I realised I had hardly even seen myself *dressed* – how would I feel if I saw a boy's body in a mirror, legs covered in hair, wearing a skirt? Would it cause me to think again, to attempt once again to deny these feelings? As if I hadn't tried and failed many times before.

What was the difference between me and an alcoholic, a drug user, a sex maniac? The thoughts ricocheted around in my head, sending me at times to the depths of despair. Dressing gave me pleasure and some degree of peace, yes, but the feelings it brought out in me were still confusing. How I would have loved to be able to talk to someone about this. But I felt there was no one.

There was a real incident repeated regularly at this point in my life: I cycle towards Declan's house and to the large black rubbish bin, placed as usual on a small semi-circular section of path close to a main road, outside a small office complex. Well away from my house or anyone who might know me. I quickly stop the bike and get off, glancing around like someone about to commit a murder. In some ways I was. For in the rucksack were the few feminine possessions I had managed to acquire over the previous year and which I had managed to keep hidden in the bottom of my wardrobe. Today was to be the last day I would ever see them. I was determined to stop dressing. I remembered the feel of the pretty green mini skirt I had rescued from a charity bag, the little black dress which I had 'forgotten' to pass on to my sister from a friend, a few other small items which had meant so much to me. All were in that bag. With a sigh I put the treasures carefully in the bin, placing the bag as if it was a loved one who had just passed away.

But of course, the desire, the need didn't disappear and a little while later I again had a skirt or a blouse hidden away. Just like my dreams, probably never to see the light of day.

Shortly after I left the hardware store and then tried my hand at insurance brokerage I got the opportunity to take a position in the Land Registry (later the Property Registration Authority [PRA]), a safe and secure government job, very rare in the recession-hit early 1980s. From the outset, I found the civil service everything I expected it to be: bureaucratic, conservative and not a place for the faint-hearted. Thinking about the slightly humorous warnings of my father when I was deciding whether or not to take the position I was delighted to see that I had been part of a batch of new recruits, mostly in or around my own age, and we could hang around together without worrying about the older staff. Though my lack of confidence did hold me back a little I was delighted to find other science fiction fans in my department and quickly formed a close friendship with one, Gerry. Our relationship grew and I began to look forward to chatting and arguing about books and music in the relaxed atmosphere of our office. Larry Niven, Arthur C. Clarke, Yes and Genesis formed the basis of our initial discussions and I introduced him to some of the music I was being exposed to by Colum. We also started regular sessions of role-playing games, like Dungeons and Dragons, enticing others in the office to join us from time to time. But the drinking sessions with the guys after work held no attraction for me and again, I knew I was different, uncomfortable in their boisterous and alcohol-driven company. Yet I so enjoyed the time I got to spend chatting to Gerry, in the office, on lunch-breaks, on occasional nights out. I suspected that in time we were likely to become close and I hoped my enthusiasm, my passion for our common interests, wouldn't prove too much of a strain on our friendship.

Within a few weeks of joining the Land Registry, I heard of a *Star Trek* convention in Leeds in September of 1980 from my Scottish pen pal. My pen pal had written: 'It's much more friendly than a science fiction convention. And my other pen pal Helen will be there, so you won't be on your own. And anyway, most *Star Trek* fans are girls!' My room, in the Dragonara hotel, was on the tenth floor from where I had a marvellous view across the train station to the dirty coal yards and drab yellow brick buildings that comprised Leeds city centre. I had been impressed by the lovely countryside on the train journey across from Manchester where my flight had landed, enjoying the view across the Pennines, known as 'the backbone of England'. On my brief wander around Leeds the previous day I had admired the grandeur that simply wasn't present in Dublin. There was a different atmosphere here that interested me, the accents and the styles were very strange to a teenage boy from Dublin. And I felt no embarrassment in lying on the ground beside a tall office block to take a photo. I was enthralled!

Later I stood in the lobby of the busy hotel with a friend, Ray. It was our first *Star Trek* convention and we were looking at the teenage girls standing nearby, some in skimpy, tight fitting, uniforms which I found attractive on a number of levels. I thought, somewhat unkindly: 'I'd look better in those than some of them.' Suddenly a very pretty girl came up and introduced herself: 'Brendan? I'm Alison and this is Helen', pointing to an attractive, smiling girl who was flicking through a fan magazine. It was 10.05 a.m. on Saturday 20 September 1980, a time and date that lived on in my mind for the rest of my life.

Two years later, we stood on the platform of Glasgow train station waiting for Helen to arrive from Leeds. We were attending Alison's wedding. Our little group had become close friends, attending quite a few *Star Trek* conventions and even visiting each other's homes. The train arrived and a multitude of passengers came towards us. No sign of Helen. Then I saw her. She took my breath away. Dressed in a lovely floral skirt and plain top, low heels and a fashionable trench coat swinging open she walked towards the group, smiling. I could barely get the words out.

'Helen! You look fabulous! *Wow.*'

Helen began to laugh and said: 'It's all thanks to Weight-watchers and I wanted to look good for this lovely occasion.'

I kept glancing at Helen, looking at the transformation, not just in her appearance but also in her manner and confidence. She was a different person.

Soon after we gathered in the church, surrounded by ranks of tall and good-looking firemen, there to honour their colleague, Alison's future husband. Helen and I were grinning as our friend Alison was escorted down the aisle. It had regularly occurred to me that it was just possible that I might never get married; I didn't think I had the personality or looks to attract women, they just seemed to want me as their friend, not boyfriend! Self-doubt, always. But there was also something beautiful about the ceremony, two people so obviously in love committing to each other, would I ever experience it?

The ceremony over, the party moved to a nearby hotel for the reception. Of course, traditional haggis was on the menu, but having tried it at a convention the previous year I wasn't likely to be tempted again. Ray and I were talking about the latest *Star Trek* film when Helen came into the crowded room. She sat between us, moving us apart. 'Make room, make room,' she said, knowing we would appreciate the obscure science fiction reference. She exuded confidence. Ray saw Stuart, Alison's new husband, nearby and made his way over to him, leaving us alone.

'Weddings are really romantic and this is even more so than most.'

Helen smiled and said 'Yes, lots of couples getting together. It's surprising what happens at them ...' and left the sentence hanging.

She moved a little closer and said: 'That was a very passionate kiss Stuart gave Ali at the ceremony, wasn't it?' My train of thought was broken as I looked at Helen. She was smiling again, leaning slightly into me.

'Yes it was,' I said. 'I was wondering when they were going to come up for air! It was ...'

We looked at each other. Something changed. Suddenly our eyes met in a different way, a spark seemed to jump between them. I leaned towards her. Our lips met, initially gently, then more forcefully. I placed my arm around her and pulled her closer. Tongues clashed and my heart quickened.

The kiss seemed to last only a second, then I heard Ray's broad Birmingham accent: 'Hey guys, get a room!' and there was nearby laughter. We released each other and opened our eyes, surprised to see Ray, Alison and her new husband Stuart standing beside us, and with what looked like the entire room focused on our little corner of passion.

'If you could let go of Brendan for a moment Helen, I'd like a little help with something?' said Alison. The two women moved off towards the bathrooms, leaving me star struck, and Ray grinning in their wake.

'What just happened?' I asked myself, possibly even aloud. A few minutes later Helen returned with a smile. My heart pounded as she sat down beside me again and we continued where we left off. It was a life-changing evening, friend turning to lover, taking me by pleasant, very pleasant surprise. My mind was focused, clear. This was a very special woman.

Our relationship developed over the next few months. We found it hard to keep our hands off each other, even in public. Helen kept running to the bathroom, nervous and excited at the feelings I was causing in her. On my first visit to Leeds we made gentle love, the first time for both of us. As we lay in each other's arms in the warm aftermath something within me was telling me that Helen was the one who I would spend the rest of my life with.

A few days later her period, which was always regular, was a little late. But it arrived the following day and our role as parents had to wait for quite a few years. We felt alive, energised and optimistic, so totally in love and looking forward to the future, together.

THREE QUESTIONS

Age: 22

Helen's usually busy and bustling family home was quiet for once. A large three-storey terraced house set in a hillside suburb of Leeds, she shared it with a sister and brother, two other siblings had already moved our, and her parents. But for some reason everyone was out, and we had the opportunity to explore each other in comfort and privacy. Tonight would be question three.

The first was when I had asked her to marry me. I performed in the traditional way, laughing nervously and going down on one knee on the wet ground, terrified that she would reject me even though she had pretty much agreed in advance, giggling as I had raised the subject the previous day. There was really little doubt in either of our minds that we were right for each other and following her soft yet enthusiastic Yes to my question we celebrated with a flat coke and an awful science fiction film that was memorable only due to the occasion.

The second question was when I had the equally terrifying prospect of having to ask her father for permission to marry Helen. He had always treated me well but there was a family story that he chopped a man's hand off in the Second World War when he served in the Royal Air Force in India. I didn't want something of mine chopped off for having the nerve to ask for his daughter's hand in marriage! But he agreed, of course, delighted for us.

And to question three: Helen closed the door, locking it. 'Just in case,' she said, and smiled. Her room was small with a single bed and a homemade wardrobe. And books, lots of books, unsurprising considering our common interests. There was a little incense and low lighting giving a lovely romantic setting. My passion for her was sometimes overwhelming and she found it hard to deal with. But I found her irresistible, truly a part of me, even at this early stage in our romance. I knew that our relationship, no matter what happened, was going to be a huge part of my life. I had feelings for Helen that I had never dreamed possible. As much as I had liked and desired other women, this was true love, a completely different experience. It was beyond romantic or sexual, important though they both were. It was feeling like Helen was just a discrete part of myself that had somehow been surgically removed. I seemed to know what she would say, and she felt the same about me.

Helen moved towards the bed and shyly undid her the buttons on her blouse, then unzipped her skirt, letting it fall to the floor. One of the many attractions of her for me were her stockings, and today they excited me even more. This question, the final of the three and the one that was to define our relationship from this point on was on my lips. I was afraid to ask it, afraid of rejection, afraid of the effect it might have on her. I had thought about it in advance, thought about how I could phrase it so that if she was horrified or upset I might laugh it off as a joke, but I was almost too nervous to ask it, and that was going to ruin my plan.

'God but you look sexy tonight hon,' I said, reaching for her and kissing her.

'Are you all right?' she asked, perhaps sensing a different emotion in my body. 'You seem nervous ...'

'Well I have something to ask you but I don't want to upset you. It's just something I want to do that you might not be comfortable with,' I said.

'Well, the only way to know is to ask me,' she said, looking anxious, the passion waning.

'It's about your stockings, I like them so much and I'd love to wear them while we make love.'

There, it was out at last, the secret I had kept from everyone my entire life. I looked at her with an equal amount of fear and hope.

'Oh,' she said, cautiously. 'Of course, I don't mind.' Lots of possibilities had probably run through her mind when I said I had a question, maybe some strange or unusual sexual practice, but this was not something she might have thought of. The effect on me was immediate, I felt as if a huge weight had been lifted from my shoulders. She sensed this and perhaps she wondered if there was something more to it than just a little bedroom play. But soon the passion reignited, and we explored each other fully, relaxed and comfortable in the privacy of the empty house. The remainder of the weekend together was even more wonderful for me than usual. The experience of finally telling someone had energised and excited me in so many ways. It had lain hidden deep within my core for most of my life. Now I had shared at least part of my innermost desire with the woman I knew I would spend the rest of my life with.

When I got back to Dublin the following week I thought about the weekend, and the direction our relationship could take now that some of my secret had finally been revealed. I tried to keep busy while I was away from Helen, always preferring to have too much to do rather than too little, leaving as little time as I could to dwell. I felt, however, that a new chapter of my life had begun.

But although I could go and buy my own female clothes, I knew that I didn't want to risk pushing too far. I would have to be satisfied with the odd occasion when I dressed in her lingerie, or sometimes in private in my own room at home, and I knew the excitement of the romance we were discovering and sharing would be ultimately more fulfilling, more important to me.

Yet on my own, away from Helen, I felt the urge growing more and more. The few women's clothes I had were still hidden at the bottom of my wardrobe. The embarrassment on both our parts would be too much if my mother found anything feminine hidden away and I certainly didn't want to ruin my relationship with her, or Helen, the two most important women in my life. At least now that I had a fiancée I could pretend that Helen had left the clothes there on a previous visit.

I sometimes wondered if my father too had some deep, dark secret. Did everyone? Was there something, some desire, some longing that most people hid for most of their lives, only exposing it accidentally or with those they truly trusted? If the sensationalist headlines in the tabloid newspapers were to be taken as true then some of the secrets were appalling. How would he react if he did find out about my occasional cross-dressing? I had never been the typical son, whatever that was, and I certainly had never exhibited any of the usual male teenage behaviour. Did he suspect? Or was it a case of just not wanting to know, even of respecting my privacy? Would he see me as weak, a lesser person, because I couldn't resist this urge?

There were other things on my mind at that time apart from dressing and it gave me great pleasure to be able to tell my parents about Helen and especially our mutual interest in science fiction and *Star Trek*. They were delighted at the prospect of having a daughter-in-law and I travelled to Leeds early in 1982 to be greeted by a thin covering of snow on the back street near Helen's house on the outskirts of Leeds. We were celebrating two events: Helen's twenty-first birthday (for which Declan's brother Enda had carved a beautiful wooden key) and our official engagement. The engagement ring was a lovely three diamond setting, delicate and not too flashy, costing £237. I had wanted to spend much more on it but Helen wouldn't let me. It was just perfect for her finger. Like my bride-to-be.

As we wandered around the crowded house, all three storeys filled with clumps of people, family and friends mingling and wishing us well I thought back to the many times I had lain in bed wondering if I would ever meet someone special, someone who I could spend the rest of my life with. Tonight I was annoying that special person by clinging to her too much, not quite believing I had found her. But she was putting up with me, knowing that I wasn't the best in crowds or at parties. Helen's parents enjoyed a celebration like this, and I was doing my best.

We had no plans for a wedding date at that point; Helen was studying radiography in an east Leeds teaching hospital and my job as a civil servant wasn't readily transportable. And the north of England in the early 1980s was not the place to go to look for work.

Sometimes I looked at this amazing woman who de-served the best, yet she was getting me. For some reason she thought I was rich, despite my assurances that I was anything but, yet I suppose to a student like Helen at that time anyone with a job seemed rich. I knew she would progress further in her career than I was likely to in mine – she had a passion and a caring nature that made her perfectly suited to her chosen profession, whereas to me my career at that time was secondary to my hobbies and interests. It paid the bills.

So, it would be a few years before we could think of marriage. But in some ways we didn't mind. We managed to see each other every month at least, sometimes twice, travelling by boat or even by plane, taking turns in showing each other the respective sights of our cities. The time together was even more precious as we knew each brief interlude would end all too soon. Most of the time we would be happy just to lie together, listening to *The Moody Blues* or *Bread*, reading Garfield comic books and howling with laughter, just enjoying the feeling of being one.

Yet we knew we were building a solid foundation for our relationship, one that would endure once we managed to get together in the same country, wherever that turned out to be. I reminded Helen on occasion of what Asimov said about challenges: 'It has been my philosophy of life that difficulties vanish when faced boldly'. We were facing those difficulties together, yet physically apart.

There were a few people in my life who were important to me and who I could call friends. Increasingly so was Gerry from my workplace. Through our regular games of Dungeons & Dragons I saw the diverse natures, the intelligence and wit of all of the players, and I was delighted to be in their company. They were so different, and I was the common link. What was it that attracted me to them, and vice versa? Different relationships and yet similar too.

And on the periphery, Colum. Very different. Yet was there a deeper connection between us that I just wasn't allowing myself to see? Was I gay too? I was desperate for information, for someone to talk to. I knew I couldn't let Helen know of more of my doubts, she had been so understanding when I brought up the subject of dressing a little during our bedroom play, I couldn't raise other issues as well before our wedding. But who could I talk to?

Any time I started thinking about men sexually I became confused. I found it so difficult to accept any personal attraction I might have for them. What was it that defined our sexual orientation, what made some people attracted to the same sex? Being engaged to Helen caused any transient thoughts on the subject I might have to be hidden deep within the core of my mind and I simply couldn't face them. Yet they were still there.

***

The morning was cold and crisp. 'Perfect for a parade!' I said, grinning as Helen wrapped up warmly in a scarf, gloves and boots, looking wonderful as we went to catch the bus to the St Patrick's Day parade in Dublin.

Sometime later we were positioned nicely in the city centre and I stood back to get a better angle for the photograph of her on the crowded street. 'Ok, look like you're enjoying yourself …' I called as she made a face at me and turned to look at another float going by, grinning. 'A T A security …' blasted out, again and again. I snapped the shutter on my new camera, sure that I had the perfect photo. Seeing her in the viewfinder I fell in love with her a little bit more.

It took a while for us to finally get together in the same city – lots of trips across the sea, then up and down to Cork where Helen took a job at the Regional Hospital before she took a position in St James's in Dublin. Then we started searching for a house, eventually finding a quiet housing estate just outside Templeogue in south Dublin. We signed the contract on the day the Space Shuttle *Challenger* exploded, a joyful day for us personally of course but tinged with considerable sadness.

We were delighted to finally have a place where we could actually be together after four years of seeing each other infrequently. There were quite a few frowns and some comments from relatives but that certainly wasn't going to stop us living together before we got married! The wedding date approached quickly, and Helen was desperate to get a dress. She chose one from a boutique in Dublin city centre, only to find that it had gone out of business when she went to pick it up. Fortunately, my father knew the owners of the shop and managed to get the dress from them. Helen kept it carefully hidden from me, following tradition. She told me of the many times she and her sister had dreamed of weddings, of bridal dresses and handsome princes. Well handsome I wasn't but at least I was a prince of sorts. It appeared that one translation of my name from Irish was literally Prince Stinking Hair.

I agonised over who to choose as my Best Man. My best friend was undoubtedly Declan and I had another wonderful friend in Gerry. Both shared so many of my interests, knew me so well but of course neither knew my deepest secret. In the end, I chose Gerry. It could have been Declan who remained a true friend throughout my life, providing support and advice at all points. Both attended the wedding and Gerry was a wonderful choice.

We had some difficulty in deciding on our wedding

guest list. Having booked a barge for the reception, we were limited to forty-six people and we had a large number of friends and family that had to be left out. I was surprised that so many were willing to travel from Ireland to the wedding, but then I was the first of my family's generation to get married – and it was an unusual and tempting reception. My parents' generation, growing up with 'The Troubles' in Northern Ireland, found it difficult to come to terms with the idea of their son marrying an English girl, despite the fact that they found her very pleasant. I suspected there might have been talk amongst the wider relations, wondering why I had to go abroad to find a wife. Again, I felt I was being different, but at this stage of my life I was getting used to it and part of me liked it.

In late August 1986, I stood at the altar with my bride-to-be walking up the aisle to become my wife. She was stunning in her beautiful dress and we giggled when the priest commented on the length and passion of our kiss at the end of the ceremony. Well I had never kissed a married woman before I told him and I wanted to enjoy it.

A few hours later, our wedding barge made its way serenely down the Leeds-Liverpool canal. Helen and I had just had our first argument as a married couple when I stood on her bridal train as we went down the steep steps onto the barge. As it pulled out of the dock we saw children running along the tree-lined banks, yelling happily at the wedding guests who were just starting their drinks. When we appeared at the prow of the barge the children called to us to kiss, again and again, eliciting cheers. I loved every minute of the occasion; never one for the limelight, I discovered that being the centre of attention, with everyone wishing us well, was actually quite a lot of fun.

Helen and I turned to our guests for the speeches. It had been a wonderful service, the church in Beeston almost full with family, friends and neighbours. I was thrilled that her brother Bernie and a good friend of his, Paul, had performed at the ceremony, providing the musical accompaniment with their guitars. I looked forward to having the opportunity of getting to know Bernie more as a brother-in-law. Now it was time to thank everyone for making the journey from near and far to wish us well.

I stood up to make my speech, with just a few short notes that I had hurriedly written that morning. 'I'll be fine, I'm used to speaking in public,' I had said when the suggestion was made a few days earlier that perhaps I should work on the most important address of my life. But now, standing up in front of all my family and friends, I froze. Then I remembered that everyone was here to celebrate our special day and I relaxed, the words started flowing and I got a few laughs. 'The most difficult thing I've ever done,' I said later, embarrassed that I had forgotten to compliment my stunning bride, being reminded by Declan at the end!

Following the reception, we went back to Helen's parents' house to change for our trip to London where we would spend our wedding night, and from there it was off to romantic Paris for a ten-day honeymoon. After the hectic and pressure-filled (but fun) past few weeks I was looking forward to spending some time with my best friend and new bride, and we had a new Garfield book for the train trip down to London, to ensure the 'funnymoon' as we had taken to calling it, got off to a good start.

A delay on the trains left us too late to check into our hotel and for some reason rooms were difficult to get. But a very small room was discovered and offered to us when it was explained that it was our wedding night. Very small? More like a broom cupboard, certainly not what we expected when booking but it really didn't matter. We were married and enjoyed the night regardless. We shared a couple of glasses of champagne in our salubrious narrow uncomfortable bed, but still enjoying the feeling of being married.

The following day we took a hovercraft to Calais and a train to the wonderful city of Paris where we enjoyed the (too short) ten days exploring the wonderful city, sightseeing and enjoying the lovely cuisine. I found the language difficult, lacking the confidence to really converse, and once again was I impressed with Helen, this time because of her language skills.

Helen had planned a trip to see the Eiffel Tower on our first night, only a short Metro trip away from our hotel. She was grinning as we walked, hand in hand, towards a steep set of steps at the Palace de Trocedero.

'Ok I want you to close your eyes and let me guide you … It'll be worth it, this is the place to see it, and it will be magical in the dark. Ok … now!'

I opened my eyes and saw the beautiful creation of Monsieur Eiffel ahead, lights twinkling on the beams, standing proudly, stretching towards the stars and dominating the south of the city spread out in front of us. It was, as Helen had promised, magical. We kissed, emotionally enjoying the atmosphere and the knowledge that we had so much more of our married life to look forward to. Paris was a city we returned to repeatedly, finding new wonders each time and our honeymoon was everything we hoped for.

Yet once I had time, almost too much time, to think, I found myself again being drawn to the small bag of lingerie that I kept in the bedroom. Once or twice I would wear it, sometimes with Helen as we were intimate, sometimes on my own. Always I felt guilty and confused, wondering what these desires were. Each time I thought about them I tried to push them to the back of my mind, focusing on Helen, science fiction, stamps, the cat, the house, work … anything but dressing. My life was good – we had money, a nice house, lots of friends and interesting hobbies. Yet still I had to dress.

4

Wedding bells and bouncy baby

Age: 23–38

Following a trip to the 1987 World Science Fiction convention I received a call from an old committee member and a few weeks later the first meeting of the new ISFA was held in a pub on Camden Street. I soon found myself immersed in the business of planning and running a growing organisation.

***

An enigmatic call one afternoon from a good friend ('You can't tell ANYONE who the guest is!') led to us appearing in the audience on *The Late Late Show* later that year when William Shatner was a guest and RTÉ needed a few 'Trekkies'. A few words from us on camera, a couple of brief shots of us grinning as we shook Shatner's hand yet as I wandered around our local supermarket the following day it was clear that we had been noticed and remembered, leading to some humorous interactions with the staff members.

'Ireland is such a small country, isn't it?' I mentioned to Helen later. 'Hard to keep anything private …' That experience taught me well for what was to happen later in my life.

***

It had been a stressful day. Work had been very busy, followed by an awkward committee meeting about the future direction of the ISFA. I eventually got home to find Helen playing with the cat and my exhaustion and frustration evaporated. She looked so well, dressed in a pretty skirt and top and I couldn't stop myself from running my hands over her, causing her to laugh, squirm and complain. As the evening drew to an end I was tempted to ask if I could wear a skirt or one of her dresses. Then I became annoyed with myself, realising that if I did ask, I was likely to ruin the happy atmosphere that evening. I was going through phases of frustration and longing, but usually I managed to keep my desires within, not allowing them to surface in case I upset her. I knew from her obvious reluctance at times that she disliked the sight, even the thought, of me expressing my femininity in any way. Yet I needed the outlet. Sometimes. And tonight, again, I bit my tongue and hid my longing. But I feared that it was going to explode at some stage and what would be the consequences?

Our life together went on happily, revolving around science fiction, gaming, stamps, our cat and work. Helen was so creative, from art to writing and, later, cross-stitching. She inspired me in so many ways. Yet as I felt I wanted to explore my feminine feelings more I was faced with the reluctance of Helen to participate and I usually backed down. A little bedroom play and rare brief periods with a skirt or dress on my own left me more frustrated than satisfied. I often wondered about my feelings, continuing to read about cross-dressers in the newspapers, but they still seemed to be associated with the gay scene and there seemed hardly any advance on the lurid headlines of the 1970s. The gay scene was something I wasn't interested in and where else could I go? I felt different but still didn't know what I was. At times, as the feelings became more intense, I often fantasised about dressing fully, with make-up, high heels and long hair. But they remained just dreams.

My parents began to wonder if we were going to have children. Helen began to get a little broody, seeing the approach of age thirty. But I was reluctant, seeing only the negatives of having a child – the cost, inconvenience and change to the happy routine we had. I had never let myself appreciate children, never feeling in the slightest that I should be allowed to be a parent, with the responsibility that entailed. Was I being selfish or was I just scared? I had never really believed I could get a job, have a girlfriend, get married, get a house. I had felt children were an annoyance more than something to be treasured but as time passed I began to find myself thinking about them more. When Helen was asked, as a child, what she wanted to be when she grew up, she answered: 'A mummy'. I knew she would be amazing but how would I be?

My sister Shirley had been in the US for a few years but was now moving back with her husband and two children, one a young baby. She and her new family regularly joined us on Sundays for the family dinner with our parents. I found holding her young baby, Becky, to be nerve-wracking in some ways, yet also very right and natural. Shirley had given me the honour of making me a godparent and I enjoyed the special time I had with her. Something within me was changing – I found myself thinking about when we could have one, how it would affect our lives and what joy it would bring

On a visit to the city centre one day, I asked Helen: 'Hey hon, do you mind if we go in here?' We were passing an upmarket boutique with party dresses, skirts and tops that I had seen many times and never had the courage to visit.

'Oh, ok if you want to,' replied Helen.

'What do you think of this one?' I asked, holding up a skirt.

'Too short for me, and I'd never wear pvc/leather anyway,' Helen replied.

'Do you mind if I get it for me? It's not too expensive …' I asked nervously.

'Oh, if you must, just don't wear it around me,' she said, annoyed.

'Thanks hon, I won't. It's just that I love the feel of it and I'm tired of trying to fit into yours.' That was intended as a compliment, an acknowledgment of her success at losing so much weight but she'd left the shop, obviously upset. I brought the skirt to the counter, reluctant to look the assistant in the eye, but she was too busy chatting to her colleague to pay me much attention and I walked out of the shop clutching my prized possession, determined to try it on at the first opportunity.

We went to a party at a neighbour's house that night and were quite late home, but I just had to try on my new skirt – now! So I gently eased the skirt over my hips. It felt wonderful, right, and I began to daydream, thinking more of what else I could get to complete the outfit. Although I had picked up a few cheap items from charity shops over the years this was the first time I had gone into a boutique to buy something off the rack. As I lay on the bed I thought of what it would be like to have actually gone in and tried the skirt on, asked the assistant for advice. I wanted so much more. But I couldn't. I was thirty-two years old and surely should be beyond feeling like this, should be concentrating on my career, my family and thinking about acting responsibly. Yet this seemed natural, seemed right to me.

Lost in thought and the feelings running through me I didn't notice Helen come in.

'Oh my god,' she said, 'that's horrible,' and hurried out of the room. My heart missed a beat – did she mean the skirt, or the sight of me in the skirt? When I had changed back and made my way downstairs, I found her in tears by the sink.

'Just leave me alone, just go,' she said. Should I have asked her first? But why should I have to ask her permission to do this? I felt it was only a little fun. There was coolness between us for days and I was frustrated and annoyed by her reaction. I knew there was no point in trying to talk to her about it or the broader subject of dressing – neither of us knew enough about being trans, so we just didn't have the words. Later Helen would say how she was 'blinkered' and unable to process her concerns and worries but at the time we just struggled through. At times like this the enormity of moving forward in any way, to continue exploring who I actually was, seemed like a journey I simply couldn't take.

Helen's reaction was one that she would have on many occasions as explorations of my feminine side continued. I wanted to move faster, do more, experiment more, both with her and on my own. She found it difficult to accept. I knew how hard it was for her, she understood my needs and tried so hard to accommodate them. I attempted to edge forward ever so slightly, not even contemplating the effect on us if I had to stop. Years later I discovered that the transgender population is the most likely to consider and actually attempt suicide. It was a dark time for us both but we knew that the love between us would see us through. It had to, as I couldn't imagine life without my best friend.

Perhaps to take my mind off my worries and to give myself a new challenge I decided to avail of the opportunity to undertake a full-time diploma in Land Surveying in the Dublin Institute of Technology, starting in 1993, fully sponsored by Land Registry. I was delighted to finally be going to third level education. I immediately felt the pressure, but I quickly found that I enjoyed the experience of formal learning again. Being older, I got some respect from the other students – and even the lecturers. It was a very mathematical course though and it was always going to be a challenge for me with only a B in lower level in the Leaving Certificate but the year had started at first principles and I found I could easily keep up. My college friends were as usual mainly women; there was a girl in her late twenties, the brightest in the class, I got on particularly well with. Many aspects of the course that excited me, but I also found it terrifying, conscious of the fact that if I didn't pass, I would have to refund my department the fees! But the ignominy and embarrassment would be much worse.

A few months into my second year in college Helen was just about to walk out the front door, looking gorgeous in a short green skirt and fashionable sandals when she turned and said: 'I have something to tell you, but it'll wait ...'

I had been busy getting ready for college, lost in a world of coordinates and translations. I stopped suddenly, sensing an excitement, nervousness, in her voice.

'Something tells me that this is big, and you can't leave me hanging like that,' I said.

She walked back from the doorway, closer to me, and smiled and said, 'well I don't want to ruin your day!'

Now I was very curious, and I was just about to start guessing when she quietly said: 'I'm pregnant.' The words I had been wondering if I would ever hear were hanging in the air as we hugged, jumped up and down and cried. The responsibility of the future began to weigh heavily on me immediately and I felt as though I was in shock, whilst at the same time being ecstatic.

And what a sense of timing! I had passed first year with distinction, but it had been stressful, and I was facing into a second year where a minimum pass mark of 60% in every subject was required to progress to the final year. Now I had the added worry of a pregnant wife.

As soon as the twelve-week milestone of pregnancy was passed I started to tell my classmates and some of the lecturers in the hope of getting some sympathy and leeway from them! Of course, who I really looked forward to telling were my parents ... they were equally thrilled, treating Helen with kid gloves from that point on, counting down the days to one of the biggest moments in all our lives.

And around six months later, on a glorious July day our life was completely changed with the arrival of a 9lbs. 7oz. baby girl. We had discussed names so when she was presented to Helen by the mid-wife early in the morning after eight hours of labour we looked at each other and Helen said: 'It's our Jenny!' Just an hour later I left the hospital as the staff had to clean up both mother and baby and do various tests and basically told me to go away, almost forcing me out the door. I really didn't want to leave! So at 9 a.m. I made the short walk to Bewley's in Grafton Street to tell the staff who we knew well of the birth and to have my breakfast. It had been a long night and, as exhilarated as I was, I was also exhausted. But the day was lovely and sunny, and that's how I felt I should describe my wonderful daughter.

Two weeks later on a beautiful summer's day I placed

my daughter carefully and quietly into her pram, trying not to disturb Helen and our other baby, our cat Gandi who was asleep on her lap. I pushed the pram up the drive and took Jenny on her first short walk around the neighbourhood, feeling incredibly proud and somewhat emotional at the feelings coursing through me. And feeling amazed that, with no training and actually very little knowledge, here I was with another human being whose life I had been entrusted with. 'You need a licence to drive a car,' I thought, 'but you don't need anything to create a new life!'

I treasured every moment I spent with our new daughter. She was prettier, more intelligent, and happier than any other baby who had ever been born. So I believed. And so I still believe! But then so does every parent about their child. It was a joy being with her, seeing her react to my silliness, laughing and gurgling, then, as soon as she possibly could, trying to form words. She was a challenge in so many ways, yet such a lovely challenge.

Our Saturday trips to town were a highlight of the week, a way to de-stress after a busy week. Breakfast in one of the city centre restaurants followed by a wander around the shops. As she grew up Jenny showed interest in reading and ended up with at least one book every week. Early on we promised her that if she ever wanted a book we would buy it for her. She held us to our promise for years. It was clear from the moment that Jenny began to talk that she was clever, she seemed to love words and regularly surprised us with comments. A constant barrage of 'why' from our daughter, amusing and entertaining our friends and us, transformed our quiet Saturdays.

As we wandered, I found myself increasingly hoping, needing, to talk to Helen about clothes and make-up. I so wanted to share this part of me with my best friend, hoping she would understand. But it was clear from her reaction that she just couldn't, didn't want to, understand. She saw me looking in the shop windows at clothes that she simply would not have worn and said so. But surely she knew that it was for myself that I wanted them. I felt frustrated. Who could I share this with? I found myself thinking about dressing more and more. I worried that my work was suffering, I knew I was losing interest in science fiction, in Dungeons & Dragons, even in some of my friends. This was something I had to address in some way. But how?

We had just come home from one of our regular Saturday trips to town and I suggested some intimacy with Helen. Jenny was asleep in her pram downstairs, so I went to the bedroom to change into something feminine and called to Helen. She walked into the room as I lay on the bed, mind elsewhere, thinking of her overnight in the hospital on-call later, the baby, the upcoming European science fiction convention we were organising – the last thing she wanted to see was her husband in a skirt looking ridiculous. She stormed out, slamming the door, and I could hear her cries as she went downstairs. Then Jenny woke, crying, and suddenly what was going to be a little fun had turned into a horrible row. When I went to comfort her after changing, she screamed at me: 'I married a *man* not a woman! Just leave me alone.' It was the first time she had used those words and again I saw the huge distance we both had to travel if I was to become truly the person I was inside. I just hoped Helen could remain on the journey with me.

The situation was becoming difficult for both of us. Now that the stress of college was over, I had time to think and the more I considered it I realised that dressing was becoming increasingly important to me. It must have been clear to Helen that something was changing within me, and it was also clear that she wasn't happy with the direction it was taking. I was becoming moody, snapping at Helen over inconsequentials, feeling frustrated and ever more depressed. 'Our life is good' I would tell myself, trying to rationalise my feelings and persuade myself that I could do without dressing. My sleep was disturbed, I was tired all the time, annoyed at myself and taking little pleasure from anything apart from Helen and Jenny. I had always worried a little, not quite getting the whole idea of life and adulthood but had managed to struggle through to this point. Yet was it all going to end somehow in tears? I couldn't imagine life without Helen, but did I have the courage to continue with life? I could see that, despite the arguments, there was concern in her eyes at the stress I was feeling and that she was afraid that I might do something dramatic. Yet we simply couldn't or wouldn't have the discussion that we knew we had to have and our life continued, as parents and spouses, somewhat bumpily.

We had left Jenny at her dance and singing classes and had an hour to relax and read in a nearby coffee shop. Now I was wearing tights under my trousers regularly and enjoying the feel of them against my smooth legs, always carefully shaved. As I was sitting down, I noticed a well-dressed couple at the next table who smiled at me. The man glanced down, clearly seeing the tights under my trousers. He smiled at me again and I felt a thrill, repeated shortly afterwards when the man looked down and smiled at me again. The couple got up to leave and again the man looked at me. 'Goodbye have a lovely day', he said to me. It was the first time I had ever experienced an actual attraction to a man, but the combination of knowing he had seen the tights and his looks excited me. What was the attraction? Was it sexual? Had it been a form of acceptance? Of acknowledgement? I wondered if, just possibly, he dressed too and was also searching for answers, for someone else to confide in.

I was distant for the remainder of the day, trying to come to terms with the minor encounter and wondering if I was making more of it than I should. There was little doubt that my appearance and my mannerisms were intentionally more feminine, veering towards androgynous on occasion and this also caused a little friction with Helen. I was taking a lot of care in my appearance and clothes though remaining on the male side of the gender divide outwardly. Inside was very different however and as time passed I was certain that this path was the right one for me.

The incident with the attractive guy and his reaction to me changed me, slightly, in a different way too. I felt I had taken a step further towards … where? Before, I had been unwilling to accept the possibility that I might be bisexual but I realised that while my outwardly male *persona* Brendan was horrified at the thoughts of being with a man, my ever-developing female self was becoming curious.

When I bought a computer we suddenly had the possibility of accessing the beginnings of the internet through the noisy dial-up modems that were appearing. Access was so slow that trying to find anything at all was frustrating and most of the time we used the computer for email and word processing only.

But as I sat in the dining room one night, baby asleep in bed, our white deaf cat wandering around Helen's legs as she finished the dishes, I saw something different, a reference to transvestites. I clicked on the link and was brought to what seemed to be a collection of chat rooms devoted to gay men, lesbians and transvestites. I chose one that seemed to be for transvestites and cross-dressers and clicked on the Enter button.

'Please enter the name you wish to be known as in the room'.

I stopped. I had never given a female name any consideration. I was also nervous, what if someone in the room knew me, and I gave away something that could identify me? Helen was by the sink and I called to her.

'Hey hon, have you heard of chat rooms on the net? I've found one that's related to dressing and I'd love to talk to someone else about it. What do you think?'

She came over and looked at the screen.

'Well you need a name and if you don't make it too close to your real one then you should be fine. What name do you want? Brenda is obvious.'

'No, too close and besides I don't like it. I can't do anything with James – Jamie? – no, how about Phillip? – Philippa?'

'Oh, that's nice, yes go with that. Has a nice ring to it,' she said. So I went to the opening screen again and typed Philippa as my login and started asking questions of the others within the room. Emotion flooded out of me as I found others like me and I really realised I wasn't alone in having these feelings, desires and dreams. Someone asked: 'Where are you from Philippa?' and I replied with tears in my eyes at the use of my new name, my true name. The others in the room seemed so much more knowledgeable than me, so experienced and capable and I probed as many as I could with endless questions, my initial reticence quickly evaporating.

An hour later I rose from the chair and tidied up, then went to bed, curling into my wife with our daughter asleep in the bedroom next to us. My mind was filled with possibilities and I hardly slept. It felt like everything up to that point was just the prelude to my real life. I was approaching forty and I was Philippa.

5

A NEW BEGINNING

Age: 38–40

I woke up the following morning, ecstatic. I was Philippa. The name was mine. I felt as if I had been truly born again. Yet I had to properly discover this beautiful stranger who finally had a name. I turned over to Helen and said: 'Thanks so much for last night, it really meant a lot.' She smiled slightly and went to get our little four-year-old ready for her crèche, leaving me to think. Last night had been such a huge moment for me, for how many people get to choose their name? In the cold light of day I could have had second thoughts and I wondered if Helen realised what choosing the name had meant to me. When I heard Jenny's happy laughs as she was pulled gently from her bed, I wondered what the future would bring for us as a family. But as I cycled into work, enjoying the autumnal sunshine and the wind on my helmeted hair I let a little shriek of joy escape. It was a feeling I later came to describe as a 'wow' moment, when suddenly everything had crystal clarity and I truly believed in the future. It had to be with those two beautiful people and it had to be as Philippa.

A few weeks later I sat dozing on the couch, thinking about the coming weekend when we planned to go to see the new *Star Wars* film on the biggest cinema screen in Ireland the following day with a group of friends. I was also thinking of what questions I could ask in the chat rooms later, maybe when Helen had gone to bed. I was learning of the terms for people like me, from transvestite or cross-dresser to transsexual. Operations were talked about, sex reassignment surgery, recovery and the legalities of name changes. The many and varied terms used in the trans community which evolved it seemed from day to day. There was also advice about the practicalities about going out in public and how other trans people had come out to their friends and family.

The house phone rang. I answered to hear the voice of a neighbour of my parents. 'Brendan? You'd better come across quickly. Your father has been taken ill. It doesn't look good I'm afraid so be as fast as you can.' A frantic phone call to a local taxi company and a short time later I was standing in my mother's kitchen, surrounded by neighbours and family.

'What happened?' I asked.

My father had suffered what appeared to be a massive heart attack. He had been suffering from a lingering cold for some time and combined with weight issues, stress and a poor diet the inevitable occurred. We drove the short distance to the hospital in a daze, worried and emotional. Eventually we found the ward and a doctor took us to a quiet room.

He addressed my mother: 'Unfortunately Mrs Ryder there was nothing we could do. He appears to have died immediately. It was a massive heart attack. I'm so sorry.' We looked at each other in shock, in disbelief. It seemed unreal, a bad dream that we just wanted to wake up from. I felt the room spinning and thought I would pass out but managed to reach over to hug Shirley and Mum.

On the way home later, I thought of Jenny and Dad.

They had idolised each other. Would she understand? How do you explain death to a four-year old? Helen and I had no idea of how to tell her. But somehow, we had to find the words.

Religion had never played any part in our lives – it had taken over two years for us to get Jenny baptised. But when it came to telling her about her beloved Granddad the following morning all we could say was that 'Granddad has gone to heaven'. In that terrible moment, at one of the most difficult moments of my life I turned to religion. Was it the easy choice? The right choice? The only way for a child to understand? It wasn't the time for us to consider the bigger picture, it was a time to focus on Jenny, Mum and the wider family. Everything else could wait.

Jenny wasn't able to grasp what had happened, but she still managed to sing a favourite song of my father's at the end of his funeral a few days later. In all the sadness of that time, I was happy that for the final years of his life he had experienced the joy of being a grandfather to such a wonderful child and I was proud of being able to give him that, if nothing else.

I thought about my father a lot in the months after his death. We never had very much in common, I was too bookish for him, I think. But I had respected him and appreciated the interest he took in my projects and hobbies. He had introduced me to music and took me to my very first live music concert. He suggested my career in the civil service. He teased me, exasperated me and encouraged me. He had given me everything a parent should give and also gave me the space to allow me to find myself. While I had always been my mother's child, constantly looked to her, sought her approval and admired her femininity, I sensed my father was perhaps more willing to look deeper and was less concerned with what others thought, willing to attempt to understand. I would miss him terribly.

After the dust had settled and some semblance of normality returned to our lives, I found myself being drawn back to the internet chat rooms to find out more about transgender (trans) issues. 'Transitioning', changing to living permanently in your preferred gender, was a term that I had not heard before but something that I began to see mentioned. Trans was an umbrella term for all shades of moving between the gender spectrum and I was somewhere on that spectrum. In my daydreams I started to imagine a different future, a different life for myself, because online I found there were people who had successfully managed to do just that, to continue in their jobs, in their marriages and to retain most of their friends and family. But the more I read the more I realised that these people were the exception rather than the norm and that most in fact lost their partners and close family. It was a long way away for me, but I determined to ensure I kept my marriage, job and family with me if I ever had the courage to move forward with this huge change. Because the one person I did not want to hurt on this journey of discovery was my best friend Helen.

My coffee breaks in work were usually spent on my own, reading. But I was finding it so hard to concentrate on anything else besides the thoughts and hopes of transitioning. The more I discovered about the possibilities the more I became excited. I found myself with tears in my eyes, anxious to move forward but desperate not to upset Helen and Jenny. I longed for understanding and acceptance but nothing was guaranteed.

Something in my life had to give. Science fiction had played a huge part in my life and perhaps it would play a part later but for now I knew my involvement with conventions, magazines and fandom had to end. Science fiction had given me Helen, Declan and so many happy memories. But I needed to find me, the true me. That would take time.

***

Jenny was at the window waiting for the car to pull up. She was full of chat as usual, commenting on the dogs being walked, the leaves being blown by a strong wind and asking endless questions as only a four-year-old can.

'Grandma will be here in a few minutes Jenny,' called Helen. 'Put your coat on.' As usual on a Sunday we were going to my Mum's for the afternoon, dinner and listening to her talking about her regular golfing outings. At sixty-five she was still playing golf, having only taken it up at the insistence of my father a few years before. It was her only social outlet and so it was important to us to be as much of a support as we could. Sometimes she simply didn't understand the pressures of our life, the demands of work, of Jenny and of needing time together as a couple but we wanted to be there as much as possible for her at this difficult time.

Today I was in a bad mood though. I had put on stockings under my trousers as usual. Helen saw them, and, obviously annoyed, commented that they looked stupid. I became upset. Helen made another comment about the stockings, Jenny started coughing and I just freaked, furious and kicked the wall, frustrated. Then I recovered and looked at the wall. I began to laugh. I had kicked with such force that the thin plasterboard had broken. Helen came down and looked at it.

'What happened?' she asked.

'Eh, don't worry, just a little accident. I'll sort it out later,' I answered, somewhat sheepishly. I saw in her eyes that she understood, at least a little, of what I was going through. She kissed me and smiled.

Thinking back to the incident I could see how people could commit acts that they wouldn't dream of in the cold light of day. I had felt feminine in that moment I had put the stockings on. Despite the disturbed night, all the minor problems so far, I felt feminine. My head was ready to explode from the pressure of these feelings, then I thought of how far we had already come on this journey. By taking it slow, by introducing the concept gradually, I hoped that people, and Helen in particular, might be able to see this was not simply a fetish or a little fun but an integral part of me, something I simply could not change.

When we returned home that evening, I looked at the paltry amount of female clothes I had. A skirt or two, some underwear, one old dress, a tiny amount of make-up. No shoes, no jewellery, my hair was awful and not at all feminine, but how could I justify getting a wig – and where would I get one? If I was to move forward with this fundamental aspect of who I was, who I wanted the world to see, then I needed to plan. Helen came into the room and kissed me. Trying to understand how much I loved her was trying to comprehend the size of the universe. We were enjoying our life, we both had reasonable jobs, no serious debts or demands and our wonderful little girl was giving us so much joy, each day seemed to be something new and entertaining from her.

My mother was always keen to babysit Jenny so Helen and I would get to go out perhaps twice a week. These moments of togetherness, me acting the idealistic romantic and Helen putting up with my sometimes-extravagant gestures and public demonstrations of affection. We talked about our hobbies, our shared interest in science fiction of course, but she also developed an interest in cross-stitching after a trip to a craft shop in Leeds some years previously and over the years the walls of our house became adorned with her beautiful work. I was just stunned by her creativity, if a little frustrated when she became so immersed in her projects that she would ignore me! Another of her creative outlets was making jewellery and she could produce lovely earrings quickly which, once I got my ears pierced, I tormented her to make for me. She was endlessly talented, whatever she decided to focus on.

Meals out sometimes accompanied by a trip to the cinema were our usual escape from parenthood for a few hours. But Helen wasn't a night bird and usually wanted to go home around 10 p.m. Of course, we were delighted to be going home to our little girl who would entertain us with stories of her night with Grandma.

During this time, I started a mental list. Helen was always amused at the lists I made; I would have great intentions which never quite came to fruition. But this list had to be finished and every item crossed off. For my sanity. It contained the outline of my future life.

The internet was leading me in one direction only – transition – and it was becoming increasingly important to me. Almost every time we made love I wanted to dress, and I was beginning to use a little make-up. I started to take a few photographs of myself, hating the results for the most part but convincing myself that I was improving, just a little. But as time passed I sensed a serious strain developing between Helen and I, a tension that hadn't been there before. She went through phases of accepting and then being critical of my outward displays of femininity. If I brought up the subject of transition, up to and including surgery, she became upset and more than once I heard 'I married a man not a woman' thrown at me. I sulked, unwilling to confront her face to face and for the first time I truly began to fear I might lose her and Jenny. Like so many transgender people before, the effect on their partners was sometimes almost ignored, even by the trans person themselves. I knew I had the best interests of the whole family in mind during this personal journey of discovery, but would I have to stop to save my family? Could I stop? Not for the first time I considered that what I was doing was simply selfish.

6

TRUE BEGINNINGS

Age: 41–43

I was learning so much from the internet. Regularly I would be asked by men to meet, but they had just one thing in mind. I was tempted but too nervous. One step at a time. However, one evening I was delighted by a different invitation.

Pamela, a trans woman from north Dublin suggested a lunch together.

'Oh, I couldn't!' I said, 'I'd be too afraid of being recognised. And I don't have a clue about make-up – I don't even have a wig for heaven's sake! I'd be terrified.' But then I realised that she was talking about meeting, not as Philippa and Pamela but rather in our male identities. Both of us identified as trans of course but neither of us had been out in public as the women we truly were inside. My heart pounded with excitement and fear. The net had been anonymous, nobody knew who Philippa was, there was nothing linking my virtual female persona to Brendan, no clear photos, no personal information. Once I took this step I would lose control of the situation, place my privacy in the hands of someone else. Yet that other person was doing the same. So nervously I agreed to meet the following day.

I sat at the table in the city centre coffee shop. Fight or flight, the primal choice. I looked around, trying to spot Pamela in her male guise. My guilt at being here was tempered slightly by looking at the many others sitting in the coffee shop, what secrets were they hiding? I had discussed with Helen my plans to meet Pamela, so no, I told myself, I shouldn't feel guilty. But I did.

Pamela arrived a little late, neatly dressed in a business suit. To the world we were like any other pair of men discussing politics, sport or the economy. Yet quickly and quietly we began chatting about dresses, make-up and wigs. I did let slip where I worked and was delighted to hear that Pamela was also a civil servant.

'I work not too far from you. I've looked into a lot of the legal issues with transitioning in work, though I really don't see myself ever getting to that stage. But I think I sense in you that it might be more than a little fun, more than an occasional thrill. There are many different types of transgender people and no one is the same. Be yourself.'

'Thanks Pamela, work certainly has been one of the issues that worries me,' I said.

'You won't get fired for being who you are, Philippa. But do watch out for any bullying or harassment.' My heart leapt as she quietly said my name. It was the first time I had heard it said aloud by anyone apart from Helen. I felt validated and emotional and Pamela noticed.

'Are you all right? This is the first time you've ever met anyone like yourself but believe me there are a lot of us out there.'

'It's the first time I've ever heard my name being used. It's such a small thing but it means the world to me. It makes it real.'

Pamela smiled and said, 'I'm honoured to have been the first to use it then!'

As we parted I thought to myself: 'From now on I have to be more positive, more confident of myself. I can do this.

I can be better than this.' I skipped back to work, excited at the possibilities for the future.

The more I read online the more I found that many throughout the ages had felt the feelings I had been experiencing. Gender overlap had always fascinated poets and mythmakers and the rich traditions of Hindu, Greek and the Romans regularly blurred the lines of the sexes. Indeed the Roman poet Juvenal, harking back to the Phrygians of Anatolia (who allowed men who felt themselves to be women to be castrated and live in their preferred gender) said of his fellow Romans: 'why are they waiting? ... take a knife and lop off that superfluous piece of meat'. Sir James Frazer in *The Golden Bough* referred to many ancient cultures that trained people like me from childhood to best prepare us for life as women. Many other examples exist and knowing that I was not so unique and certainly not mentally disturbed gave me some small degree of comfort.

I continued to take digital photographs of myself. I needed to show Philippa to the world and learn from others, I had to make mistakes just as a teenager girl does and find my own style and persona as Philippa. But everything was rushed. I couldn't ask Helen to take them, so I waited until she had gone to bed. Hiding again, my life seemed to be full of fear, dread and very little joy. I imagined the scene if Jenny came down to find her daddy in a dress. I had no wig, no shoes, no idea how to use make-up, no dress sense – and yet each time it seemed right. My poses were awkward, my smile forced. Outside I was far from the woman I knew I was inside. Could I really see her within the man's body in the photos? Doubts, doubts and more doubts filled my mind.

I was pushing the boundaries both at home and elsewhere. One Saturday morning Jenny came into the bedroom as we prepared to leave for her dance and drama classes. I was in a dressing gown, just out of the shower and she looked down to see my bare feet with slightly pink nail polish shining in the sunlight. My heart pounded as up to that point she hadn't seen them polished. Would she become upset and run to Helen, cause another row and would my stupidity ruin our day? But she simply smiled and walked out again with the clothes she wanted.

'She saw the nail polish. I do wish you'd stop wearing it,' Helen said.

'Oh for heaven's sake hon, it's only a little and surely it's better to introduce it this way, gradually, so that it seems normal, or at least not weird?' I replied.

'I just feel it's going too far,' Helen said. She was reluctant to discuss or contemplate the future – it was dangerous territory for us both.

I was grasping at straws, pleading inside with Helen to support me, to help make this impossible situation bearable. 'It's really difficult for me, I find it hard to concentrate on anything else at times and this at least helps a little.'

I left the bedroom before Helen could reply, frustrated. Again. I knew she would be upset. I was upset. Everybody was against me it seemed. I needed support. I needed to talk to people. I needed to hear that the feelings, the desires I was having were normal. Pamela had helped of course but usually I only got to chat to her online. I needed more. I was at a turning point but where would I end up?

The day passed without any comments from Jenny or Helen about the incident. Was it progress towards acceptance or was everything building up to a crisis where I would have to choose between becoming my true self and keeping my family? Could I make the choice and what would that be? Philippa was who I truly was within and to deny my true self would cause huge problems both to me and to my family. Yet so would fully transitioning and the impossible choice occupied almost every waking moment.

Later that day I had some time to myself as Helen and Jenny were due to go shopping after Jenny's dance and drama classes. I crossed the River Liffey, enjoying the autumnal sunshine and admiring some of the stylish women passing on the newly opened Millennium Bridge. I had heard of a shop that sold wigs to the trans community, on Abbey Street somewhere. Did I have the nerve to go in? Today? I had the time, I wasn't meeting Helen for a while, maybe I could just drop in and see how much a typical wig would cost. Recently I had felt much more confident, felt Philippa truly emerging and a new-found personality rising from the core of my being where it had been hiding for almost my entire life. It was Philippa's time. My time. I began to smile as in front of me I saw 'Snips' hair stylists and hair replacement centre.

A tall bald guy was on the till when I walked in. 'Hi, can I help you?' he asked.

"Em, I'd like to ask about getting a wig?' I said quietly, blushing slightly.

'Of course, come upstairs and we can have some privacy. I'm Laurence,' he said.

As soon as I saw the room, filled with wigs of every style and colour, I knew this was right for me. Laurence was sympathetic and understanding and I felt safe divulging my trans name.

'Oh, Philippa is a lovely name,' he said, and I smiled, loving each and every time I heard my name uttered. I wanted him to keep saying it.

I felt comfortable telling him of my limited experience in dressing and was delighted to hear that their beautician also gave make-up lessons and regularly dealt with the trans community. Laurence had picked out a few different styles and colours for me, all tending towards browns and reds.

'I want something that will look good but not dramatic,' I had said. 'Something realistic and natural.' So the gorgeous blonde shoulder length pieces were left on their stands and I came away with an unremarkable brown bob, but one that felt as if it was my own hair. I loved it, I felt comfortable and I felt right. From having a quiet afternoon to myself I felt I had suddenly progressed a huge amount to … where?

A few days later I arrived for an introductory lesson in make-up with the beautician. Again, I was made feel welcome, made feel normal. I began to see a path towards my goal and to believe, truly believe. What was next on this journey of discovery?

With my new hair, at least an idea about make-up and the very beginnings of a dress sense the person in the photographs was starting to resemble society's idea of what a woman should look like. But in my mind I knew I was only a very small part of the way to where I wanted to be. As Jean-Luc Picard said in *Star Trek*: 'If we're going to be damned, let's be damned for what we really are.'

The woman in the photographs was becoming real but a little part of me hurt when I thought how I was doing this essentially alone whereas teenage girls had years to perfect their look, to make many mistakes and learn. They got advice from their friends and peers, but I had no real friends to help. Yet.

The photos I reluctantly shared online received compliments and I glowed, thrilled at any little boost to my confidence. Usually the compliments came from other trans women but the men in the chat rooms, 'admirers', were in most cases only there for online 'fun' and to make suggestive comments. I became annoyed but as I chatted I found myself beginning to wonder, allowing myself to think about them in a different way. As we talked I began to see each compliment, each sexual suggestion as a reinforcement of my feminine self. A little thought began to germinate: what would intimacy with a man be like? Could I enjoy it? Could my sexual preferences, which had been so firmly 'straight' until now, change so much to even consider men seriously? Had they always been there, just hidden, even from myself? Was the emergence of Philippa, my true self, the reason for the beginning of the changes in my sexual orientation? And would that be cheating on Helen? When we married I knew I would never, ever cheat on her. I hadn't. But I hadn't for a moment believed that my desires would extend to men. I was reminded of a quote from Gore Vidal: 'Sex is a continuum – you go through different phases along life's way … and if you don't, you've been sort of cheated.' And from my hero, Bowie: 'it's true – I am a bisexual. But I can't deny that I've used that fact very well. I suppose it's the best thing that ever happened to me.'

My attraction to men was secondary however to my gender identity, though there were commonalities. My friend Pamela told me about a club called Gemini where trans girls could dress and socialise and we arranged to go together. So in early December 2000 at 6.15 p.m. I stood nervously waiting for her on a wet December evening under the historic clock at Clery's in Dublin city centre. 'Surely she should be here by now?' I thought. She only worked around the corner. The minutes ticked by. I was so looking forward to the evening, apprehensive and excited. I expected Pamela would introduce me to people, we'd dress and chat for a few hours then we'd go home. It would be nothing for Helen to be concerned about. But for me it would be another huge step.

I spent ages trying to decide what to wear (not that I had very much to choose from) and trying to get accessories. I found that Marks & Spencer's had generous size 8 shoes (I was a 9 in 'male mode', and that was a size larger than available women's shoes generally). I had two outfits, basic make-up and various other bits and pieces that were carefully arranged in a large sports bag with a towel over them, just in case someone happened to see inside while I was in work.

At 6.40 p.m. I decided to ring. No answer on Pamela's mobile. I tried the house phone, hoping that nothing had happened. Pamela answered. She had missed her train and decided not to come. I was distraught. My big night ruined.

'Can you tell me where the club is? I'm so keen to go and I don't care if I'm on my own.' The club was on North Frederick Street, just beneath a video shop. Only five minutes' walk away.

The street was busy but poorly lit. Bed-sits on one side and a few run-down shops on the other didn't make it the most inviting place. I saw the video shop and an open gate which led to a set of metal steps. As I started to go down the steps there were a few shouts from nearby and I hesitated.

'Big decision, girl,' I thought. 'Do you really want this?'

But I had questioned myself and considered all the options and possibilities many times before and would again. Transitioning always seems to be a series of decisions and each one seemed more difficult than the previous. But I had decided, for tonight at least: this time was my time and I carefully made my way down the steps to the basement door.

I rang the bell. No answer. I could hear laughter and music. I tried again. A lace curtain twitched and I saw a face look out. A minute later a woman came to the door and opened it.

'Yes?'

'Hi, I'm looking for the Gemini Club? I'm Philippa,' I said nervously.

'Well you'd better come in then! I'm Emer, it's lovely to meet you Philippa.'

That moment lived in my memory for many years as Emer very quickly became a close friend and *confidante*, my closest in the trans community. I was about to be seen by a lot of people. Anyone could be there – friends, work colleagues, even relations. My anonymity was about to be taken away in a few steps. But, with pounding heart, dry mouth and shaking hands I made my way into a room with a small bar, crowded with men and women, a smoky, noisy place. There was a heavy mist of perfume in the air. Perhaps ten girls and a couple of men were arranged on couches or at a small bar, laughing and talking. The girls were mostly dressed in short skirts and high heels, the men obviously flirting with them. Then out of a side room came a tall woman who introduced herself as Lorraine. She was dressed in a fabulous black gown and heels with dramatic make-up and big hair. I felt somewhat uncomfortable. What was I supposed to do? Emer, who was dressed in a knee-length skirt and pretty top, seemed to sense my discomfort. 'You can change in either of the rooms on the left, just claim some table space and get organised. Take your time.'

So I walked in to the first room, a narrow, crowded space with two trans girls in various stages of undress. I excused myself and nervously opened my bag, finding a little space in front of a mirror and began to apply my make-up. I couldn't look at the other girls, I was blushing and embarrassed. An hour later I was dressed in a black skirt and white blouse, low heels and some clip-on earrings, ready to face the group outside. I stepped through the door, anxiously, hoping I wouldn't be laughed at. Some of those I had seen seemed to have so much more experience than me and I felt inadequate. Emer was the first to see me.

'Wow,' she said, 'You look great Philippa!' Heads turned at the bar and complimented me. My spirits rose. Lorraine, who had been chatting to another girl, stood up and said to Emer: 'So hon, are we heading out for something to eat?'

Emer took her coat from the back of a chair and moved towards the door.

'Are you coming then, Philippa?' she asked.

'Me?' The group laughed.

'Yes you hon,' said Lorraine. 'Grab your coat and let's get going. Why do you think we're still here? We were waiting for you!'

'But where will we go? I look awful, I have never been in public before, what if someone sees me …?' I babbled.

Emer laughed and said, 'We'll look after you, we stay in safe places for girls like us, we'll get you back in one piece and you might even have some fun!' I was tempted, but terrified. With a shock I realised that Emer too was trans. 'Girls like us'. The words immediately made me part of the community. Only on the internet had I seen trans girls who looked as well as her. And although I had thought about going out in public at some point, I had wanted a lot more experience with make-up, I needed to find a style that suited me, and most of all I desperately needed confidence. What would Helen say when she heard? But the excitement of the moment, the possibilities of the night ahead, decided me.

'Ok,' I said cautiously, 'but I don't have a coat. I really wasn't planning on going out.' A coat was magically acquired and suddenly I was one of three women making their way to Emer's car, conveniently parked outside the club.

As we drove down O'Connell Street past Clery's clock I felt like hiding. My heart was pounding. This was an incredible experience already but the possible ramifications of what I was doing began to hit me hard. It was so much further than I had intended going tonight when I stood waiting for Pamela only a couple of hours ago. Lorraine and Emer were busy chatting in the front of the car; it was clear they were long-time friends, and I was delighted to have been invited out with them. My head was spinning. We arrived at the car park and suddenly I had my next big test. Walking in public. At least the rain had stopped and despite the time of year, it was warm.

'Just relax and enjoy the experience,' whispered Emer, sensing my fear. 'You'll be fine!'

The area was busy with Christmas revellers, all caught up with their own celebrations and as we walked along the street no one was looking at us.

Emer said, 'we're going to pop in here for something to eat, it's the IFI – have you been before? It's very gay-friendly and open-minded.' We walked into the busy, noisy space, and I felt relaxed as we found a free table where we continued to chat.

An hour later, we made our way towards the back entrance of the Clarence Hotel. No one had stared at me, there had been no nasty comments, and I felt good. Emer was lovely, keen to make me feel comfortable, and complimented me on my choice of outfit and accessories. Lorraine was very witty and had us laughing with stories about many other outings. I did get a laugh though when I told them of my previous experience being dressed 'en femme' in public, accidentally, in a school play when I wore one of my mother's long cardigans that looked like chainmail (to some degree) as I played the part of a rather feminine Roman centurion.

I discovered that most of the girls in Gemini stayed there all night, happy to dress and chat. They would sometimes go to a gay bar as a group, spending a few hours there before going back to the club to change and go home. That was at most what I had in mind when I arrived, and I was still amazed that I had found the courage to go out with the two other trans women. But I was getting even more certain now that it had been the right thing to do.

We moved from the crowded Octagon Bar in the Clarence to a gay pub, The Front Lounge on Parliament Street. It too was packed, but we managed to squeeze in beside a group of gay guys and I smiled when one of them turned and complimented my shoes.

Emer and Lorraine suggested going to one more pub before heading back to Gemini to change for the trip home. I sensed that they were doing this as much for me as for themselves. It was clear they had been out many times before and although it seemed such a short time since we had left the club almost three hours had passed. As we left the Front Lounge the doormen smiled and said 'Goodnight girls' and my heart jumped. I was so ecstatic at the comment that I didn't see the small step to the street and fell forward, ending on my knees on the ground and hitting the side of a parked van with my hand, setting the alarm off. Lorraine picked me up.

'Well that's certainly making a dramatic exit!' joked Emer. 'Let's pop across to Reid's, if you're still on for it? You can clean up there.' We crossed the busy street and made our way in, sitting at a small empty table I regained some of my composure.

'I have a spare pair of tights, I'll pop to the loo to change,' I said.

'I'll go with you,' said Emer, anxious to look after me and we squeezed by groups of tipsy party-goers down the narrow stairs to the ladies. The queue was long, well out the door, with a mixture of late teens and older women gossiping and chatting. Suddenly, for the first time that night, I felt exposed, even out of place. I felt this was a step too far, especially as I was still in a little shock from my mishap. Emer sensed my discomfort and said, 'Let's leave it, it's just too busy. We'll be going soon anyway and you look fine, the tights aren't that noticeable.' I was almost disappointed not to be able to experience the women's toilets for the first time but it was a step too far.

We finished our drinks and made our way back to Emer's car. My knee hurt, my tights were ruined and my pride was bruised but I was walking on air.

A little while later, after I had changed out of my female clothes, Emer dropped me at the entrance to our estate and I walked in the door of our house, full of excitement. Helen was still up.

'Wow, what a night!' I said.

'You had a good time then? What's the club like?' she asked.

'The people are nice, there's a great atmosphere. Two other girls and I went out for something to eat and a few drinks …' and I recounted the various incidents of the evening. Helen looked horrified.

'You went OUT! I thought you were staying in the club! What if someone from work recognised you, think of the embarrassment and the possible ramifications. That was not the agreement, and was going too far. I'm annoyed.'

I felt deflated, the exhilaration dissipating rapidly. 'It seemed the right thing to do, the two girls I was going out with knew the scene well and I felt safe.'

'That wasn't the agreement. You told me you were staying in the club.'

'Well I'm sorry hon, it was a spur of the moment thing. It was mainly because Pamela let me down, I'm sure I would have done as we agreed otherwise.'

Helen turned away as she said, 'I give you an inch and you take a mile. You have to be careful. But,' she said with a slight smile, 'I'm glad you enjoyed yourself', I could see she was surprised at what I had done but I was delighted with her reaction, filled with love for her and at her understanding of my journey. How difficult this balancing act was, keeping Helen happy whilst still moving forward on my personal journey of discovery as Philippa. It was only going to get harder on everyone, family, friends and work colleagues, if I decided to progress to hormones and surgery. I often thought of a series of spinning plates and considered the effect on me and my family should even one of them fall. I could lose Helen and Jenny. I could be forced from my job. Socially isolated and friendless. It made me so annoyed to read or hear of people dismissing trans people, indeed the entire LGBTQ+ community, as making a life choice. Who would willingly undertake this journey unless they had to? My eyes filled with tears as I thought of the difficult path towards my future. I was filled with doubts and worries, the stress eating away at me inside, counterbalanced by the hope for the future and living the rest of my life as Philippa, after gender-affirmation surgery as it later came to be known. Tonight had shown me that was my path, though it had lain hidden in my subconscious for years.

I curled into Helen that night, so grateful for my wonderful life-partner. I was determined to keep my family together and with me on this journey. I would keep the plates spinning.

I walked nervously into the office early the following day waiting for a comment. Nobody paid any attention as I sat at my desk and the day continued as normal. My fears, the absolute certainty that I had been seen out the previous night and was about to be ridiculed, were unfounded.

As I sat in a coffee shop later, on a break from work, a U2 song came on the radio. Bono sang 'Girl with crimson nails has Jesus round her neck ...' I had been that girl last night, wearing a necklace with a cross and red nail polish. With tears of joy in my eyes I skipped back to work, grinning. 'You can DO this girl' I thought to myself. *Wow.*

I was excited by my two new trans friends and the discussions we had in the noisy bars. I had discovered more in three hours with Lorraine and Emer than I had in months on the internet. I sensed a connection with Emer especially. She seemed to understand me, to see where I was coming from and, more importantly, even in the few short hours we had been together, where I wanted to go. It was clear that, if and when I wanted to progress, she, and Gemini, were the links I needed. I so wanted to share my excitement with

Helen, but it was clear from the reaction after my evening out that she was still uncomfortable and upset. And I couldn't blame her. In her position, would I be any different?

Emer and I sent each other Christmas and New Year texts. She was always on my mind and I was delighted when she agreed to meet again shortly after Christmas. So a few days into the New Year I emerged from the dressing room in Gemini in a black skirt, white blouse and heels, with a small handbag and coat.

One of the other girls in the club commented, 'Very nice, off to work are we?' I blushed a little and laughed.

'I wish! But not for a while yet. I have a long way to go before I'm ready to go full-time, if I ever do. No, I'm just meeting a friend for something to eat, maybe a drink. See you later? Oh, and what time can I come back here?'

'Don't worry, there'll be someone here.'

'Thanks so much, that'll make things a lot easier.' My phone beeped, a message from Emer saying she was outside.

'Loved the little skip you gave as you left the club, are you happy?' asked Emer as I got into her car.

'Very, thanks so much for meeting me. I couldn't wait to get out again. The club is quiet and it's much more fun being out in the real world, seems right for me.'

It was brighter than my first time out and I felt more conspicuous. My stomach churned. It was difficult to walk with the little confidence I had developed over the past few weeks and my head was bent as we made our way through the narrow street. Emer quietly said, 'If you walk like that it attracts attention. You look great, keep your head up and smile.' I clutched her hand. Here I was, second time out in public and so emotional I felt I would faint. 'Thanks so much Emer. This means a lot.'

The staff in the restaurant were attentive, flirting a little with us and we laughed at their antics. On the walk back to the car Emer suggested a photo. Pointing to a bench she motioned to me to sit 'in a ladylike manner'. As she took the photo she said: 'Ok, now this time look like you're actually *enjoying* yourself!'

I laughed. 'I am, I am, honest' but the comment had the desired effect and I found myself laughing and smiling in the chilly January night.

Later that week we arranged to meet again and Emer amused me by suggesting we use it as a photo-shoot, bringing me to the huge Christmas tree in O'Connell Street and then to the courtyard in front of my workplace. 'Just think,' she said with a glint in her eye, 'after you've transitioned you can show all your colleagues this photo and let them see what you were doing!' I thought about her words. 'Transition'. Was I really going to live full-time as a woman, have surgery? Or was this a passing phase, albeit one that had lasted a very long time? Every time I thought about this aspect of my life, I felt guilty. It was eating me up inside. I wanted to stop for Helen, for Jenny and all those that I was affecting. Yet every time I dressed, it felt so natural. I knew this was my true persona, the one I knew had to be shown. I fell asleep after our lovely evening, worried, upset and frustrated. Again.

Yet with much of my waking thoughts so focused on discovering Philippa there was the also the wonderful routine of family life with Helen and Jenny. I lived for the weekends when we could be together, go to the parks and feed the ducks, go to bookshops, museums, art galleries and department stores – all part of being an ordinary family. The endless questions emanating from Jenny – I'm pretty sure at one point she asked why was the sky blue. Helen and I almost fought for her attention at times until, twenty minutes later and exhausted, we passed her between us! It was a joyous period in our lives.

But, joyous as our lives were I still lived for the evenings where I could chat to my online friends and learn about the path I hoped lay ahead. One evening I entered my username and password and was brought to the opening screen of one of my regular chat rooms. Not too much happening tonight, one or two trans girls, two admirers or curious guys. My profile picture was one of the few I was even vaguely happy with, from a trip out with Emer. It always attracted admirers and tonight was no different. A guy from Nottingham, Phil, introduced himself with 'wow!' and I started to grin.

'Nice opening,' I said, 'hope it's referring to me.'

Phil: 'Lol, but of course ...' and quickly the conversation developed, but not the usual way these sort of conversations did. There was a genuine politeness, a sense of typical English manners. I realised that here was someone who could listen, was interested in something more than talking about sex and seeing explicit photos, something I simply wouldn't dream of taking. A very pleasant hour passed, and Helen was calling me to come to bed.

'Same place, same time, tomorrow?' I asked, a little nervously.

'I wouldn't miss it for the world,' replied Phil, and a friendship was formed unlike any I had had before. Phil was a gentleman, a lovely guy who was willing to spend ages chatting about anything but at every opportunity would compliment me, encourage me and support me. I found myself looking forward to the nightly virtual encounters, which on occasion lasted two or more hours, revealing more and more about myself, both verbally and visually on the webcam which I had recently acquired. Phil would ask me to walk, complimenting my figure and poise, and I felt empowered, my femininity affirmed and strengthened.

***

So here I was, at the beginning of a huge journey of discovery. And what was in my wardrobe? Mainly clothes I hated the sight of, that, every time I put them on reminded me of who I wasn't, of what society was expecting me to be. A man. That had to change, and quickly.

But I hadn't a clue what suited me. I wanted to look attractive, desirable and even sexy sometimes. All those looks are learned over time, usually in a woman's teenage years. But those years were far behind me and I had a lot of catching up to do.

Helen cringed when I wore anything above the knee but thanks to my regular cycling I knew I had good legs and wanted to show them off. So short skirts and dresses became a part of my range, especially for nights out. But daywear was another area altogether. For that I was taking my lead from Emer. She would look at the average woman in the street of a similar age and aim for an appropriate look. And so did I, erring on the conservative side perhaps a little too much sometimes. Allied to the problems of choosing what to wear was the guilt attached to spending too much money. I didn't want the money I was spending as Philippa to be another issue between Helen and me. So I went to charity shops occasionally, haunted the sales racks and looked for bargains.

Shoes were so difficult to find in size 9! How I longed for my feet to be even just one size smaller – was it too late to bind my feet in the oriental manner now I would wonder. Hands and feet and the Adam's apple: the three things that were very likely to betray the trans woman who wanted to *pass*. At least I could get the Adam's apple reduced through minor surgery (though luckily mine wasn't too prominent). But feet and hands I could do nothing with.

Then there was the night before the night out. Painting my toenails, shaving my legs. Trying on outfit after outfit, getting frustrated and upset, trying to be quiet and not disturb Jenny in the adjoining bedroom. Accessorising the outfit from my small collection of cheap jewellery with clip on earrings and large bracelets. Packing everything carefully in a large sports bag, possibly two bags if I needed a coat.

All these accessories for a simple night out may seem extreme to anyone reading this. Yet these feminine signifiers all added to the image I needed to display to reduce the likelihood of someone seeing me as male. At this stage of my development any negative comment would have the potential to send me back into my shell, into the 'closet'.

I sensed this journey was not going to be an easy one, either emotionally or practically. But it was one I had started and had to continue. For my sanity.

I continued to meet other trans women, learning from them and indeed teaching them some of my acquired knowledge and tips. One of the most important friends was Karen who lived in south Dublin. I arrived at the Dart Station with my large sports bag, spotting the white car with Karen waiting outside. We had met online first, then had a 'business lunch' together where we talked quietly about our secret lives. I had sensed another kindred spirit in her, and she had been kind enough to offer to bring me to her house to continue our discussions.

We hugged briefly, a silent embrace which said so much. As the car pulled into the large, gated driveway I surveyed the impressive three-storey detached house.

Karen opened the front door and said: 'you can change upstairs, there's a spare bedroom with an en suite. But have a glass of wine first.' She opened a bottle of white wine and handed me a crystal glass with a thin ribbon around the stem.

'Very elegant,' I remarked.

'All my wife's work, she's the creative one,' laughed Karen. We sat in the beautiful, ornate drawing room beside a roaring log fire and I felt comfortable, safe and content, knowing that here was a like-minded person who I felt I could share my most intimate thoughts with, who understood my fears, desires and anxieties. This was the first time I had felt this way and I realised that Karen was fast becoming a close friend. My nights out with Emer were still terrifying, my mind full of worry that I would be seen and recognised by someone from work, or worse, one of my family. Then there was the fear of verbal or physical abuse, always a danger to the LGBTQ+ community. Tonight was different and finally I could totally relax.

After a short chat about generalities, Karen suggested that we change.

'After all, that's the reason you came here!'

'Not at all,' I said. 'It was mainly to see you!' But of course, I did want to dress, and I was shown to the spare bedroom, beautifully appointed with an ornate mirror and a large bathroom. 'This is perfect Karen,' I said, 'see you in about an hour!'

She closed the door, leaving me to organise myself. I was nervous, wanting to impress her. I sensed, even at this early stage that for a number of reasons I was probably going to go further than her – her family and business life suggested that discovery of her *femme* identity could be disastrous. She had to make do with the odd evening at home, perhaps with friends like me, and could not risk going out.

So I appeared sometime later in a new dress and heels, having attempted to put into practice the lessons I had learned from the beautician in Snips. I had also picked up a pair of small gel bra fillers from one of the department stores which gave me somewhat more of a female shape! I wasn't entirely happy with the results, knowing that some of the specialist medical providers sold much more authentic prosthetics but I was unwilling to spend upwards of €200 on them. Karen was very impressed with my efforts however and I beamed with delight.

Later that evening, after more wine and food we settled down to some serious discussions about our respective situations. Karen was keen to emphasise to me how lucky I should consider myself.

'My wife knows I dress a little, I sometimes get to wear lingerie in bed, but there's no way she would entertain me going out in public, or meeting others. She would be furious. You have a very understanding partner in Helen.'

'I know,' I replied. 'I try to be as honest and open with her about the situation, but I can't tell her everything. I know I have to take this further, the more I discover about it, the more certain I am. And I find recently I'm becoming attracted to men – that's something I've never really felt before and it both scares and excites me.'

'Would she consider a threesome? Maybe that would be a way to have you both satisfied, and still share intimacy?'

'I don't know, I doubt it. I'll ask her at the right time.'

But I really felt that it was very unlikely that Helen would entertain the idea. She had enough to consider without this concept being thrown into the mix. Peg, Karen's wife, was unaware of the deep intense feelings she had about dressing. As the conversation deepened, I began to realise that, while I was certain of where I needed to go, she did not. Or rather that she simply couldn't or didn't need to go there.

'Coming more and more to the forefront of my mind is the certainty that, ultimately, full transition and surgery is what I have to have. I won't go too far initially, I'm willing to take it slow. I'm only forty, reasonably healthy. People transition much later than this. But if Helen ever says 'stop', I will stop. Or at least try to. I really don't know if I would be able to, maybe I would have to try electro-convulsive therapy or something, like they used to do on gay men.'

'Think about what you really need, rather than what you want though,' said Karen. 'Don't do any more than you need to at the moment. With Jenny at the age she is it could be awkward.'

And the thought of Jenny, and the potential effect on her, was uppermost in my mind. I would have hated our relationship to change fundamentally, for her to come to even despise me for what I was attempting to do. I felt that was unlikely, I was quietly confident that the intelligence she was beginning to show in abundance would get her through my change. It was a risk I had to take anyway, for my sanity, and as the evening turned into early morning, I opened up more and more to her, coming close to tears and appreciating her understanding and wisdom.

As I left the lovely house and hopped in a taxi home (reluctantly having changed back to vaguely male mode, though not really caring how I looked at that point) I thought about how lucky I was to have two amazing friends in Emer and Karen. They were approaching the situation from different points-of-view and I was thus able to see all possibilities. With such good friends, I knew the path forward would be easier.

Every time out with Emer was a learning experience. Her poise and elegance, her confidence, dress sense and femininity inspired me. In ways she reminded me of my mother, with a similar sense of humour. She amazed me with stories of her experiences, her trips away for weekends, even of flying to London and visiting some of the clubs there. I was in awe of what she had achieved.

Seeing her walk down the street, nobody passing a second glance at this seemingly ordinary woman going about her ordinary life taught me more than any amount of thinking, reading or talking could do. I so wanted to achieve what she had managed. I was only at the beginning of my journey however, and Emer had been out in public for many years. In some ways, seeing her and listening to her adventures, I wondered if that would be enough for me. Would I, like so many on the internet and some I was just hearing about in Ireland, have to progress further? The vast majority didn't fully transition, hiding their feminine side all their lives. Could Emer and I transition together? I felt so close to her at times, a friendship that was deeper due to our shared pain, our shared desires to be our true selves. Who would achieve their dream first, or would neither of us? Because she, like me, had concerns and worries: of family, job and friends. Through this lifestyle she had lost a lot already and I was beginning to see changes in the relationships I had. The future, for both of us, was uncertain.

The subject of men would often come up and she laughed when I told her of my kiss with a guy a few weeks earlier in one of the gay bars. 'Did you really almost faint? Did your knees really give way? You're such a teenager!'

We would giggle like schoolgirls. Because in some ways that's just what we were, exploring our desires and our femininity, as if hormones were coursing through our bodies like never before.

And our femininity was to get a very public display shortly afterwards with an invitation to Alternative Miss Ireland in the Olympia theatre, the venue for the largest annual LGBTQ+ event in the country, an opportunity for a party and a major fundraiser for various charities.

'Just one thing,' said Lorraine, who had invited us, 'we're going to a party atmosphere, so maybe dress up a bit? Sometimes your look is a little, shall we say, formal, maybe even secretarial?' I grinned and started thinking about what I could get.

So a few weeks later I walked out of Gemini in my new outfit, feeling wonderful. A short black pvc dress, fishnet tights and 4" heels.

Hopping into the taxi a few minutes later I got the first positive reaction of the night: 'So where are we off to tonight darling? And can I come too?' asked the taxi driver, paying lots of attention to me fastening my seat belt in the back of the car.

'Well if he sees up my dress it won't be very exciting,' I thought, wearing as I was a tight girdle and two pairs of tight pants to give me shape and to hide the offending bulge of my upsetting male anatomy. But I appreciated the furtive glances he was taking in the mirror. I hopped out of the car and went to cross the road, suddenly realising that there were two lines of traffic coming straight towards me. I felt so good in myself that I was not at all surprised when both lines of traffic stopped and I calmly crossed, smiling at the reaction of my friends on the other side.

'Jesus Christ, Philippa! No wonder you're stopping traffic in that outfit!!! When I said "dress up a bit" I wasn't expecting that!' one of the group said. My friends laughed and we started towards the Olympia theatre. As I walked along the street, seeing the glances and hearing the (mostly positive) comments about the group I realised that I did enjoy the limelight, did enjoy the attention and even the thrill of the unexpected. I was going headlong towards – where? – but I was enjoying the ride.

The show was amazing with lots of drag queens and kings, some very professional, others just there for a bit of fun, all competing for the titles. It was also my first experience of trans men, seeing them both on stage and at the bar. But it was also a night to be 'fabulous' and the majority of the drag queens there were pushing the boundaries, each trying to out-do the other in terms of frock and make-up. Lorraine may have been shocked to see the transformation from quiet secretarial Philippa to (somewhat) drag queen, but I wasn't out of place here. Yet I knew that, for all the enjoyment I was getting from the looks, comments and occasional touches, this was just playtime. Tori Amos said in one of her songs that 'some of the most wonderful people are those who don't fit into boxes.' The boxes were exploding tonight.

The night passed too quickly, and I had too much wine. As usual Emer left me home, teasing me over my giddiness. Falling into bed at 3 a.m. Helen sleepily asked: 'Did you have a nice night?' and I smiled as the room spun and said, 'Yes!'

Yet how did I know I was truly female? The only experience I had was of being me, whoever or whatever that was. Was I male? Was I female? Was I being told by society that I was male because of what was between my legs? What about what was in my mind? And what was in other people's minds? Were they so secure in their identities that they never allowed themselves to consider alternatives? I remembered hearing a statistic that said that 10% of men had tried on women's clothes at some point in their lives. It was confusing, upsetting and yet exhilarating.

Looking at my body and the offending bulge between my legs I knew I didn't hate it. But I did wish it wasn't there. Apart from anything else it ruined the nice smooth lines of dresses. I began to really want it gone.

Emer suggested a trip to see the Garda band in the National Concert Hall a few weeks later.

'Dress up a bit, it'll be a high-profile evening, it's for one of the children's charities. Just for heaven's sake don't wear that pvc dress!'

'Oh I have something in mind,' I replied and started the planning process, thinking about the dress I had bought in a refurbishment sale from a shop in Grafton Street the previous week. As I learned more about the practicalities of the lifestyle, I realised just how much needed to be considered before a night out. I would regularly worry about my clothes choices, worry if the shoes matched the outfit, was terrified about make-up: despite my brief lessons it seemed an arcane art, and I knew I was no magician! Then there was the need to enhance my feminine shape and subdue the male attributes. False breasts, tight girdles and of course my 'crowning glory', the lovely wig I had bought a few months previously. To others it may have seemed as though I was trying to be something I wasn't meant to be. To have to alter my body so fundamentally to show the outside world who I was inside, was it simply living a lie? I didn't believe so. And I also knew that the person I wanted to portray, as with Emer, was of an ordinary woman going about her ordinary day. I didn't feel the need, as some I knew of, to construct an amazing shape which moved and jiggled in all the right feminine ways yet took hours to put together. I admired anyone who did but that wasn't for me. No, my goal was to be 'passable' in as short a time as possible. Like any other woman.

As soon as I met Emer she said: 'No way we're not getting piccies tonight, sis.' We set up the camera on nearby pillars and walls, enjoying each other's company and feeling the bond between us strengthen even more, laughing with the passers-by who looked towards us. We walked towards the venue, seeing lots of smartly uniformed (and attractive) gardaí and a large crowd of people making their way through the main doors. I was worried I might have overdressed but no, I was blending. We were getting some looks but nothing out of the ordinary.

'Ah, NOW I see the problem with ball gowns', I laughed as I tried to settle into my seat in a ladylike manner. A good-looking and tanned foreign guy in the seat beside me smiled and said: 'Well you look fabulous my dear', and I smiled back at him, feeling a thrill run through me.

Following the concert Emer drove to a quiet spot to allow me to change back.

'Thanks for a wonderful evening sis,' I said, and hugged my friend, my *confidante*, my soul mate. I hated the change, was reluctant to let anyone see me in anything but *femme* mode, but practicalities entailed compromise. Others were compromising much more, and I had to give a little too.

Emer smiled as she read my mind and said: 'I can still see Philippa within you, she will always be there. It was a pleasure being out with her again', and I walked up the driveway, smiling yet with tears rolling down my cheeks which was happening more and more often. This was such a rollercoaster, I had to stay on the rails.

7

PROGRESSION

Age: 44

My online relationships were important to me, but one more so than any of the others. I felt a true connection with Phil from the north of England. He was exactly the sort of person I needed at this moment, one who could appreciate me for who I was now, would never ask about my past life or indeed even my plans for the future. He just seemed to enjoy hearing of my boring days and my increasingly exciting and adventurous evenings.

Tonight Phil had a surprise coming. I sent the images from my trip to Alternative Miss Ireland to him and I waited, impatiently, for him to respond. And waited. And waited.

'Well? Did you get them?' Still nothing.

'Phil? Have you fainted? Phil?' Then I saw he was typing, and I started to grin.

'Philippa …'

'Yes Phil?'

'Philippa … wow!'

I was grinning broadly now, almost shaking with excitement and desire. He always loved the photos, loved seeing the sass exuding from his online girlfriend and he complimented me on every pose and every pout. His messages were humorous, witty and kind. They were what I wanted, needed, to hear every night, all night.

My confidence was growing every time I spoke to Phil and, as I was getting out so often now as Philippa I wanted to keep track of the outfits I was wearing. I felt like a teenager at times! I began keeping lists, and planning in advance for my nights out, now perhaps three times a week. In my notebook I would sometimes write my thoughts about each trip out, my feelings and exhilaration at being myself for even a few short hours. It might have seemed somewhat immature, but I had to acknowledge that I was essentially finding my femininity, mining my inner core to find the true person within. I needed to develop my sense of style. I had to learn. I had missed my female teenage years for the most part, now I had to fit them in as best I could to my busy 'male' life.

With Emer's photographs of us almost every time we went out together, I could see how I looked and carefully examine myself with a very critical eye. When I compared myself on my first trip out with my more recent trips I was happy with the progression, I felt more confident and also thought I was becoming more *passable*, meaning that I wasn't going to be seen as anything other than the woman I truly was. I was still nowhere near where I wanted to be though, so I booked style consultations, anxious to discover the woman underneath the upsetting male exterior. To some, even at that time, the desire to 'pass' as female (or male) to others was irrelevant and indeed often provoked arguments. For we were being ourselves and shouldn't have to conform to what society would accept as a woman or a man. Yet for me, for my own personal safety and comfort, my mental well-being, I wanted, needed, to pass.

Another area that I needed help in was make-up. Snips, the beauty and wig salon, had taken me to a certain level but I wanted to get super confident and competent. Beauty salons were plentiful in Dublin, but I chose Make-Up Forever where I had heard from others that the make-up consultants were very understanding. I was far from the first trans person they had dealt with and they tried to respect my privacy by giving me the lessons in less public areas of the shop or at quiet times. And gradually I saw the change, began to understand the techniques and even to enjoy the act of applying make-up. It was depressing to enter the beautician's in male clothes with barely anything feminine visible and then spend an hour talking about make-up techniques and styles. Yet even in male mode my name, when the consultant used it, made my heart soar and I left after the lesson smiling and with a happy skip. It was getting better. Yes, it was getting better.

And yet, for every step forward there was the push-back from Helen, my own fear of discovery and the possible ramifications. At one point Helen saw me writing in my diary. I had just come home from a typical night out and I was buzzing. But it was clear from her face that she didn't feel the same way.

'Listen, I don't want to have a big argument, but I do think you're moving too fast. I've put a few thoughts down in this letter, have a look at them and see what you think,' she said, and I immediately felt my defences rise. We had always found it difficult to discuss my transition, she simply didn't want to face it. I took the letter reluctantly, going to our bedroom. Scanning through it, I felt a rage rising as my brain refused to absorb the words she had written. How could she not see the pain I was going through? How could she not accept me for who I truly was? The path which I had carefully laid out in my head towards a future where I hoped we could all be happy, a path that I thought she had understood, now seemed full of obstacles and heartache for us both.

I crumpled up the letter, then tore it as I stormed downstairs. I threw the pieces on the table in front of her, saying: 'I'm so disappointed that you can't accept me, that you don't have confidence in our future together. I can't do any more for us, I'm doing this in the only way I can …' It was all I could say as I turned to go to bed, unwilling to even let her respond. I knew she was going to be upset but at that moment I really didn't care. It was going to be a tough few days and far from the last argument, the path I was taking would entail us having more. The spinning plates were almost falling.

Soon after an opportunity came to take some of the pressure I felt off, and to allow Helen some space. Emer had often mentioned how she would go off for weekends without the pressure of having to be home at a certain time, taking the opportunity to sleep in a nightdress and to wake up as herself. So she suggested that I accompany her on one of the overnights, to a small hotel in the Wicklow village of Aughrim. It would be a great opportunity for me to experiment, to plan outfits for daywear, evening and night, and would allow me to see just what being 'full-time' female entailed. The regular nights out with either Emer or going to Karen's lovely house were not enough anymore.

I suggested it to Helen, who accepted it could be helpful for me. The words she had written in her letter gradually sunk in and I honestly tried to be more aware of her situation. But I was very frustrated at having to hide my feminine side, to be expected to switch from male to female to male and we agreed that this weekend away would be useful to release the tension somewhat. I felt I needed to experience more than just a few hours as myself.

Emer arranged to meet me at a southside DART station for the drive to Aughrim. As usual I changed in Gemini early in the morning, feeling so grateful for being allowed a key to the club. My first trip on public transport awaited me and I was very nervous. But one of the many lessons I had learned over the past few thrilling months was that most people are too caught up in their own lives to worry about looking at and wondering about others. There were a few glances towards me from some of the other passengers on the platform, including a group of schoolgirls, but no giggles, no pointing, no insults. A little while later the train pulled into the pretty little station and I saw Emer waiting and smiling.

'Ok sis that was terrifying!' I said.

Emer laughed and said, 'you survived your first trip, well done. Now we can have some fun!'

An hour later, we pulled into the beautiful grounds of the country house, set in the middle of the countryside, and I smiled. I reached over to kiss Emer on the cheek.

'Thanks hon, this means so much to me.'

'You're welcome, this will be a weekend to remember.'

Having checked in as Philippa, the first time I had used my name in any official capacity, I was impressed to see Emer produce a credit card in her own name rather than as her 'brother' as we referred to our male alter-egos. We settled down in the lounge for afternoon tea, and I looked longingly at the ornate chessboard nearby but Emer had never really played the ancient 'Game of Kings'.

We changed later for dinner – I had a long flowing dress and Emer had a skirt and blouse. I felt wonderful. The staff treated us well, politely, not giving any indication that they suspected the women in front of them were anything different to the other guests. After dinner and drinks we sat in the lounge, enjoying the quiet atmosphere and the summer scents wafting in the slightly open windows as we made small talk with the other guests before we retired to our room. Emer and I were sharing a large, beautiful twin with a lovely ceramic bath. We couldn't resist temptation and we took modest photographs of each other, giggling like schoolgirls. Drifting off to sleep a while later I had a moment to think of how wonderful it would be to be sharing this with Helen. For the future, hopefully.

After an extravagant breakfast the following morning, I suggested a walk around the grounds of the country house. The rolling hills of Wicklow, the sound of a nearby stream and the beautiful early summer weather all combined to ease our worries and concerns and we were silent as we found our way back to the historic hotel. I really did not want the trip to end, being desperate to spend more time with Emer. But we reluctantly drove back towards Dublin, stopping for lunch in Rathdrum, the energetic, excited chatter of the day before being replaced by a quietness, an acceptance that shortly we would be back to pretending to be someone we really weren't. This simple overnight, something which friends and couples do without a thought, had been a very special experience for us.

As we got closer to home, I reluctantly asked Emer to stop somewhere quiet so I could change back to my male clothes. I almost cried as I did, having experienced a semblance of what full transition would be like. 'How much more we could accomplish with our lives if we didn't have this terrible secret to focus on?' I asked Emer as she pulled up to the entrance of my estate. We had said it before and would say it again. Emer just smiled sadly as we hugged.

I knew Helen could see the changes in me, my excitement at every night out, my pushing at the generous limits she tried to impose. I didn't want to risk our relationship, lose any friendships, yet I also had to try to progress as far as I needed to, as quickly as I could. The joy I was feeling at the gains I was making as Philippa was counterbalanced by potential losses – friends, family and more. Everyone told me of the difficult path transitioning entailed. Could I make it, even with the help of Emer and others? My very regular nights out (and, increasingly, more daytime trips) only became possible when I was given a set of keys to Gemini. Some of my trans friends changed in their cars but I didn't have that option, never having driven. My only choice was to either use Gemini (or a phone booth, superhero style, I thought humorously). Gemini though had its own problems as it was well known in the area and the windows of the pub opposite provided a perfect vantage point for the clientele to make fun of the girls leaving Gemini on nights out. All these hurdles to be crossed just to be true to ourselves.

Shortly after the trip to Aughrim with Emer came an opportunity I had been dreaming of. The online chats with Phil led to a definite date and we organised an overnight in Birmingham to coincide with his work and a Bolton soccer match the following day, a team that he was passionate about. Helen was aware of my relationship with Phil and what a support he had been for me but was a little ambivalent with the thought of me going to see him.

Phil, ever the humorist, wrote: 'for once though I'm going to be more excited about what happens before the match than during it,' and I could imagine him grinning as we chatted enthusiastically.

I rang the hotel, booked in my male name then organised my flight to Birmingham. When I went online with Phil that night I was excited that this momentous occasion was actually going to happen.

The date drew nearer, the discussions got more intimate, the excitement rose. I had organised with Phil the exact time and place we would meet and how the evening might go. I had my outfits ready, which I wouldn't tell him about, and was teasing, flirting and suggesting like never before. Then, just three days before the trip, he dropped the bombshell.

'Hi hon, I'm afraid I have some bad news. I won't be able to meet you on Friday. It's work, I've finished the contract early and I can't make any excuse for an overnight in Birmingham now. I'm so sorry, I know how much this trip means to us but I simply can't make it.'

I sat at the computer, devastated, unable to even reply. My doubts, guilt, nervousness about this trip had all been put behind me. It was a huge step in my progression. I wanted this so much. I wanted to be with Phil. I had told him of my deepest desires, the future I so wanted for myself as Philippa. There was no one else, not even Emer or Karen, who knew as much about me. Now it seemed he was to be taken away from me by fate. The rest of the conversation was stilted, I could hardly bring myself to type, not sure of what to do next

The following day I made up my mind. I was going to Birmingham. I was upset with the situation, but I knew I needed this weekend away and the opportunity to be myself.

I cancelled the hotel and booked a B&B near the gay area of Birmingham where I felt I would be safer. I decided to be upfront with the guy who answered when I rang to book, telling him I was trans.

'That's great darling,' he replied, 'we'll look after you and point you in the right direction.' I put the phone down with a little more enthusiasm and went to pack for the most important overnight trip of my life to date.

My outfit for the trip to Birmingham was androgynous veering towards feminine – black trousers, a tee-shirt, low heels, unisex bag. I was wearing tinted moisturiser, a little lip-gloss and perfume, which I was going to add to when I got out of the neighbourhood. Check-in at the airport was unremarkable, the security staff didn't look twice, disappointing me slightly! I was focused on this trip and I ready for whatever was to happen and going to enjoy it.

I arrived in Birmingham city centre a couple of hours later and walked out of the railway station before realising I had no idea how to get to the B&B. A lorry driver, seeing my confusion, called out to me from his cab.

'You look lost love. Where are you trying to get to?' I gave the name of the street and he said: 'I'm going that way, hop in. Save you a taxi fare.'

I was conscious that I might be about to get into a lorry with a murderer, but I actually didn't care because I felt this was *my* time. I clambered up into the high cab, which would have been a difficult exercise even without the heels. The driver was attentive to me, eyeing my legs in the tight black trousers. I was a little confused, wondering if I was passing as female and thus attracting him or if he was gay and attracted to a femme guy. 'Have a lovely time darling', he said having left me to my B&B and I crossed the road smiling broadly. A nice start to the trip, no matter the reason.

Walking in the door I was greeted by two men, who

introduced themselves as Fred and John, the owners. I was keen to change, to show them as little of myself in male mode as possible, and so anxiously climbed the stairs to the attic room. It was very small, but fine for my purposes.

'Just a minute darling,' said John, disappearing into an adjoining room and returning with a large full-length mirror. 'Now you'll be able to see just how gorgeous you will look later!' and I laughed, feeling, again, that I was on the cusp of something wonderful.

I took my time changing, anxious to impress Fred and John. I dressed in a knee length skirt, pretty blouse and low heels then grabbed my handbag to go down to the small lounge. Fred was behind the bar and looked twice at me before saying, 'Lovely, darling! I didn't recognise you at first! Hey John, get the champagne out!' The two guys, obviously partners, were utterly charming and seemed to enjoy having an Irish girl to entertain.

After a quick lunch I took a trip around the vicinity of the B&B, doing a little shopping in a designer mall and enjoying just being myself. I also felt a little lonely and maudlin, thinking about who should have been with me. Maybe next time.

I decided to go blonde for the evening, an adventurous change to my usual look. No secretarial Philippa tonight. A knee-length red dress (with a revealing split) and some chunky jewellery completed the outfit. I lay on the bed, relaxing, thinking about how I would manage the evening. I wanted a little romance, a little flirting. I wanted attention, compliments, above all the assurance that I was attractive and desirable. I wanted intimacy. Sex. It was time for Philippa to lose her virginity.

'You're quite desperate,' I thought with a smile, 'but

this is your time.' I thought of Helen and Jenny, at home, wondering about me. I knew Helen would be furious if she found out, but I suspected she knew that my nights out weren't entirely for meals and talking, that perhaps I also had a little fun with men. Because sometimes I did have a few kisses and cuddles on my nights out back in Dublin but never more than that. I simply couldn't let it go further and after every minor encounter my guilt dispelled any possible joy I had gained from the attention of the guy the previous night.

I hated myself for what I was about to do, more and more thinking of staying in my room, maybe going for a drink downstairs and playing safe. But my desire was too strong. Again I thought of Phil, and my upset and regret over the situation with him weighed on my mind. All combined to somewhat dilute my excited mood. But I quickly recovered and began to concentrate on the finishing touches.

As I walked out of the B&B I got the first comment of the night, a 'gorgeous, honey, you'll definitely pull tonight!' from a couple of guys walking hand in hand on the opposite side of the road and I skipped along towards the club that had been recommended. As I squeezed through the door I realised I hadn't eaten since lunchtime and my stomach was beginning to rumble.

I found an empty high seat in the busy bar and placed my sparkling water on the table nearby, taking in the surroundings and the clientele. The split on the dress revealed a lot of my leg and I saw a few men and a couple of women glancing over, appreciatively I hoped. It was mostly couples in the bar, along with a few camp guys holding court around tables, entertaining small groups with extravagant gestures and amusing anecdotes. I was enjoying the atmosphere but increasingly thinking about how hungry I was. I moved to get my coat from the back of the chair. As I was about to leave an attractive middle-eastern looking guy smiled and said: 'You are leaving? But I was going to buy you a drink.'

'Oh, well maybe I can stay for one drink. But I need to eat!' I replied.

'You can eat after we make love,' said the guy, introducing himself as Hamad.

I laughed and said: 'You are very forward!' delighted at the attention from this tall, good-looking guy. As we attempted to communicate, he moved closer to me, gently running his hand along my leg, slipping his fingers into the high split.

'You like?'

'Yes,' I replied softly as he leaned into me and kissed me. The communications between us became physical and I enjoyed his hands exploring my body, his kisses becoming more passionate. 'Hamad,' I said, giggling, 'this is lovely but I have to eat! We can go somewhere afterwards.' He looked annoyed and I saw that tonight was going to be purely sexual, a meeting of bodies not minds. I thought of stopping there but he was very attractive and I wanted him.

We shared a pizza in my room, not quite the romantic meal I had hoped for and again I thought of stopping, thinking of Helen and the possible results of my infidelity. But I wasn't strong enough to resist this desire and our passion took hold. We had what was, for me, wonderful, fulfilling and affirming sex, not once but twice, with this strong, well-built and attractive Iraqi who had no idea where Ireland was. Afterwards we lay in each other's arms satiated and quiet, the room a mixture of sweat, sex and uneaten pizza, our clothes strewn on the floor.

After two hours I managed to get him to leave, promising I would drop back to the club when I had tidied myself up. I was pleased he wanted to continue the evening with me but I felt the language barrier was too much. I didn't want the night to end though and I went to the other recommended club, being chatted up by a couple of women and a waiter, enjoying the attention but no, the intimacy, the act I so desperately had wanted, needed, to experience had been amazing and being unfaithful to Helen with other women as well was something I was definitely not going to do.

I fell into bed much later, exhausted, fulfilled, validated and happy. It had been an incredible experience, the Birmingham scene was a little different to Dublin's in the size and intensity and I was certainly not short of opportunities or attention, from men and women. Grateful for my reluctance to drink too much, especially considering I was in a strange city, my head still spun as I fell into a deep sleep.

I was keen to get home, to Helen and Jenny. I thought of Phil, and how the night would have been with him. Very different I knew. I was becoming depressed and worried, feeling like a slut in some ways yet also thrilled. I was over-analysing the situation as I was wont to do with everything, so I forced myself to get out of bed, showered, put on a little make-up, jeans and a top to wander downstairs for breakfast.

Fred, one of the owners, was there and smiled when he saw me.

'So darling, how did we get on last night? Enjoy yourself? Do you need a hangover remedy?' I laughed and assured him I didn't.

'It was a super night, I enjoyed myself. Let's leave it at that Fred!' I said with a wink and he laughed loudly. A few minutes later he laid a substantial vegetarian breakfast in front of me and I luxuriated in the comfort of the empty bar, bouncing along with the restaurant's soundtrack, which, consisting of Genesis, Yes and Bowie seemed to be tailored to me! I had my camera and got a photo with Fred and John by the large Christmas tree, giggling as I attempted to set the camera up on auto.

I arrived home later that evening and I was disappointed to find the girls in bed, asleep. I kissed Jenny and slipped into bed beside Helen, trying not to disturb her.

But a few weeks later everything changed between Helen and I. Following a regular check-up with my GP I discovered I had Chlamydia, a common SDI. I had to tell Helen, for her own wellbeing, regardless of the possible effects on our marriage. I hated myself for what I had done, hated the situation she was going to have to face that I had created for our lovely happy family. I hoped that she would forgive me but I would absolutely understand if she couldn't. I was bisexual, a very difficult situation for anyone in a marriage.

So one evening after work as we sat in the lounge, Helen in her usual chair and me on the couch I nervously raised the subject. I could sense a gulf widening between us. I could not hold it in any longer, far more than the truth of the simple infection emerging and I began to talk and explain, to plead and appeal for forgiveness, the words flooding out like a torrent. Helen sat opposite, shaking. I felt the tears run down my cheeks. I tried to make her understand my feelings, how I had to explore my attraction to men, reassured her that it was only with men and that

I would never think of being with another woman. Still silence from Helen. Then finally she spoke and her words cut through me like a knife. No, she didn't understand. No, there was no excuse. No, she didn't care that it was *only* men. It was still deceit. Unfaithfulness. Lying. Cheating. She could not understand, would not understand this betrayal. I didn't blame her. The tears flooded down my cheeks, but Helen looked shell-shocked. I attempted to bridge the gulf between us but Helen pulled away.

'Get away from me. Leave me alone. I trusted you and you broke that trust. I can never forgive you. Just go away.' I left the lounge, frustrated at everything, upset for Helen, Jenny, the future and my behaviour. Maybe I should have engineered an accident tonight on the way home. I had considered it, not for the first time. Maybe it would have been better for Helen never to know. She was disgusted at the thought that I had cheated in that way and possibly given her an STD. I went to the dining room and wondered what the next few days would hold.

A few minutes later Helen came out from the lounge and I studied her face. 'You did this to her,' I thought to myself. 'It was you, being selfish as usual. You deserve nothing, you have no excuses, none.' I went to the cupboard and took down the spare bedding, ready to organise it on the couch.

'No,' said Helen and I looked at her nervously.

'Is she going to kick me out?' I thought.

'No,' said Helen again, a little more quietly. 'Sleep in Jenny's bed tonight, she's with her friends.'

'Thank you,' I said, 'thank you,' and I felt the tears well up again.

We slept fitfully that night but woke to a new day and

a new realisation. When I went into the bedroom to dress for work Helen kissed me gently. 'We'll get through this,' she said, 'don't worry.' That kiss meant so much to me, I had been given a small ray of hope after my desperate, inevitable, stupidity. She went for her STD test (which was negative) but told me how upset and embarrassed she had felt, through no fault of hers, and she was distant from me for the evening. I felt for her, upset at having caused her pain.

To me it was still a time of uncertainty, the decision was ultimately Helen's. The chasm might not be too wide after all, but I knew there were many more arguments to have and it was unlikely to end anytime soon.

The following days saw a new normality begin. The initial shock on both our parts had worn off: what had happened, happened and there were still bills to pay, work to go to and of course Jenny to look after. Life had to go on.

We decided that I should see a psychologist, possibly as a precursor to both of us attending, to get an opinion on my progression as Philippa, my relationship with Helen and my attraction to men. Although Helen knew of my desire to keep moving forward, we hadn't discussed my full transition at any point. I wanted to do everything gradually, almost by osmosis, but inexorably moving towards my ultimate goal of living life full-time as Philippa. If I could do that and avoid too many arguments or upsets then all the better. Many trans people would simply decide on a day and arrive in to work or their home in their changed gender. I couldn't risk everything by doing that. Slow and steady, I had to compromise as others were.

The psychologist used by a lot of the trans community seemed the obvious choice. He was familiar with all aspects of the issues involved in transitioning and I was sure that my minor encounters with men were mild in comparison to what I had heard others did. Yet in the back of my mind were some doubts and worries – what if he said my feelings were only sexual? Or alternatively, what if he said I should seriously consider surgery and going full-time? Did psychologists say such things? I had never really talked to anyone who had been to one and this was a completely new field for me. Depressed and upset I may have been but I determined to make the best of the situation.

A week later I walked along Parliament Street looking for the premises. The street had featured quite a lot in my life to date and I wondered what changes the next hour was going to bring. The ISFA had met in the Parliament Inn and my first time out in public had been just across the road in one of the main venues for the LGBTQ+ community, The Front Lounge.

As I walked along the busy sunlit street I saw the sign for the psychologist's office. Happy that I was there in plenty of time I crossed the road to The Front Lounge to have a coffee before the appointment. As I walked into the relatively quiet bar, I heard the faint strains of John Lennon's 'Woman' playing, and tears came to my eyes. 'Appropriate,' I thought, and sat down smiling. It was apt that I was here at the next stage of my journey, I just hoped I wouldn't trip on the way out this time.

Thirty minutes later I walked across the road for my appointment. I was dressed *en femme*, a big step for me at that point, I had changed at lunchtime in Gemini for my early afternoon appointment, no hiding today. A sign on the door of a small waiting room requested patients of the psychologist to take a seat. I settled into the comfortable armchair, nervously fumbling with my mobile phone and wondering should I text to let him know I had arrived. A tall bearded man passed the door a few minutes later, glancing in, and continued upstairs. A little later he came back and looked towards me.

'Philippa?' I nodded. 'Would you like to come upstairs?' he said in a strong American accent.

His office was large and comfortable, two padded chairs and a desk, some flowers and an abstract painting on the wall.

'I saw you come in,' he said, 'but I thought you were a cis-woman.' I blushed and thanked him.

'So why have you come to me? You explained briefly on the phone but take your time and talk about what's worrying you.'

I began to discuss my desires and experiences to date, dressing, and going out, the deep and lasting belief that nature had played a joke on me by giving me a male body but a female mind. The depression and confusion I had felt whenever I allowed myself to think about the issue. I started telling him about my recent encounters and the discovery that I had Chlamydia, and then having to tell Helen. He nodded.

'So how long have you been dressing as a woman? Why do you do it, is it purely sexual or is there something more?' The questions were probing and, somewhat repetitive. He was taking detailed notes, studying me. It was a strange experience, but I felt relaxed and confident. I found myself talking at length about my feelings, my desires and my hopes. But also my fears: effect on family, work and especially on Helen and Jenny.

'Well, from what you're saying you are essentially a

teenage girl. And you have feminine desires which you can't handle, don't know how to handle. So don't worry, this is entirely normal for someone in your situation.' He continued in a reassuring manner and I became more relaxed, opening up more and feeling a weight lift from me. I left some time later, happier and more positive about the situation. As I progressed in this amazing journey I realised that I liked talking about my feelings, could express myself honestly with him and each time I did I felt another small step had been taken. 'Who would have thought even ten years ago that I'd be seeing a shrink?' I thought with a smile.

I let Helen know about the meeting, told her what the psychologist had said and left her to absorb the information. It was very positive from my point of view but I tried to see hers too. I suggested that she might like to see him too, or to go to someone else, to get an independent opinion on our situation. She said she needed time to think. If our relationship was to move forward, to cross this gulf, we had to be adult enough to explore all possibilities. Some of those possibilities were difficult to consider.

I found myself thinking about my situation constantly, or my developing deep friendship with Emer. I wanted to talk to her every day, at least text, to discuss the next trip out and our latest purchases and adventures. With so many texts and calls to Emer I found myself being pulled away from some of my friends and I felt the time was approaching to tell them, at least a little, about my secret life, about who I truly was and where I was probably going.

I suggested lunch in a nearby bar with a close friend from work to 'discuss something very personal'.

As we walked along the street, I carried a small bag with a collection of photographs from my recent trips out.

I asked my colleague if he had any idea what I was going to tell him, but he just shook his head.

We took our seats at the ornate table in Café en Seine, quickly ordering from the menu and I took a deep breath.

'I'd like you to first have a look at some of these photos and tell me what you think,' I said, producing a thick photo album, surprised that in such a relatively short time I had managed to accumulate so many photos of myself. 'Thank you Emer', I thought. And these were just the relatively good ones. What would my good friend think?

He was flicking through the album with a puzzled look on his face.

'So who is she? Are you having an affair with her?'

I realised with surprise that he really did not recognise me and replied: 'well, for many years I've felt drawn to dress as a woman; these are photos of me. I'm what's known as transgender. Helen knows about it and is somewhat accepting, Jenny doesn't know as yet but at some point soon we will have to tell her. I feel that as time goes on this is going to become more obvious to people, I may be seen like this by someone from work and I wanted to tell you for two or three reasons. Working with you, and the friendship we have are two. But also I did want to tell you for personal reasons so that if it does come out at work I have someone who knows my story and some of my reasons for doing it.'

He looked surprised.

'Had you no idea what I was going to tell you?' I asked. 'I thought maybe some of the guys in work might have seen the lip gloss, smelled the perfume, even overheard me talking to a friend Emer who's in the same situation as me. You really had no clue?'

'No. Nobody has said anything, that's for certain.'

I laughed. 'That surprises me, I thought at times I was giving it away and that somebody must have figured it out. But then I suppose everyone is too busy getting on with their own lives.'

He nodded in agreement.

'So what's the next step then? Have you considered the effect on Jenny and Helen?'

I nodded and told him of some of the events of the past few years.

'I'm not sure where this is taking me, but I'm determined to have as little impact on people as I can, while still being true to myself. It has been a roller-coaster ride even to this point, and I really don't know what's around the next corner.' I smiled, 'Don't worry, I'll keep you up to date', and went on to tell him of my excitement at seeing the name Philippa on a document in work. Girly, so girly, yet also so me.

As I thought about the revelation later that afternoon again, I considered the effect on others. Something so personal that had occupied my mind, on and off, for thirty years was going to be a big shock to a lot of my friends. How many would I lose in the process? I had thought of Helen and Jenny, my mother, when I told her, and the wider family of course. But friends were different. Could the relationships I had built up carefully over many years survive? I had already dropped out of science fiction fan circles, something I couldn't have imagined doing before and that was painful. From online chats with other trans people I knew that I would lose some friends but possibly gain more. And, most importantly for those who really mattered, those who I needed, I would be myself and I could move forward and be a better person in the future. I was doing the right thing. I had to be.

A few weeks later, I was surprised to bump into another person from my office in Gemini and it turned out they had been going to dress there for a few years. Quickly enough though we found that we really didn't have much in common apart from our trans situation and didn't see each other often. Later again I heard that there was yet another trans girl in the PRA but I never found out who, only knowing that she worked in a different building. I thought of the big shock I was likely to cause and how people just don't know what is going on in other people's lives. At least three trans people from a staff of over 500. I suspected there were more, and if international studies were to be believed, it could be as many as twenty-five or even fifty.

As Emer pulled up at the driveway to my house I told her about my encounter in Gemini with my work colleague. She mentioned how neighbours had seen her on occasion but she was very careful in work, not giving any hint whatsoever.

As I moved forward with my transition I was feeling more confident, but did feel the need to move away, to some degree, from seeing Emer so much. My life was very different to hers with fewer demands on my time. As my circle of friends in the LGBTQ+ community continued to expand, I had plenty of opportunities for nights out. I also enjoyed just going out on my own, looking forward to living a normal life as Philippa in the future. Yet Emer was truly someone special to me and I wanted to share my progression with her.

As I got out of the car I noticed a face at the window of a house opposite. I had decided to come home dressed tonight and felt so comfortable that I just couldn't bring myself to change. So I walked up the driveway with confidence, then fumbled to find the keys, and quietly made my way in. The light was still on in our bedroom and I crept upstairs.

'Hi hon, how was the night?' I said as I started to take off my dress.

'Oh,' said Helen, 'you came home dressed? That's a big step. What if Jenny had still been up?'

'Well I did check the bedroom light was off, and it is almost midnight,' I replied defensively.

'She's asking why you go out so much you know? Again tonight. She misses her daddy.'

'I know, and I hate having to creep around like I do, but at the moment it's all I can do.'

Helen shook her head and turned away, leaving me to consider again the effect this situation was having on everybody in my life. Our relationship had improved a lot since the incident in Birmingham and I really didn't want to risk damaging it. I lay in bed, thoughts flitting through my mind: positives: I'm being me, the true me, my mood is much better, I'm a better person. Negatives: Family – what happens when Mum finds out? What would my sister think? Helen – she's losing the man she married, gaining what? At best a sister. The embarrassment for her in work, what would her family think? And then of course Jenny: her friends, her classmates, and the ridicule she would suffer if the secret about her 'daddy' came out. Helen had alluded to it tonight: Jenny was losing her daddy, and gaining – what? Who? Work – could I lose my job? So many negatives and so few positives, and all the positives seemed to be selfish, only affecting my desires and me.

My sleep was fitful, restless. The teenagers who some-times gathered on the green behind the house were there again, shouting and whistling, and my constant fear was that they would notice my changes and start daubing graffiti about me around. So many negatives. So few positives ...

However, I had the opportunity to tell a close friend about my transition a few days later. An old friend, Colum, who had left Ireland some years previously to become a Buddhist monk, was in Dublin for a quick visit. Colum had come out as gay to me before he left and I had often thought about him, and what he would think of me now.

He rang one afternoon. 'So, are you back in Dublin? Are you a monk yet?' I asked him.

'You don't become a monk that quickly, it takes years. And there's no pressure, I don't have to do it in any specific length of time so I'm taking a break from my studies. And yes, I'm back in Dublin for a week. Do you fancy meeting for a drink?'

'I'd really love that,' I replied. 'And if you don't mind, I'd like you to meet a very good friend of mine called Emer.'

'Oooh, something to tell me?' said Colum, and I could hear the humorous curiosity in his voice, looking for scandal.

'Yes, I do, but it's not what you might think ...' I said, leaving the sentence hanging.

'Oh go on, give me a clue,' he said, probing

'No. But let's meet in a nice pub on Capel Street called GUBU. Do you know it?'

'I think so, is it not a gay pub?'

'Well I don't have a problem with that,' I laughed. 'Do you?'

The following evening was beautiful and sunny. Emer picked me up from the club and drove to the usual spot in Drury Street. It was only a short walk across the Liffey to the pub where we were to meet Colum.

'Are you nervous, sis?' asked Emer.

'I suppose I am. I was disappointed with the reaction of one guy a few months ago and I don't want to feel like I'm in danger of losing all of my old friends.'

I hugged Emer and we laughed as two guys coming towards us on the street starting singing 'Sisters ...'

Walking into the quiet pub we decided to sit at the front, being a little early. I was wearing a knee length skirt and blouse, low heels. Unspectacular. Ordinary. Normal. The words summed me up, it was the image I wanted to portray. Most of the time anyway.

Then I saw him at the other end of the bar with a guy. I felt my stomach fluttering. This was a big event for me, bigger than I had thought. Colum's acceptance of me was important, I wanted validation from someone who meant a lot to me. I made my way down to stand in front of my old friend. He glanced up, then looked away. I continued standing, a smile on my face. He looked up again with a puzzled expression. Ok I thought, time to say something.

'Hi Colum, I think you know me.' More quizzical looks, then a gradual dawning as I said, 'This is Emer and we arranged to meet here tonight?'

'Well, I wasn't expecting this! Wow, this is a surprise!' said Colum.

They made room for us at the table and we began to talk. It had been a few years since we had seen each other, and I was anxious to give him the opportunity to speak. I didn't want the evening to be all about me, but I was desperate to hear what he thought of my revelation. I let him talk first, allowing him to see me as Philippa, as a woman and yet how I was still the friend he had known those many years before. As we chatted, I hoped I was expressing myself confidently, realising that I might be overdoing my femininity. I sensed a curiosity from him but was there a lack of understanding? From the evenings out with many from the gay community I knew that acceptance was not guaranteed and that many gays saw trans as simply gay guys who liked to wear a dress. It was difficult to persuade some of them otherwise.

His friend had met me in male mode some years before and seemed supportive, interested in learning more about the transgender world. Emer and Colum seemed to get on very well, and I was content to let the conversation wander, not focusing on me too much, allowing the shock to my friend dissipate and perhaps give him time to think about what I had revealed to him. And a little while later he made one of the most perceptive remarks I had heard about me.

'Sitting here looking at you and listening to you, eh *Philippa*,' said Colum 'I know now that what I felt as we grew up makes sense. I always felt there was more to you than you were letting me, or anyone else in fact, see. I was pretty sure you weren't gay. Now I see what it was you were hiding, maybe even from yourself. But you should have *said* something!'

I explained how long it had taken me to come to terms with my identity, to actually realise what was happening and what the feelings and desires meant.

'And I *did* hint a bit! What about all the times I would comment on women's clothes, either in the shop windows or what girls were wearing? Did you not pick up on those clues at all?'

'No, not at all. I suppose in a way we were both going through a transition of sorts, I was busy coming out as gay, discovering my interest in Buddhism, having a few relationships – my life was busy and I suppose I am not exactly the most perceptive of guys. Sorry!' and we laughed.

We finished our meal and said our goodbyes. He had been such a good friend and, as with my other great friend, Declan, I desperately wanted to keep the friendship. It would be interesting to see what the future would hold for Colum and me.

My life continued in the same vein over the next few months, going out with Emer or some of the other girls regularly, two or three times a week. It was expensive, as it usually entailed a meal out, with possibly a taxi home, and paying for the use of the facilities in Gemini. It allowed me to gain confidence, in dressing, make-up and being out in public, and I found myself more and more just enjoying the feeling of being out and being myself, not attracting attention. It took quite some time before I felt comfortable using the female changing rooms in shops to try clothes on and I usually just bought something, hoping it fitted or suited me. In work I felt frustrated. I wanted to show my femininity, wanted to talk to the other women, to be even more of their circle than I was at that point. But what if it went wrong and I was ridiculed? I was nervous and easily embarrassed which of course drew attention to me.

Every now and then I felt the need for some male company, just to experience a little intimacy, the sort that Helen couldn't give. Every time I did it I felt horribly guilty, upset at the thoughts of being unfaithful again, but the pressure to do it was intense, and I consoled myself by keeping the fun to a minimum, little more than kissing and cuddling. It was the feel of a man's arms around me, or his hand on my legs, higher and higher, that drove me wild. Helen didn't want to hear about my brief encounters, preferring to accept that Birmingham had been a lesson for me and that I wouldn't betray her in that way again.

Of course, I had my desires, my fantasies, my daydreams, but in reality how likely were they to come to pass? I was reasonably happy with my weekly outings and the occasional day away with Emer. But I longed to experience the feeling of waking up in a nightdress again as I had in Aughrim, of putting my make-up on and leaving the house in a dress, walking down the road to catch a bus to meet Helen for lunch, or for a night out with one of my friends. The thought of going into work *en femme* was almost impossible to imagine. How many others could truly say that they had to hide such a huge part of themselves simply because society couldn't accept them? Could the vast majority of people even imagine what I was going through?

Helen was being supportive, as much as she could be, but there were limits. She wouldn't allow regular dressing at home, frowned on my coming home dressed, wanting to minimise the impact on Jenny of course, as I did. But I was becoming more and more androgynous in my daily life, sometimes making it obvious that I was wearing tights or stockings under my trousers. It was a, nerve-wracking but exciting time as I learned what was possible, as I pushed the boundaries more and more.

But my nights out were my escape, my chance to be the true me and to push the boundaries even further. I saw an advertisement in the gay community magazine GCN for an LGBTQ+ friendly restaurant on the Dublin's quays called Eliza Blue. Beautifully situated at the new Millennium Bridge there was a pleasant atmosphere when I went in to book a meal for Emer and myself that evening.

A camp guy with a strong Australian accent greeted me. 'Yes chicken, how can I help you?' he said

I started to grin. 'Ehh,' I started, losing my tongue and

the waiter started drumming his fingers on the cash desk.

'Come on, come on, I haven't got all day, I'm very busy,' he said, grinning and looking around the virtually empty restaurant. I could hardly get the words out: 'Emm, I'd like to book a table for two for my sister and her friend for tonight please?' I gave the details and turned to go, reluctantly. There was something about him and all I wanted to do was stay. I looked back and smiled at him. He was watching me closely. Had he guessed that the booking for 'my sister' was actually for me?

'See you soon,' he said. 'Tell your sister to ask for me and I'll make sure she enjoys herself, I'm working tonight. My name is Darren.'

'I will, she'll be delighted to meet you I'm sure' and I walked out, laughing, looking forward to the evening even more than usual.

I arrived slightly early having taken a taxi from the club and walked in, seeing Darren running around the quite busy restaurant. I decided not to bother him and sat at our table, a lovely window seat where I had a gorgeous view up along the Liffey as the streetlights began to come on. A minute later Darren came over to me. Before I could say anything, he said: 'Ok, you're a white wine type of girl. We have a lovely chardonnay. Back in a minute, chicken', leaving me with my mouth open. When he came back with the large glass of wine, I attempted to start the conversation.

'You must be Darren. My brother booked the table earlier and told me to ask for you.' Darren smiled and said, 'Yes, that's me', but gave no hint that he recognised me from earlier. Emer arrived shortly afterwards and we chatted until Darren came back to take our order. He stopped in front of the table and looked carefully at the two of us.

'Are you two sisters? You must be! Hi, I'm Darren,' he said to Emer and she laughed. He disappeared into the kitchen a minute later, grumbling at my request for the vegetarian option. 'Oh, you're going to be one of those awkward customers, are you?' he said with a mock scowl, raising his eyes to heaven. Emer looked at me and smiled.

'Have you known him for long?' she asked, and I laughed.

'Since lunchtime. This could be a fun evening.'

Darren flirted and joked with everyone in the restaurant but seemed to always make time for the 'sisters', checking in regularly. 'A tart for a tart' was his comment when I ordered the apple pie for dessert, causing Emer to giggle and agree, wincing as I kicked her under the table. I sensed a very kind-hearted person, I felt very comfortable around him and looked forward to many more meals in Eliza Blue. He was to become a good friend, always making time for me, even at short notice and, some years later, he was the cause of some very happy tears.

8

RESOLVE

Age: 45–46

For most of a year I had managed to keep surviving on my two or three nights a week out as Philippa. But the pressure continued to build. I wanted to wear something resembling a nightdress in bed. Helen relented. But the arguments continued, and each quarrel failed to find a resolution. She was giving a little, but not fast enough for me. We had a few brief discussions but Helen was reluctant to look towards the future and consider what it could mean. For me there were only two options. I was either going to have to stop entirely or move forward. Both had inherent risks to me, my family and friends. It was a very difficult time and I was sure Jenny suspected something. How could I hurt her?

We both needed support and the opportunity arose for me when, in mid-April 2005 a trans support group was set up in Outhouse, the LGBTQ+ resource centre on Capel Street. I mentioned that I would like to go and Helen agreed. 'It can't do any harm anyway, be good to get to hear other people's stories and experiences,' she said, always trying to be supportive. I hoped that I might be able to get some advice regarding her situation too.

So a few weeks later, I walked into a room with ten others and to a meeting that was to confirm the direction my life was taking. Emer was there, along with Sara. I had seen most of the others either in Gemini or on nights out.

The discussions very much centred on progression, transition, and was almost entirely made up of male-to-female trans women. I also found that my experience to date had been unusual in having the support of my wife and having the freedom to be out on a regular basis, with fewer arguments at home than many others.

The safety of our community around the streets, especially late at night, was raised and I recounted to the group my one minor incident where I had been struck on the head when going down the steps of Gemini after a night out.

'I was very worried leaving the club,' I told the others, 'I changed as quickly as I could and then stood at the bottom of the stairs, listening for any noise on the street. When I got to the top of the steps, I looked up the street for a taxi, saw one turning the corner and ran! I was absolutely terrified.'

But the incident provoked others to tell of far more serious incidents and to remind everyone of the potential dangers that our community faced on a regular basis. Through the support group I began to form friendships with others as we continued our different, unique and personal journeys together.

One of the women who ran the support group had been in touch with the national trans group Transgender Equality Network Ireland and organised a meeting for anyone who wanted to be involved. As I had been attending the support group frequently, I was beginning to realise the importance of using my privileged position – married, job, friends – I had to start working for my community. Drugs, alcohol abuse and suicide attempts were far too common amongst the LGBTQ+ populace, brought about in the main by the pressures caused by what my friends were facing daily. I regularly thought back to the arguments with Helen and the frustration we had both felt over the years. I could understand how people felt forced to such extremes. Quickly enough I found myself on the committee with other passionate people and slowly, so slowly, a little progress began to be made. I felt that the trans organisation was unlikely to be very visible in the media or at other large public events, so my potential exposure would be limited.

My wardrobe was full to overflowing. I had dresses, skirts and trousers at one end and my boring, 'male' clothes at the other end. On occasion Jenny would see the female clothes and comment that she hadn't seen Mummy wearing them. I was certain she was beginning to suspect, and I decided to move Philippa's clothes to the attic, where I put a floor, some lights and a mirror, a considerable challenge for my limited home improvement skills. It became a little haven for me, somewhere I could quietly plan my clothes for my next trip, I could dream about a future that seemed to be getting closer. I left the house in daylight at one point, *en femme*, frustrated that I wasn't moving fast enough. I began to arrive home more dressed as Philippa, ignoring the risks and the inevitable arguments with Helen. Then I would lie in bed, listening to the teenagers behind our house and worry that they had seen and recognised me and would daub graffiti around. (Many years later ironically I ended up working with one of them on Marriage Equality and other campaigns). Sleepless nights, frustrating days.

On my trips out, I could only wear clip earrings, and the choice was very limited. I wanted to wear the dangliest, most spectacular earrings that seemed to be the fashion at that time. 'All you need to do,' I was told, 'is get them pierced and then replace the stud with a little piece of fishing line. Keep it there for a few weeks and you'll be fine.'

I arrived home on Friday, the day before a holiday to Madeira, with little flowers in my ears, the smallest earrings the piercer had which would keep the holes open. Helen and Jenny both freaked and as Helen removed them there was blood everywhere. She replaced the earrings with the fishing line. Jenny was crying, saying that she didn't want her daddy looking like a scary biker. I tried to reassure her, saying it was only a joke and that the holes would close up quickly. I tried to keep the fishing line in for the holiday, without success, and my pierced ears didn't happen for a few more years.

On the holiday, I was almost always addressed as 'Madam', presenting androgynously. My hair was getting longer, coloured a lighter shade than my natural brown. My mother didn't comment but shook her head each time she heard the collective term 'ladies' being used as we sat in restaurants. I desperately wanted to tell her, to be honest with her, but I felt the time just wasn't right. Would it ever be? I found myself sometimes so frustrated that I would just say, as she found fault with something I was doing 'I'm just doing my best!' Our relationship had changed as I moved forward and that saddened me immensely.

***

TENI developed slowly and it was clear that any progress in the area of trans rights would be difficult to achieve and involve a lot of education of both politicians and the public. But in Europe trans organisations were very well established and we heard of a large European trans conference to be held in Vienna later that year. This brought problems – if I was to travel abroad, I would have to use my male passport, and I didn't want to travel in male mode. Having discussed with Helen the possibility of travelling to the conference I made an appointment with the psychologist I had seen before, to get a diagnosis I could produce at passport control. I was nervous, wondering how he would view my progress.

I had three meetings with him, explaining the increasing but still limited support I had from Helen, how many people I had told, my many outings and the beginnings of my work with TENI. He delved into my past, asking about my childhood influences and when I talked about my love of music and mentioned Bowie in particular he laughed and said I was one of many trans people to be influenced by him.

On my final visit he handed me a letter, a diagnosis of Gender Identity Disorder (GID). He had also sent on my details to Loughlinstown Hospital, the only centre for GID treatment in the country, and told me I would get an appointment with the Gender Identity team in a few months. I was amused by the term as I certainly didn't feel 'disordered' but it was the next step in my journey and I was ecstatic:

> The bearer of this letter ... Is a patient in this clinic, diagnosed with Gender Identity Disorder (302.85). As part of an on-going treatment regime, in accordance with International Standards of Care for this disorder, the patient publicly presents cross-dressed; this includes wigs, clothing and other items. Activities include travel outside Ireland. Your discretion is dealing with this patient is appreciated.

Travelling to the European conference, which resulted in the establishment of Transgender Europe, as Philippa and presenting a male passport caused little more than a raised eyebrow. To me though the act of handing over the document was in essence a sort of 'coming-out' and each time I felt violated that this very personal information was being shared with total strangers.

The conference was held in Vienna's City Hall, a hugely imposing and impressive building, and the programme of events was very political and rights oriented; while I hadn't exactly expected make-up lessons I had expected it to be more general and I was initially a little disappointed. But I learned over the coming days that trans activism was far more militant than in Ireland at that time, more demanding. And more vocal.

> *Nature chooses who will be transgender; individuals don't choose this.*
> Mercedes Ruehl, actress

When calls came for the formation of a Steering Committee for the newly formed Transgender Europe I found myself asking the assembly to accept my nomination. First TENI, now TGEU I thought as I walked back to my seat. But I was delighted at the opportunity to become involved on a bigger stage. As the weekend progressed, I knew it was a pivotal point in my development and indeed in the development of some of my friends who had travelled to the council also.

Steering committee meetings were subsequently held on a regular basis around Europe. Travelling to distant cities for the meetings I would regularly think of Emer and how it would have been wonderful to have her sitting beside me, discussing what we were going to do, the sights to see and flirting with the local men. I sensed however that this visibility and commitment would be a step too far for her, somewhere she and many within the community simply could or would not go. In my work with TENI and now

TGEU I had to try to make it a little bit easier for them.

The steering committee meetings usually had an emphasis on rights and legal issues, no talk of support or services for the community, and I again realised the different emphasis of TGEU and TENI, and on how broadly the majority of the TGEU members interpreted the term transgender, taking it to mean anything from drag queen/king, transvestite or cross-dresser to someone who had or intended to fully transition, medically and socially. I knew that such a broad definition would sit very uneasily with some back in Ireland who viewed the issue as a purely medical one, 'born in the wrong body' as the cliché went, and would be unwilling to accept a more inclusive definition.

Coming back through Dublin airport from TGEU meetings I was always *en femme*, despite still having to travel on my male passport. The meetings gave me the opportunity to learn more about the legal and medical side of transitioning, and of course, give me the opportunity to be myself, truly, for an extended period of time. They were helping my progress immensely.

On one trip I was struggling with my suitcase which had a damaged wheel. So I didn't notice a small shelf near the escalator, and my elasticated bracelet caught, flying apart, beads scattering everywhere.

'Hope it wasn't expensive, dear,' said an elderly woman behind me and I grinned – 'Penney's best,' I replied, and made my way to passport control. The queue was short, plenty of staff dealing efficiently with the crowds. I always loved coming home to Ireland, and I handed over my male passport with a smile. The official glanced at it, looked at me and scowled, throwing the document back at me without a word. I took the passport and carefully placed it back in my handbag, pointedly saying: 'Thank you, and Happy Christmas.' All I got back was a grunt and more scowls. I was furious, my good holiday mood evaporating, and I made a mental note to complain through TENI. His behaviour had been unprofessional and unacceptable and infuriated me.

Walking into the Arrivals Hall and seeing all the smiling faces waiting for their loved ones I made my way to one of the coffee shops. I was too early to go home as it was unlikely Jenny would be in bed and I sat down feeling a tinge of sadness. Protecting her was paramount to me and if I had to deny my own wishes for a little while longer then I was willing to do so. But the time would have to come soon when 'the terrible truth', as some saw it, would have to emerge.

The appointment letter for my initial consultation with the endocrinologist in Loughlinstown arrived shortly after Christmas. It was for February, six weeks away, and I was emotional as I read and re-read the three short lines. I showed it to Helen having texted Emer.

'So, how do you feel about it? Should I go? Don't forget what I said, if you feel I'm going too far or too fast just say so and I'll try to slow down or even stop.'

Helen looked at the letter, and it was clear she realised the implications. 'No, you have to go. It's right for you, that's obvious. It's just that I'm sad at the prospect of being on my own in my fifties, having lost my husband and essentially living with my sister.'

Ouch, that hurt a lot. I was taking a big step and I felt it would be better to work through it together, my best friend and me. But it wasn't the first time she had expressed those feelings. I longed for her to fully accept me and hoped that we could continue our romantic and sexual relationship.

I knew I was never going to stop loving her – maybe she could see through the exterior to the person beneath? Time would tell.

In addition to trans issues, I had learned that the endocrinology department also addressed issues of obesity and other conditions associated with hormonal imbalances. I didn't want to stand out, though obesity was something that wasn't an issue for me, fit and relatively toned as I was. I was no different to anyone else with a minor medical issue though even that thought, following the TGEU conference, was controversial as most of the Europeans did not consider trans to be related in any way to the medical, and especially not the psychological, field. The argument was that trans people had the right to express themselves in any way they wanted, and they shouldn't have to ask permission or expect any special treatment. As much as I agreed with that viewpoint, I would do what was required for me, from a purely selfish point of view.

I took the day off for my appointment in Loughlinstown, dressing as usual in Gemini, then caught the bus past my workplace keeping my head down hoping none of my colleagues would happen to be getting on. What a way to come out in work!

A few hours later and I was truly on the path to medical transition, if not quite on hormones. The endocrinologist was matter of fact, happy with my physical condition but surprised me by asking how quickly I expected to be going for surgery. I was nervous and a little tongue-tied, 'Well I'm not entirely sure. I want to take it slowly and I want to start hormones as soon as possible but I don't really have a time frame in mind for surgery.' I explained how I wanted to give people time to come to terms with my changes, to try to bring people along with me as so many couples ended up separated as a result of this and I really didn't want to be in that situation. He indicated that I would be placed on a very low dose of hormones initially which would be increased depending on how my body reacted.

I knew the process would be long. I had heard from others within the Support Group that there would be twice-yearly health check appointments in Loughlinstown, blood tests and various other meetings and consultations, with psychologists and psychiatrists. Then, once I felt ready to proceed to surgery there would be all the paperwork associated with having surgery paid for in the UK by the HSE. Then the long recovery. Some said it took up to a year for the body to fully recover from the invasive trauma of the operation, with up to twelve weeks off work. Would I cope? Would Helen and Jenny cope? Work? Family? Friends? Again doubts. But again, I felt it was something that I had to do.

Soon after my trip to Loughlinstown, I heard of a fundraiser which was being held in the Mansion House for Katherine Zappone and Ann Louise Gilligan to fund their fight to have their Canadian same-sex marriage recognised by the Irish state. I suggested to Emer that we go, knowing she was always someone who enjoyed something a bit different. The case was at that time under appeal to the High Court and the LGBTQ+ community, 'the Pink Pound', were being asked to help in their legal costs.

I had a wonderful ball gown (worn the previous year to the Concert Hall) and sensed another opportunity to get it out of its protective wrapping.

Emer chose to park that evening in the nearest public car park, directly underneath my office and I was very nervous as I swung my legs out of the car, saying: 'what if the security guys recognise me and record me on cctv? I could be a star when I get into work on Monday!'

Emer just laughed. It was a beautiful summer's evening and I felt wonderful as we walked along the city centre streets. I was with one of my best friends and going to a safe, welcoming and accepting space. It was going to be a good night.

The Round Room in the Mansion House was full of attractive tuxedo-clad men with equally attractive women in some stunning dresses. As we entered the beautiful room Glória, Ireland's LGBTQ+ choir, were singing a funny song and the audience were entranced, some singing along with them. We were seated at a very large round table with ten others, all straight couples it seemed. The meal was enjoyable, the company entertaining and there was no hint from any around the table that they suspected we were anything other than two women out for the evening. Indeed, at one point, while Emer was in the ladies one of the women asked me something: 'I can see there's a spark between you, I was wondering if there was a romantic element to it ...' she asked, smiling. A bit taken aback I wasn't quite sure how to respond but managed to get out 'Well, we're very good friends but we're both married ...' All eyes at the table turned towards me and one of the guys said, with a glint in his eye: 'Ooohhh so you're lovers and your husbands don't know!'

At that point Emer came back to the table, looking a bit confused as all eyes turned towards her and as she sat down I whispered in her ear: 'Listen hon, we're lovers, married to men who don't know about our relationship – just run with it, I'll explain later ...' Emer grinned and said 'ehhh,

Ok?' Before I had a chance to say anything else Katherine and Ann Louise came over to our table and thanked us all. We were a little star-struck but managed to exchange a few words with them and they both became friends some years later when Katherine became a senator and then ran for the Dáil in our constituency, being appointed a minister.

The weather had deteriorated to heavy rain during our lovely evening and we ran back to the car park, laughing at the situation we had found ourselves in. But as she dropped me at my house (having stopped to allow me change out of the ball gown) I looked at her, thinking lovers we may not have been, but she was somebody truly special in my life, who had helped me progress so far, so fast. I looked forward to many other amusing and wonderful evenings with her.

Having to change to male clothes before going home was always painful to me but it did bring some light-hearted moments too. One of my good friends, Sara, dropped me home and allowed me to change in her car in a nearby car park before going into my house. Getting back into her car after 'the change' elicited 'who the fuck are you and what did you do with Philippa? POLICE!!!' We fell around the car laughing, though I was almost in tears too. Because her comment, intended humorously, held so much truth. It felt that Philippa was being murdered every time I changed back to my male persona. But I knew it was getting better. Slowly, so slowly, it was getting better. I climbed the stairs smiling, to kiss my amazing daughter as she slept, thinking that 'Philippa' was becoming the norm and 'Brendan' was gradually fading. My sense of humour was important in getting me through this difficult time and was often commented on. 'May as well look on the funny side,' I would reply, 'moaning won't help much!'

A few weeks before my next consultation with the endocrinologist I was called for a bone density scan. I changed in Gemini, wearing a skirt and top for the trip down to the hospital. It was a lovely spring day and I felt positive, happy at a little more progress, dropping my head only briefly this time as I passed by my workplace on the bus. I asked Helen what the procedure for the scan would be and so was quite relaxed as I got on the scanning table. The machine chugged as I was moved through and the radiographer called out 'Now miss, don't move as the machine scans, it will sound loud and may vibrate but that's perfectly normal.' I was relaxed and happy, especially as the radiographer had used the right prefix. I had been unsure when I arrived at the hospital for my first appointment what to do about my name. My historical medical records to this point were all in my male name, and surely there should be some reference made to that, but the secretary was happy enough to accept me as Philippa James, the name I had taken to using, the referral having been made in that name by the psychologist.

The scan finished and the radiographer asked me to move off the table then said, 'Oh, just wait a minute. Oh, we'd better do that again. 'Em, would you be wearing a suspender belt with metal clasps?'

With some embarrassment I admitted I was, 'I couldn't find any clear tights so just grabbed these!' and the assistant laughed.

'Don't worry, you'd be amazed at some of the metal objects that people have on them. So if you could remove the suspender belt before we do the scan again …?' and I complied, feeling rather ditsy. Helen would kill me if she ever found out.

Whether the radiographer knew of my trans situation

or not, a stereotypical example of what some people think of as trans I certainly did not want to be, and the sexual implications of wearing a suspender belt embarrassed me. But every experience was a learning one and I just resolved to think ahead next time!

A few weeks later, I arrived back at the hospital for my next consultation. It was the day before my forty-fifth birthday and I was excited at the prospect that the next day I might be starting a new life.

'Miss James? Can you come this way?' the secretary called to me and indicated the door. The consultant was sitting at a table as I entered and looked up briefly. 'Hi Philippa, I've reviewed your results and everything seems fine. Now normally we don't prescribe hormones without having some sort of idea as to your transition plans. When would you see yourself going for surgery?'

Surgery. Every time I heard it my heart jumped. It was of course my ultimate goal, as far as the medical aspects of transition were concerned, and of course I had thought about it – but when? As soon as possible but how could I give a date when the majority of my family, work and friends didn't know about this alter – true – ego? I realised that the consultant was still waiting for an answer as I hesitated.

'Well in all honesty I don't know. I would hope to be looking at perhaps three years, but I'm taking this transition very slowly as I want to ensure that as many people stay with me as possible. I have a daughter who doesn't know yet, along with my wider family and I need to inform my workplace as well.'

I began to get worried then, was he going to refuse me hormones because I hadn't progressed far enough?

'That's fine Philippa. There is a limit as to how long you can be on the testosterone blocker Zoladex, so we won't put you on that yet. However, you can start on a very low dose of oestrogen immediately, and let's see how you do.'

The HSE had a reputation of being very cautious with regard to hormonal treatment; in most European countries the dosage would probably be twice what Loughlinstown was prescribing. Yet I was delighted to be on the medical path at last. And at least I didn't have to undergo the two-year 'real-life test' before treatment began, like some countries required. I could request a higher dose later. The consultant filled out a form and handed it to me.

'We'll see you again in three months' time to assess your progress.'

He shook my hand and wished me well and I left the room grinning from ear to ear. It was too late to get the prescription filled at that point, so I went home to tell Helen the news.

The following day, my birthday, I sat in a café with my lunch in front of me. The staff in Boots Pharmacy in St Stephen's Green had been very friendly, no strange comments or looks as I asked for the prescription which lay on the table in front of me. I took out one of the blue pills, looking at it carefully. Yes, there were risks: to my health, to my marriage and maybe even to my job. Yet it was what I had to do, this little pill could help me show my true self to the rest of the world. I placed it on my tongue, took a sip of water and swallowed. The next stage of the journey had begun.

A few minutes later, I got my phone out and sent emotional text messages to Helen and my friends Emer and Sara. Sara replied immediately, mock annoyed that I had managed to get hormones first as we were at roughly the same stage in our transition. Emer was as usual very supportive and happy for me, as was Helen. I sat at the table for a few more minutes, imagining the effects the drugs were having on my body and hoping for breasts before I left for home. A memorable forty-fifth birthday.

Soon I began to notice that my nipples became very sensitive and a little painful. There also began to be tightness around them, as if something was developing. Which of course it was, my breasts. The area became very tender, and if Helen cuddled into me at all I would groan at the discomfort, but all the while smiling. The daily blue pill was having an effect, and soon I began to see a definite swelling. I felt I had sunshine in my stomach. I downloaded a log from the internet to chart my progress, planning on measuring the changes in my body but soon forgot to keep it updated. It was far more preferable to start transitioning at a younger age and I knew I was never going to develop the way I really wanted to. But I also felt that I was getting the best of both worlds with this path. I had the honour and delight of having a wonderful relationship with Helen, getting married and becoming a father to an amazing little girl. Now I had the opportunity to experience at least some of the joys of being the woman I wanted to be and knew I was. Yes, the best of both worlds. I was still me, the person I had always been.

Now that I was firmly on the medical path to transition, I felt it was time to start the process of progressing formally at work. I was unsure as to how to inform my HR department and so I first decided to discuss the situation with my union representative, someone I had known for many years. He had noticed a few changes in my appearance and had wondered about the reason. Having told him, he commented on my bravery, suggesting that I talk to the Employee Assistance Officer (EAO), a civil servant who remains independent from any department and acts as a confidential counsellor for employees.

I was tempted to turn up to the EAO meeting a few weeks later *en femme* but I didn't feel it was appropriate first time round. At this stage I was more confident and well used to telling my story and I was comfortable explaining how I wanted to minimise the disruption to the office and progress without causing any problems, for other staff, management but most especially for me. I made clear that I was aware of my rights, thankful of my experience with TENI and TGEU.

The EAO official looked at me, looked at the 'man' who sat in front of her and smiled, commenting on how the usual discussions she had dealt with were alcohol, drugs or gambling. She asked about my female name, anxious to start using it. As the meeting progressed, I became aware that she was unaware of many of the issues relating to trans and needed some clarifications. Although not as obvious as with some people, she also seemed to be confusing being trans with a person's sexual orientation.

As the session ended, she commented how she would like to meet me as Philippa in a future meeting. The short walk through St Stephen's Green on my way back to work saw me skipping and grinning. The afternoon had meant more to me than I had expected, and I was excited at the prospect of getting everything formalised. Up until this point my double life was spent most of the time in male mode with regular but all too brief forays out as my true self. But over the past year that balance had begun to change, and I knew the next few years were going to be an exciting time.

I felt very guilty with regard to Declan, my oldest friend. Our friendship had yet to be tested by the revelation of myself as Philippa. How would he react? I hoped and expected he would be positive. Yet I couldn't be certain. I didn't want to risk the friendship just yet, managing to stay in touch with phone calls and occasional nights out. But now I wanted more with him, a link to my past, a past at least some of which I was anxious to retain. As I considered my two closest friends, I also thought of my mother and sister, and the wider family. How could I tell them? Depression and frustration: despite the distance I had travelled to that point, all I needed was acceptance and understanding.

These issues, and more, were regularly brought up at the twice-monthly TENI facilitated Support Group meetings. It was of huge benefit to me to hear them aired, by others as well as myself. We all wanted wisdom, a way to navigate the very difficult path we were on. We sought advice from those who had transitioned previously. My transition to date had been good and I tried to show that it was possible to those who were starting out in the process. So many seemed to want everything immediately, frustrated at having to wait, having to continually deny who they were, and I completely understood. Yet I also wanted to show that the slow and gradual route I was taking might just be better for some. But hearing of those who had attempted suicide, the drug use, the alcohol issues that this situation caused reinforced in my mind just how important it was to continue to inform and educate wider society about the issues affecting my community.

As with others in the support group I found the effect

of my hormone regime to be two-fold. My moods were much better in general, far more positive, I felt more optimistic and certain that I was doing the right thing. But I also found myself more emotional, likely to find my eyes welling up at random moments of joy, simple things such as seeing babies smiling and playing the evocative strains of beautiful melodies such as that of Tori Amos, Sigur Rós, Yes or many others. Music had been my saviour over the years as I came to terms with the changes in my outlook and desires and I expected it would always be.

Another reason to be positive were my regular trips to TGEU Steering Committee meetings which took me all over Europe – the expenses were mostly paid as the group was getting a small amount of funding. It was almost as if everything was conspiring to ensure that my transition would be as smooth as possible. The trips increased my confidence and security and being around others in the same situation allowed me to see what was possible, what could be achieved.

Training sessions were held in Manchester, meetings in Vienna, Berlin, Copenhagen, and elsewhere. The work was considerable, but the rewards were plentiful in knowledge and friendships. However, I was always a little nervous travelling to the meetings, going through passport control where I essentially 'outed' myself to every official who looked at the 'male' passport, then at the 'woman' presenting. In most cases, I would get a slightly curious look but during a trip to Berlin I feared I was about to be turned back and refused entry.

As usual I gave over my male passport. But the look on the security official's face was frosty as he looked at it, then me.

'This is not you.' I produced the letter of explanation, my 'diagnosis', and passed it through the hatch. He read it, shook his head and passed both letter and passport to a colleague. No smiles or laughs, they consulted quietly and gave occasional glances in my direction. The queue behind me was building up and I was becoming annoyed and anxious. How ironic that I, a trans activist, fighting for rights, might be refused entry while travelling to a trans activist meeting.

After what seemed like an eternity of discussion and examination, they slowly handed me back my passport and letter, waving me through whilst all the time watching me, no hint of amusement on their stern faces. I was very uncomfortable and stressed, but pleased to get through to the lovely city that was Berlin and ensured I told my TGEU colleagues of the incident as soon as I arrived.

***

Of course as Jenny matured and approached her teenage years, she began to be out with her friends more, shopping in the city centre or just hanging about in the nearby parks. But she always wanted time with us, her kind nature being remarked upon by all who met her. She seemed as happy to be at home with us as with her friends. The closeness of our relationship reminded me of the relationship I had with my mother growing up at that age. Jenny and I were on a similar wavelength and our childish giggling would sometimes erupt at inopportune moments leaving Helen to shake her head at us, grinning nonetheless. For those few moments of bliss I could forget the worries and stress I might have been feeling and just enjoy the company of my two best friends in the world.

As my transition progressed, I became very conscious of my facial hair. I hated shaving! Going out at night inevitably entailed a close shave and it seemed so different to who I was as Philippa. Electrolysis and laser were the standard treatments, and luckily my growth wasn't too dark. Some of the beauticians I went to offered laser treatment and having talked to other trans women for advice, I booked a series of six treatments. I expected to need more, the usual course being twelve or more, but I was anxious to see what improvement there would be. The treatments themselves, using an IPL laser, were painful but manageable and I endured the pain with a smile, knowing it was making me more like the person I wanted the world to see.

The following year I went to a different laser clinic for another series of treatments, where they also prescribed Vaniqa, a cream which would reduce the growth and lighten the colour of the shadow. I had found that, on occasion, especially in the evening, the growth was more noticeable, even if I shaved. And passing as a woman was hugely important to me. Transitioning involves so many changes, so many potential pitfalls, which could derail the entire process. The further I moved along that path the more I realised how difficult it was. I felt it vitally important to portray clearly and unambiguously to the world that what they saw was nothing less than a woman but was that simply bowing to society's expectations? It mattered to me though and showing that woman well involved a lot of work and commitment. To anyone who thought this was taking the easy way out, giving in to my feelings and pretending to be someone I wasn't I would clearly and emphatically list all the hoops I had to jump through to get to where I desperately needed to go.

Another major area for improvement were my teeth which had been a mess following an accident when I was a teenager. I was extremely self-conscious about them and reluctant to smile. So, biting the bullet and looking forward to a big bill I had a lot of dental work carried out over the course of nine months. The results were excellent and the smile, which had been hidden for many years, now reflected in so many ways the happiness I was feeling inside.

At one point, I was wandering around the house, tidying up and feeling quite frustrated at the mess that three people could make. I stopped and smiled. 'Hey hon,' I called to Helen. 'How do you find my moods since I started on oestrogen? I feel happier and calmer, my mind seems much clearer.' Helen agreed and said that she had always hated the moods that I got into, when I gave her the silent treatment rather than having the good screaming match that she would like.

'Now it feels like you're content inside, that you're more the true you. No, I'm happy with the changes!'

A few weeks later I went to see the psychologist again, at his insistence 'just to keep a check on your progress now that you're on hormones' he had said. When I arrived I was pleased to be able to chat freely, indeed I was encouraged to. He was unsurprised to hear that I felt I had a clearer mind, felt like I could do anything. It was a common feeling he explained. Most trans women expressed the same sentiments. I felt on an upward curve, as if I was heading towards infinite happiness …

Although I was on a path to transition of my own timescale and choosing, I realised that the upcoming meeting with the human resource manager in my civil service department was a turning point. It wouldn't be true to say that there would be no going back, yet once I 'came out' to the HR manager I felt it would be difficult and embarrassing to step back. I was in drab mode, of course, as I walked through the doors of the main office of my department, the other side of the city to my usual office.

I walked into the bright room, seeing the female HR manager at the desk by the window. A little small talk and then we moved on to the serious issue.

'The EAO has told me a little about your situation without going into detail, so I'm here to listen to whatever you need to tell me,' she said, reassuringly. 'Is everything all right?'

I smiled and said: 'yes indeed, it's nothing serious ... well, not really anyway!'

I took some photos from my bag and put them on the table between us. 'I'm transgender, this is me in the photos and I am currently undergoing hormonal treatment with a view to having surgery in the not too distant future. I've taken everything slowly and with as much consideration for other people as I can up until this point, so I'm just informing you of my plans and to see what procedures I have to go through to complete the transition in the PRA from who you see now to Philippa, what legal changes are required and so on.'

I sat back, waiting for a reaction. She looked at the photos, complimenting me on my style and general appearance.

'Well, eh, *Philippa*, this will be an interesting situation. First of all, I'd like to reassure you that we will support you fully through your transition. I haven't heard of anyone else in the civil service doing this so we'll be keen to ensure that the process goes smoothly for both you and us. One aspect that immediately springs to mind is bullying and harassment, has there been any indication of that at all?'

Once I assured her that there hadn't been she moved on. 'And the other issue that I've just thought of is bathrooms. It could become a little awkward.'

'Yes, already I feel uncomfortable using the male toilets and once I complete my legal change I will expect to be using the appropriate facilities. I obviously don't want to cause any problems but I do have to consider my own mental wellbeing. Using the male toilets is stressful and upsetting for me now, and likely to get worse as I get closer to transition. I expect to be completing my Deed Poll name change in a couple of years or so, and we have that length of time to get things in place.'

'Yes, we have time,' she said, 'and we have to consider other people's feelings as well, but we'll work it out. Perhaps the disabled bathrooms may be an option. In the meantime, is there anything else you want to discuss?' I informed her of the regular hospital appointments that were now required, and how I needed to present as female at the hospital for my own mental wellbeing and she assured me that if I got a medical certificate from the consultant for each visit I could take the entire day off, which should help me relax.

'Your sick leave is very good anyway so there's no problem there,' she said. We shook hands and I made my way down the stairs with my hips swaying and a smile on my face. But I was less than impressed with the suggestion that I use the disabled bathrooms. I was not disabled, and to even consider using them would feel like a betrayal of everything I was working on with TENI and TGEU. But another small step forward at least.

When I got back to my desk later, I saw a group of my work colleagues, all male, stood around heatedly debating an issue. I felt drawn into the conversation and stood up saying in a slight falsetto voice: 'Well, really I do feel that it should be done *this* way', and gestured in a very flamboyant way, turning and walking away to silence from the group. A few days later, my colleague who sat behind me made a comment about the incident. I smiled and said: 'So have you guessed about me then? Did that twirl give it away?' He looked embarrassed. 'No, guessed what?'

'Oh well, if you don't want to know then fine,' I said, feigning mock annoyance, 'but I think you've guessed.' I was grinning broadly now. He was someone who I got on well with and I felt that telling him would be another step forward, yet a safe step. It was also obvious that he was curious about me, and I felt that there might be an element of denial on his part too, that perhaps my 'gaydar' was picking him out.

'Oh I'm going to tell you anyway, because you've guessed a lot of it. I'm not gay, but I am transgender', and I went on to explain my situation and my plans for the future. Again, I had to explain the difference between sexual preference and gender identity, and I felt, every time I went to explain what trans was that I had to first state that I wasn't gay. My sexual preferences were my own business. It was comp-licated enough explaining about the change to my gender without trying to explain about my bisexuality too.

His reaction was a little disappointing, but then the majority of men had been the same. He seemed awkward and unsure of what to say. I was relaxed however and put him at ease by saying that shortly everyone would know as my transition progressed to a point where I started wearing skirts and dresses to work. I got the impression that this was something he simply could not comprehend, and I was disappointed. I saw I still had some way to go with preparing the office for the big 'shock'.

I began to tell other close colleagues about my plans. During one coming-out lunch I told my colleague how I wanted to stand on a tall building and shout to the world 'I'm PHILIPPA!' There were tears in her eyes as she squeezed my hand and asked how I could sleep with the stress and the pain. 'Because I know I'll get there. It's what sustains me, that belief.'

9

DISCLOSURE

Age: 47–48

Einstein had said: 'Life is like riding a bike. To keep your balance you need to keep moving.' I was certainly moving, flying even. My transition was going as well as I could have hoped. Yes, there were problems, delays and arguments but overall, and certainly compared to others, I was progressing towards where I wanted and needed to be very quickly. Yet … despite all the positive comments, the compliments and the seeming acceptance I worried about the path ahead. I still had to tell my mother, my sister, some friends. Could something still stop me? I tried to put myself in their shoes. How would I have reacted if an effeminate man came and told me that 'he' was really 'she' if I hadn't had to face it myself? Ireland had moved on since the 1970s and attitudes towards the gay community had improved yet there was still so much further to go. And trans rights had even further to go. The media were still quite likely to 'out' trans people with lurid headlines and as my profile grew as part of TENI and TGEU I feared being the subject of their gaze.

I found my interest in sex unaffected by the mild dose of oestrogen though I knew that would change dramatically after I started on Zoladex, the hormone that suppresses testosterone production and brings it down to a normal female level, although that was in the future. I was keen to retain intimacy with Helen but we both now wanted a male touch, and I knew that Helen was reluctant and even unable to participate fully with me now that my female body was developing, my breasts grew and my skin softened. Even my shape was changing a little, fat was being redistributed somewhat and I was increasingly happy each time I looked in the mirror. At one point I was desperate enough to suggest a threesome with a man, hoping that might bring us both some relief. She freaked at the suggestion and it caused days of silence and tension between us.

But I felt so much for Helen, understanding her reluctance and resistance and yet frustrated that she could not accept me fully yet. I simply couldn't be what I knew Helen wanted me to be yet she showed her love for me in so many different ways. We had so much in our relationship, this was just one challenge in our incredible love. I was positive we would get to the end of this journey, this mutual transition, together.

***

The trips to Europe for TGEU meetings continued on a regular basis, as did the work with TENI. I was elected to chair of TENI and was delighted to be able to welcome a couple of enthusiastic new committee members who were to help take the organisation in the direction it needed to go. Cat and Leslie were a breath of fresh air and the make-up of the committee now allowed a lot of work to be done which simply could not have been completed previously as the rest of the committee were struggling with their own issues around gender identity. TENI grew into a broader organisation, trying to cater for and address lifestyles and choices that it wouldn't have been able to in the earlier years when there was a much greater emphasis on surgery and male-to-female issues. From the outside it might have seemed as if we were splitting hairs but the differences between cross-dresser, transvestite and transsexual, and their accompanying needs and requirements, caused huge friction within TENI and to a lesser degree TGEU. Funding for TENI became a real possibility and with the help of Cat and Leslie a very strong proposal was presented to The Atlantic Philanthropies that was ultimately successful. TGEU struggled on, achieving much politically but also enduring a lot of disagreements and faction-fighting.

Many of my colleagues in the various groups told of how they had lost close friends over their trans status. I was concerned that perhaps Declan could be lost to me. He was my oldest friend. We had shared so much together since we discovered our common interests in boys' hobbies such as chess and science fiction. He always made me want to be better.

I had felt over the past years, as I explored my female identity, that Declan had been left out. I was nervous of telling him, for fear of his rejection would hit me very hard. Intelligent people still had deep-felt beliefs and opinions that might run contrary to a more broad-minded attitude, and the LGBTQ+ sphere was something we had never touched on.

On one of our regular evenings together we were sitting chatting about the usual stuff, playing chess in my living room. Helen and Jenny were in bed and I thought to myself that now was the time. Now or never. I took a deep breath and said: 'Dec, I have something I want to talk about with you. It's a difficult thing to say but it involves who I am and what I want to do in the future. You have been one of my very closest friends and I feel now is the time to tell you. Indeed, I probably should have done it some time ago.'

Declan looked up from the chessboard, concerned. I reached over to take the photo album out of my bag.

'For many, many years I have felt there is a part of me that I haven't been able to express, a huge element to my basic self that has remained hidden from the world and even to some degree myself. But over the past few years I have started to explore this, and what you see in the photographs is the result ...' I passed over the photo album which contained some of my favourite images. Declan looked carefully at each one.

'I should say Dec that of course this is me. The female name I've chosen is Philippa, there's a story attached.' Declan continued to look through the photos and I began to get a bit worried, but when he looked up there was emotion evident on his face.

'Wow,' he said. 'This is a surprise. It's nothing like I thought you were going to say, but now that you say it, yes, it makes so much sense. Wow.' We both laughed and moved from the table to sit side by side on a couch.

'Now that I know it makes so much sense. I have felt over the past few months, maybe longer, there was something you weren't telling me, and I felt our friendship was suffering. I knew you would tell me in time, when you were ready, but I had no idea that it was this! I'm genuinely happy for you, ehh, *Philippa*, and that's going to take time to get used to, and I'm honoured you have told me.' We embraced, both with tears in our eyes and laughed again.

'This will be so interesting,' said Declan, 'to see you progress. What are your plans for the future? I'm sure Helen knows?' and I nodded,

'Yes, and is very supportive, but not Jenny. Not yet.' We moved back to the table and the chessboard.

'I think it's important to tell her sooner rather than later,' he said. 'Kids are very receptive, especially when they are young. As she gets older and starts to have her normal teenage issues this will be more difficult for her.' I knew he was right but Jenny was the one person in the world that I feared most in telling. Rejection by her would be a devastating blow.

'Thanks so much Dec for being so understanding. I look forward to being able to go out with you as Philippa soon.'

'Yes, I'm really looking forward to that,' he said.

I went to bed with my head full of ideas, hopes and emotions. A huge step forward.

I felt a wave of emotion wash over me – it had all happened so quickly, I had been building up to telling Declan for so long, desperately wanted to tell him, now he knew and here we were planning a night out together. Each person I told and who accepted me made the journey more bearable. The few who hadn't accepted me were becoming irrelevant. At times during my transition I felt I was in such a hole that I could have gone spelunking. Declan's acceptance had me soaring amongst the stars.

A few days later I met him as Philippa. A meal and then a film passed in a blur. Declan had always been kind and considerate but seeing him now treating me as a woman impressed me so much more. He was polite and attentive, and I was enjoying his company immensely. Even with a long enjoyable walk as we looked for his car afterwards, with me joking about my feet in high heels and Declan looking increasingly embarrassed only added to the fun.

The subject of Jenny had come up on the way home, again.

'She's a clever kid, it'll be a shock, but children are very adaptable and accepting. The earlier you tell her the better.' This was what I was hearing from so many people.

'And how about your Mum, does she know?' asked Declan

I shook my head. 'No Dec, I'm afraid of what it might do to her. She's not very accepting of change, she would find it very difficult to accept me I imagine.'

'Yes, but you have to live your life. If you keep it all in you're only hurting yourself and, eventually, everyone else because you'll be so stressed out. Her feelings about the issue are irrelevant, you have to be yourself. You're her child. She should accept you.'

We chatted for a while longer, changing the subject as it was becoming difficult. I thought later about Declan's words. Was it time to start asserting myself a little more? I lay in bed, excited but also thinking of the huge challenges ahead.

Shortly afterwards I organised a night out with both Declan and Gerry from work. There was to be no going back for me from now on, and again I thought of what some friends had to endure, a divide, a chasm between their desired self and their 'real-world' life, which could never be crossed. Both of these men knew me very well and both now had the challenge of seeing a part of me that they had not known of. This transition was more than just a personal one, it affected so many others. Everyone needed time to come to terms with it, to cope with it in their own individual way, perhaps never actually accepting. It was a seismic quake in the relationships built up over the course of my life.

Yet sitting in the restaurant it was in some ways as if nothing had changed, we were just three good friends out for a night. I could see with Declan it had however, he was attentive and gentlemanly, at one point making me laugh by standing up as I stood to go to the bathroom. I dragged them both (willingly) to a nearby gay bar, Dragon, where cocktails, music and lots of chat followed and I enjoyed their reactions as I described 'the op' and some of the aftercare. Gerry had talked about seeing the procedure on television, all the gruesome detail, and I was amused to think that it was something I really hadn't seen, yet here I was expecting to be on the operating table in a few years. They quizzed me, asking if I was afraid if I saw it I would change my mind? I knew it wouldn't.

***

One of my regular TENI meetings had dragged on and I was just getting ready to go home when my mobile phone rang. It was Helen. 'Jenny has been asking where you are and why you're out so much. I think she's worked out the situation or at least most of it. It might be time to have *the conversation.*'

Helen's words chilled me. I could hear the italics in her voice, there was no doubt as to what conversation we were going to have. It was a *conversation* I had been dreading, knowing it had to happen but hoping it never would, that Jenny would realise and accept me more by osmosis, by my constant hints and gradual shift from male to female appearance. Never one for confrontation (did that make me weak?) this was really something I didn't want to face.

An hour later, I opened the front door. Helen greeted me and said, 'Jenny is upstairs getting ready for bed. She has guessed, she's a clever kid. You've been quite obvious recently and I think it's reached the point where she needs to know. It may be difficult, but I think it's for the best …'

I nodded. 'But just one thing …' and I looked at Helen.

'Thanks for everything so far. I couldn't have come this far without you. It'll all work out, don't worry. Jen has a good head on her shoulders and will cope with the news.' But even as I said the words my heart was fluttering, my voice unsteady, a sick feeling in my stomach.

A few minutes later our twelve-year-old daughter came downstairs to give me a hug before bedtime.

'Hi Jen, listen there's something Mum and I want to talk to you about. Come into the lounge and we'll have a little chat.' There was a look of worry on Jenny's face as she sat on the sofa. I could see from her face she was upset; did she really know what was to be revealed? Imagination can play tricks on the mind, sometimes elevating the commonplace to the dramatic. This definitely counted as dramatic.

The room was quiet, cat asleep in front of the fire, the usually busy road devoid of traffic and the universe seemed to be contriving to increase the immensity of the moment. Helen and I sat either side of Jenny, holding her delicate hands in ours.

'I think you have guessed most of what I am going to tell you,' I said nervously, 'but we both think it's time that we tell you the complete truth.'

Jenny looked emotional, as if she was about to cry.

'For many, many years, really since I was a little boy, I have felt different. It has taken me a long time to find out why, but over the past few years I have realised what it is that I am feeling …' and I went on to describe some of my nights out, the work I was doing with TENI and TGEU, the reasons for so many trips away. As I spoke I watched Jenny and was overcome with emotion. The news was obviously painful to her but she was coping. When I finished talking Jenny nodded.

'I knew most of it, sometimes letters would arrive for Philippa and I knew they were for you. And I had seen the clothes in your wardrobe, the bigger shoes. So I really did know.'

Such wisdom from one so young.

'This is something we will work on together,' said Helen. 'Dad's not going to do anything more in the near future, you can settle into school and then we'll see where we are. Is that ok?' Jenny nodded.

'I was afraid you were going to get divorced and our family would be split up. I couldn't take that,' said Jenny, her voice quivering.

'Jen honey that is not going to happen. And before you go to secondary school in September, we'll take you to a woman who deals with children in difficult situations, who can help you get through this.'

Jenny nodded again and moved to get off the sofa.

'Can I still call you Daddy though?'

'Of course, baby,' I said, 'as long as you want!'

'Hey,' said Helen, 'we've come this far, and we'll get through it. We'll work it all out, don't worry, it'll all be alright.' We stood up and had an emotional family hug, squeezing each other tightly.

Jenny was on the stairs to her room when she turned and said: 'you have to be who you really are. I love you.'

'That's some kid we have,' I said to Helen who turned to give me a gentle, tender kiss. I knew I would do my utmost to keep my family together. If it were a choice between my family and my dreams then I would choose my family. Tonight had been such a huge moment for us all and Jenny's lovely acceptance of who I truly was had given me such hope. As Helen and I sat side by side in the still quiet room we were still holding hands, smiling. I lay in bed that night thinking about all the challenges I faced, we faced, but we would face them together, united, as we always had been.

***

Some furniture was due to be delivered sometime that day, so I had arranged the morning off and Helen managed to get home by lunchtime to allow me to get to work. We sat on the couch together, having a quick lunch before I cycled into the city centre. It had been an amazing summer with regard to my gradual transition and I was in a rare place mentally: I was happy and confident.

'So, I was thinking about next week and maybe going out for a meal with our good friend Margaret. We could get Mum to look after Jen.'

Helen nodded. 'Yes, it's been a while since we saw Margaret. That could be fun.'

Now for the big question. 'I was thinking it could be Philippa who went out with you. You know I bumped into Margaret a few weeks ago in Outhouse at the Gay Trekkies group and told her about myself …' My heart thumped as I struggled to get the words out. Our mutual friend had come out as lesbian some time previously and I thought the common ground between us might reassure Helen.

Helen was shaking her head. 'No. I couldn't do that. Don't ask me that. The day I go out with you in public is the day that I fully accept you. I don't see that happening.'

I felt my heart sink.

'That's very harsh hon. You're giving me no hope. I've told you I won't progress if you don't want me to, now you're saying you can't see yourself ever accepting me?' I found myself getting annoyed and upset.

'I've tried to do this as slowly as I can, but the time has come for us to start going out together, I feel. If you're telling me there's no possibility of you ever accepting me then what's the point in me going on? I may as well give up on hormones and stop going out. I always said I wouldn't allow this to break us up...' Helen was also upset.

'Just leave it. I meant what I said. If we ever go out together then I've accepted you. It's too soon.'

***

As so often happened, I lay in bed that night restless, worrying and fearing the future. So often I felt on a knife-edge and a comment one way or the other could badly affect me, tipping me towards positivity or negativity. Was I being blind to reality? Was the seeming acceptance being shown by Helen likely to be withdrawn? I had to be true to myself, yes, but at what cost? Helen was my best friend, my soul-mate. Why couldn't she see through the outer shell to the person beneath? Was I being unfair?

But a few weeks later, the opportunity arose again. Margaret had phoned me about the night out and had mentioned how she'd love to see Helen too. So I mentioned the call casually one evening after dinner. Perhaps Helen had had time to think about the situation since our discussion. It was so important to give people time as difficult as it was for me.

'Ok, I suppose it's time we went out,' she said. 'How about going to Tante Zoé's? It's been a while.'

'So I'll come straight from the TENI meeting? I'll be en femme? Because that's how Margaret wants to meet me?'

'Yes, ok, but you'll have to change before we pick up Jenny from Mum's.'

'Yes, I'll figure out somewhere to do it,' I said, barely able to get the words out and smiling broadly.

A few days later following the TENI meeting and wearing jeans, heels and a colourful blouse, I made my way to meet Helen and Margaret. Helen was sitting at a table in the restaurant, with her head in a book and didn't see me come in. I sat down beside her, thinking how like our daughter she was in her love of reading. Shortly afterwards we were joined by Margaret. Hugs all around and we settled into our chairs for a very pleasant evening.

The conversation touched on LGBTQ+ issues but was equally likely to turn to Jenny, *Star Trek* or opera, Margaret's passion. Helen seemed relaxed, at ease and in the taxi on the way home a few hours later I asked her how she had felt during the day. Did she feel conspicuous being with me?

'Not at all. It felt natural, normal. Nobody gave us a second glance. It was a good night, and lovely to see Margaret again. But leave it at that, I don't really want to talk about it.' Give her time, give her time, I told myself.

I slept fitfully that night. This had been such a huge leap forward for both of us that my mind would simply not quieten, excited by the possibilities. This was a major hurdle crossed, the sort of moment that made the difficulties and the pressure more bearable. The evening would live in my memory forever.

A few weeks later, I suggested to Helen that she come with me to meet the TGEU committee who had travelled to Dublin to meet TENI. I was surprised and delighted when she agreed and we had a very pleasant night chatting and sharing stories with the large group in a crowded Japanese restaurant, a night Helen later said was a major turning point and instrumental in showing her that our life together could really work. It was a long way from the sentiments she had expressed just a few short months before. Everyone needed time to come to terms with such a huge change in my outward appearance and if it took me many years to accept myself how could I expect others to do it overnight?

We were in town on Saturday as usual, Jenny just back from her dance and drama classes, and going for lunch. As we walked through the shoe department, I saw a pair I liked, thinking about the upcoming TENI party. Helen and Jenny were nearby, and Jenny came over to me.

'Ooooh, nice,' she said, 'they'd suit you, with a nice black dress.'

I felt my eyes well up with tears, looking across to Helen who had heard and was smiling. I found my size in the shoes (being sandals I could just about manage with an 8) and bought them. Whether I wore them or not, the support and acceptance shown by Jenny made me feel so proud and emotional. I could never throw that pair out! Jenny had by now seen a few photos of me as Philippa and had even seen me coming home dressed at one point. She seemed increasingly comfortable with the situation, though I was aware that there was a line I could not cross with her yet, of going out in public with her or being seen by her friends. But I was confidant that time would come. There was no real hurry. Slowly, gradually, by osmosis. My mantra. I had waited this long and I could wait longer. Couldn't I? Her initial fears, of the break-up of our lovely family, of Helen and I splitting up, were foremost in her mind and she seemed much happier knowing that we were unlikely to get divorced. We hadn't gone into detail with Jenny about the actual details of my transition, feeling that it might upset her. But her support and understanding helped me so much.

At one of my appointments in St Colmcille's Hospital in Loughlinstown, I asked about progressing to the next stage, of taking the testosterone blocker Zoladex. This was a big step as it implied that I was thinking of surgery; the consultant was reluctant to allow patients to remain on Zoladex for more than two years due to the perceived side effects. I was considering my future as Philippa, the most immediate being my name change the following year and I felt now was the time for further physical progress. Having listened to me talk for some time about my plans, the consultant agreed and filled out the prescription for the next step in the process.

A few days later, I received the first injection from my GP, Edel. I had told her some months previously about my trans status, in preparation for my progression. I wasn't surprised to find a kind-hearted and understanding person, somewhat helped by the common gender between us. It seemed much easier for women to accept me transitioning to female than for men to accept that I was leaving the privileged male gender as some men saw it! I enjoyed chatting to Edel and it was interesting how she had always picked up on the times when I was upset or stressed, usually due to arguments or disagreements with my mother, the lack of understanding shown by people being a source of amazement to her.

But today was a joyful one and I grinned as she inserted the large needle into my stomach. 'Bye bye sex drive' I said aloud, causing Edel to laugh.

'It won't go completely you know?' she said.

'Oh I know, it's just it has caused me trouble in the past and I'm looking forward to it being a bit reduced.'

'Let's see how you do anyway, don't want it disappearing completely,' she said with a smile.

***

Initially the effect of the testosterone blocker caused a strong increase in libido, as the male body fought to keep the sexual urges going, but after a few weeks I noticed that my desire was decreasing. On one level, I did miss the intimacy and wished, once again, for a way for Helen to accept me fully as a woman. I wanted her to hold me, to caress and kiss my developing breasts, to gently stroke my now considerably softer skin and smooth legs. But the remaining visible element of my male anatomy was a complication that spoiled the clean lines of my body. No, Helen was doing her best, I knew, and intimacy between us as women would have to wait until after my operation.

***

So much happens an Irish kitchen, so many discussions and arguments and over the years, it had been a place of joy and happiness for my mother and I as we developed our relationship. It overlooked a large back garden which was surrounded by large laurel bushes. Today however there was an autumnal chill in the air and I was looking forward to getting in front of the blazing fire in the lounge.

I was starting to clear up after dinner when my mother said: 'I want you to stop wearing make-up. It's making you look too feminine.'

The comment took me by surprise. I had been wearing my usual androgynous clothes with a hint of make-up for the regular Sunday afternoon trip to my mother. Jenny was in the other room, Helen was working on-call, so it was just the two of us in the kitchen. I sensed this might be the moment, took a deep breath and said: 'Well, that's the intention.'

My mother stared at me.

'What do you mean?' she asked, a curious quiver in her voice.

'Well Mum, there's a reason I have been wearing make-up and slightly feminine clothes. Many years ago, I realised that I had certain feelings, that I wasn't comfortable being male and so I went to a doctor to discuss it. Basically, I should have been born a woman, and I'm now taking steps to become that woman. Slowly and carefully.'

My mother sat opposite me, shaking her head.

'I can't accept that.' I was a little shocked at her vehemence.

'Well, that's how it is. I was unhappy for many years as I grew up because I didn't recognise or understand the feelings that I had. It was very difficult for me, keeping it from you and Dad. I so wanted to say something but because I didn't understand what I was feeling I couldn't say anything.'

My mother looked at me in disbelief. 'You mean you've had these "feelings" for years? That's ridiculous. I would have known. You couldn't have hidden them from me.'

'Nonetheless Mum, it's true. I have been dressing since I was in my early teens. I used to wear Shirley's school uniform when the two of you were out. But let's not talk about it anymore, I want to give you time to think about it. It's not something to be worried about, it's much more acceptable now than it used to be.'

My mother shook her head.

'No, it's ridiculous. I don't believe it. What about my reputation? What will the neighbours think? What about my family?'

And then almost as an aside, 'what about Jenny? What about Helen? Have you not thought about them?'

'What about me, your child, Mum?' I desperately wanted to say but instead I replied: 'of course I have Mum. Both Helen and Jenny know and fully support me, as I had hoped you would. But I see how difficult it is for you.'

'This stays here, in this kitchen. No one outside is to know. I will never accept this, it's ridiculous. What about my reputation? And the neighbours and family?' she repeated.

We sat at the kitchen table in silence and finished our drinks. What more could I have done? How much longer could I have waited to tell her? I was forty-five, not getting any younger. I was very upset but really not surprised. I tried to put it down to her generation's view of life, but still it hurt, terribly. She, her style and femininity had been so important in my seeing who I truly was. Was she to 'blame'? No, but having her in my life was hugely influential and went a long way to making me who I was, sitting across the table from her.

The following day I rang my mother to chat. The call was a difficult one for both of us. But another bridge had been crossed.

We would regularly bring my mother out for lunch at weekends, and often as we walked into restaurants we would be greeted with: 'Good afternoon ladies, table for four?' Of course I was pleased, being acknowledged again as female despite being dressed in my usual androgynous manner but it was always clear my mother was less than impressed, visibly wincing at each interaction and at times it became too much and she would say: 'Oh for God's sake can she not see you're a man! She's just not looking', not realising that her lack of acceptance was hurting me as much as my external changes were hurting her. Both she and I were clearly longing for the return of the relationship we had enjoyed some years back but it was likely to take time, if ever.

There was still hope for our relationship I felt. At one point she said, more kindly: 'I think about you and worry about you every night. I just wish you would go back to the way you were, the way you were born.'

'But that just isn't me Mum', nevertheless as I spoke her head shook and I could see her lip tremble. Grasping at straws, I suggested she see our mutual doctor.

'No,' she said. 'This stays between us. I certainly don't need someone to tell me what I know. You were born a man. You are a man. This stays between us.'

I couldn't let the moment pass however. 'Mum, with the changes I'm undergoing it will come out at some point. It's much better to deal with the situation now, while you have a chance to control it, rather than meeting me in town some Saturday with Ann and Pat (her sisters). If I'm seen by them wearing a dress, how can we explain it in the middle of the street? Wouldn't it be much better to have it all explained beforehand when we can control it?'

The arguments continued, almost every time we saw each other. Time, give her time I told myself again. My journey of discovering the true me was going to hurt some people yet I hoped people would come to see that the path I was taking would be better for all in time. The wonderful relationship we had as I grew up was at serious risk.

***

At home, we were handing around presents early on Christmas morning as usual.

'Oh, what's this hon?' as Helen handed me a large present, grinning.

'Well, open it!' I carefully undid the wrapping and took out a beautiful handbag. This was the first time that Helen had really acknowledged me as Philippa at Christmas and the handbag was a wonderful affirmation of me and more importantly how she saw us as progressing as a couple. But it was also a pivotal moment because it was given to me with Jenny present who was grinning as she saw my joy at the bag. An ordinary Christmas had turned into a memorable one and again I was emotional and so grateful for the two wonderful women in my life.

With a lovely family Christmas over, I faced into the New Year with more optimism than I had felt in some time. I had discovered through my work with TENI and my visits to St Colmcille's hospital in Loughlinstown that there was a defined path to follow to surgery. The initial psychological diagnosis was only the first step. It had allowed me to begin basic hormone treatment. A psychiatric confirmation of my 'condition' was required, along with the 'real-life' test where I would have to begin to live in my desired gender permanently for up to two years, change my name by Deed Poll, then apply for funding from the HSE. From my discussions with the psychologist I found that my very public work with TENI, TGEU and the amount of time I was actually out as Philippa would count a lot towards the real-life test requirement. I was confident that as soon as I wanted surgery I could have it, as long as I could get funding. I was unwilling for a number of reasons to try to fund the surgery myself, feeling that as a tax-payer with a recognised 'medical condition' that I was entitled to be treated as I needed to be.

However, getting a referral to a psychiatrist was more difficult than I imagined, and I mentioned the requirement to my GP. My local psychiatrist was coincidentally at the hospital where Helen worked and it was a straightforward process, though not quick, to get an appointment. Early in 2008, I turned up for my appointment.

The waiting room was crowded. Until this point, I had not cared about the requirement for a psychiatric diagnosis but here, in the waiting room, were people whom I could not identify with. Here I felt as though I was being seen as having a mental issue, a disorder. I felt upset at having to be here, justifying my very identity to some stranger.

I was shown into the consultation room to meet the psychiatrist, confidently entering the space that could define my future. The psychiatrist began his assessment. 'So Philippa, I'm to give a report on your mental health and your suitability for Gender Reassignment surgery. The main reason of course is to ensure that there is no other underlying cause or reason for your desire to progress to surgery. So tell me about yourself and how you come to be here …'

Forty-five minutes later I left the room, having recounted my story – yet again – and ended with a warm handshake from the psychiatrist who confirmed that, in his opinion, there was no other underlying cause for my 'condition' and that he was satisfied that I was *compos mentis* and ready for the emotional and physical trauma that surgery would cause.

The official letter arrived a few days later and I showed it to Helen.

'See! I'm *not* mad!'

Helen just shook her head, looking amused, and commented that she didn't fully believe the diagnosis. It was another step forward. The letter stated:

On examination she was fully dressed as a female with a lady's trouser suit, cosmetics, jewellery and a fair wig. She sat back throughout the interview and was relaxed with good eye contact. I found her very pleasant and personable, she spoke well. It was all coherent and relevant with normal tone and volume and female pitch. Her affect was reactive, her mood was normal, she denied any sustained periods of high or low mood over the years and she denied any excessive worry.

She had no sense of any external influence or control on her, no thought insertion, she felt all her feelings and thoughts and actions were hers, and she had no sense of any kind of paranormal activity or spirits or different dimensions. Overall, there is no evidence of any psychosis.

***

Jenny's acceptance was vital to me and I anxiously looked towards her when anything about my transition came up. It was going to be a difficult time for her as she progressed through secondary school with exams, friends, boyfriends and lots of new challenges. I so hated being one of the challenges, a problem to overcome, but as I saw her develop into a strong and confident woman I felt she would cope. Her occasional comments about me, always positive or humorous, were wonderful. Going out with her and Helen for a meal, to the cinema or even shopping and seeing her acceptance of my very feminine appearance meant the world to me. And on the rare occasion we bumped into her school friends I ensured I stayed in the background, as I did in general with her school activities. I felt so sad at having to essentially be invisible, but I knew it was for the best for us all. In time it would change.

***

I approached the airport gate, noticing an older and stern looking security official checking passports. I handed my passport to him, somewhat nervously.

'I'm sorry Madam,' he said. 'This appears to be, ehh, your husband's passport? Would he have yours?'

'Ah, excuse me. If you wouldn't mind reading this certificate …' and I produced my letter from the psychologist stating that I was trans and explaining my situation. It was one of the few times I had ever had to produce the document and it was somewhat battered from being in my purse for perhaps three years. The security official's face softened, and he smiled.

'Madam, thank you. That is perfectly fine,' and he lowered his voice. 'I wish you well on your personal journey.'

I nodded, barely able to speak, tears in my eyes at receiving such a lovely comment.

'Thank you so much,' I managed to utter and made my way down the gangway to the airplane, tears rolling down my cheeks. It was one of the most memorable moments in my life to that date. Simple things, simple words. Acceptance.

***

Later that year we travelled to the US on one of our visits to see The Mouse in Disney.

The airport security official approached me, saying: 'Excuse me madam, would you mind if I just checked you. It's a random process and your seat number was chosen. If you could give your passport to my colleague …?'

'Of course,' I replied as she began to pat me down. As her hands moved up my legs her colleague yelled to her: 'Mary, wait! That's a GUY!'

The security guard jumped back from me, horror apparent on her face.

'I'm so sorry, ehh, sir …?'

Her face was flushed, and her colleague looked concerned. I just laughed and said: 'that's quite ok, it happens all the time. Can I go and catch my family now?'

I picked up the carry-on bag, took my passport from the flustered male guard and made my way down the gangway to the plane, breaking up in laughter as I recounted the incident quietly to Helen who just shook her head, grinning.

'They were just worried about a lawsuit,' she said. 'You know how litigious the US is! How *could* they mistake you for a woman with your long blonde hair, heels, make up and girly blouse, honestly …'

***

Foremost in my mind as I moved forward were Helen and Jenny. Their support and understanding was making this process all the more possible and I couldn't imagine the difficulties I would have had without it. And all the time I saw Jenny undergoing her own amazing transition from child to young woman. Young, capable, beautiful. Intelligence, humour and wit. I wanted to reassure her, to tell her that I saw the end of my journey making our family a stronger, happier one. Most of me believed this, yet part of me also worried that it could yet go badly. I desperately wanted to talk to her about what we were both going through, exploring our new bodies, our new emotions and sensations. But I settled for simple answers to the occasional questions or comments she would make, knowing that the time would come when we could discuss this part of our mutual lives together.

***

I enjoyed the Sunday morning workout in the gym, glad of the opportunity to vent my frustrations on the equipment.

But my mood was still a bit low as I wandered through the cosmetics hall of Brown Thomas. 'Coffee,' I thought and decided to try the new restaurant on the top floor.

The waitress smiled as she took my order. I felt comfortable, my mood improving. My phone bleeped, a text message. Probably Helen or Jenny. No, it was a message from an unknown number. Looked foreign. I nervously opened it.

'Morning chicken.' Only one person called me 'chicken', it was Darren, the waiter from Eliza Blue who I had known well before he moved back to Australia. The text went on: 'I hope you're well. I've been thinking of you recently. As you know I've become a Civil Minister and last night we had a little Naming Ceremony for our friends. It was very respectful, honouring the difficult path some have had to travel. I hope you didn't mind me naming you Philippa. I wish you'd been here to witness it, but maybe we can do it again when I get back to Ireland.'

As the waitress placed my coffee on the table she looked a little concerned but didn't say anything. I wiped the tears from my face and tried to regain my composure. What a beautiful message to get, to know that, on the other side of the world, totally unprompted, someone cared so much for me.

I was still seeing my wonderful friend Emer on occasion and as she was driving home through my estate she saw teenagers on a street corner, commenting: 'what if you had to walk by them on your way home after getting the bus?'

'Could be a problem but I'd just keep my eyes open and make sure I was on the opposite side of the road hon.'

'Yes but if they saw you, read you and followed you home ...?'

'Sis, I worry about that every day and every night. The last thing I want is to cause problems for my family, or anyone. I do realise the potential ramifications of my path, but what can I do? I'm taking it as slowly and as carefully as I can. It's a reasonable area, little vandalism or antisocial behaviour so I'll just hope. I'm not going to stop because of something that might happen, but probably won't.' I knew Emer was just being sensible and pointing out the potential pitfalls and problems, as Karen had done some years previously, and I thought about Emer's words when I lay in bed trying to get to sleep. Everything was going well, no problems with work, Helen and Jenny supportive and hopefully my wider family coming around in time.

As if to reinforce my fears I heard a gang of teenagers walking down the road, talking loudly, then going to the green area behind the house. I eventually fell into a fitful, restless sleep. I might have progressed a long way but there were still pitfalls and concerns.

**

I walked into the beautiful eighteenth century Unitarian church on St Stephen's Green on a wet and cold evening in mid-November 2008. It was the annual Transgender Day of Remembrance ceremony which usually attracted about twenty-five people, organised by my friends Sara and Adam, and another trans woman, Lynda.

I had been curious about the church for many years. It nestled in between two office blocks, looking very incongruous, but its solidity lent it a permanence missing from the surrounding modern constructions. It was majestic and dominated its neighbours.

A bearded gentleman introduced himself as Bill Darlison, the minister of the church. I saw a few of my friends sitting in the pews and made my way to them, reaching out to squeeze Emer's hand.

The service was dignified, as I had expected knowing those involved in its organisation, featuring a little music and appropriate readings. But what was affecting me, and deeply, was the church. The peacefulness, the beauty and the majesty of the building had a calming effect on me, and I found myself thinking about aspects of my life that I didn't allow myself to think about normally. My mind was always running at full speed but here I found it could drop down to walking pace and I liked it.

Lost in thought it took a little time for the minister's words to work their way into my consciousness. I jumped, worried that people might think I had fallen asleep, though I knew I hadn't. The sermon was about trans and how important it was to embrace all diversity, welcome all opinions and beliefs.

'And if you feel like dropping in here at any stage there will be a genuine welcome for you. I love when some of the other religious leaders humorously refer to us as the 'gay' church. We really do try to live up to our name.'

***

I made many trips to the church in the coming months and years, signing up for various associated activities, which usually took place in the Lantern Centre on Harrington Street. I found my interest in my spiritual side increase and I started meditating regularly. This became a way for me to cope with the stress of my transition, as well as daily life and the upset and anguish caused by my occasional evenings with men. It became quite easy for me to find my own 'sacred space' and I meditated most nights for a period of six months, more infrequently afterwards, sleeping much better and feeling a lot calmer. I didn't consider myself religious but embraced the opportunity to explore this side of my psyche with enthusiasm. A rationalist and sceptic I may have been, influenced by both Asimov who said; 'Properly read, the Bible is the most potent force for atheism that exists', and H.G. Wells: 'if there is no God, nothing matters. If there is a God, nothing else matters.' I couldn't deny that this visit to the Unitarian church had affected me deeply.

***

Louise was a work colleague who had become a good friend and who I had told about my transition quite early on. She was keen to meet me as Philippa, so one sunny autumn evening she and I shared a bottle of wine over dinner after I had changed – at this point I was really only short of actually wearing a dress in work so the 'change' was minimal. I explained my plans for the following year – change of name, new passport and the beginning of the final stages of my transition towards surgery. I also asked her to be honest with me about any office gossip or negative comments about me, if she felt there was a need for me to explain my situation to the rest of the staff. She seemed almost as excited as me about my transition and she remained one of my best friends and greatest supporters as I progressed.

***

My LGBTQ+ activism had given me many friends but equally after my involvement in science fiction fandom, especially during my teenage years, there were a lot of friends who I had, to some degree, ignored as I transitioned. I had been anxious to reconnect in some way, to explain and apologise. Initially I told the guys involved in *Albedo One*, the magazine that had been established a lifetime before in my bedroom in 1994. But it had been quite a few years since either Helen or I had been to a science fiction convention. I had moved away, not forgetting the community that had given me so much, including my life partner, but realising that I had other issues to deal with. I felt a need to have it back in my life in some way so I decided to give a few people a surprise. I did get a slightly vicarious thrill from telling people, especially men, about my situation and seeing their reaction, in some cases close to incomprehension, even incredulity. As I became more confident in myself, I was less interested in their reaction, especially if it was in any way negative. This was my life, no excuses or apologies were coming from my side. I wasn't about to justify who I was to anyone.

So I registered for the convention as Philippa, of course. When I arrived, I greeted those that knew me by name, amused at their initial lack of recognition. As the convention went on, I sought out those who I had been particularly friendly with, explaining briefly my situation and suggesting we meet for coffee or a drink at some point if they wanted to know more. Most seemed fine, some seemed uncomfortable and I was struck again that the community that I had expected to be most accepting found it as difficult as the rest of society to accept. Maybe I could bring the two together in some way, and I began to think about suggesting programme items at conventions, noticing also that gender and feminist issues were addressed at a number of panels already, an area that was only being touched on when I took my hiatus from the field ten years previously.

10

Decisions

Age: 49

I have arrived
I am home
In the here
And the now
I am solid
I am free
In the universe
I dwell

Buddhist proverb

The changes in me had become obvious in work. I occasionally took people to one side and quietly discussed what my future plans were with them. The HR department head had been very supportive and informed me that to legally change all my details in work simply required a copy of my Deed Poll.

Some practicalities remained though: 'how are you going to deal with the solicitors who had been corresponding with your male self before your change? You can't exactly explain it all to them over the phone!' I was asked.

'Oh, it'll be a family thing, I'll just say I'm his wife or sister!' I'd reply.

So shortly after Christmas 2009, I started to take groups of my colleagues out for coffee and cakes, to explain my situation and my plans for the future. I tried to keep it light-hearted and was amused by some of the comments:

'So that explains it then', exclaimed one wit in the office. 'You've fancied me all this time and this is your way of getting a date with me! Bit extreme, all you had to do was ask …!' I promised him I'd pay special attention to him when the time came.

Many of the questions that were asked I had heard before and the answers came easily and, perhaps to some, may have seemed rehearsed. In a way, they were of course as I had dreamed of this moment for so many years, even imagining what I would wear on my first day in work as my true self. I had thought of the possible reactions, what I would say when the inevitable slip-ups regarding names and pronouns occurred. My life had been building to this point and I was going to embrace the moment.

My date was set. I would lodge my Deed Poll in early April and start using my name once it was processed, hopefully in time for my birthday, a few days later. My colleagues asked when they should start using my new name, anxious not to offend me. Having worked in the department as male for almost thirty years though I realised it would be a difficult transition for them too.

It was a beautiful sunny day when I met Cat from TENI who was to officially witness the form signing. I was excited about the procedure and what it signified. We hugged briefly before crossing the road to the solicitor's office. She was very pleasant, laughing at the description Cat had given as their profession, 'Trans activist', and was evidently curious as to the reason behind my change of name.

At the end of the brief process I reached into my purse to take out the fee of €10. The solicitor shook her head.

'There's no need, it's been a pleasure to meet you and I

wish you well for the future.' Once again I was touched by the sincerity and understanding the vast majority of people had for my situation.

Having dropped off the completed application form I decided to play the 'government employee' card, hinting that the official might process the case quickly as I also worked for the Department of Justice. And just a few days later, I got the call I so desperately wanted.

'Ms Ryder? Your Deed Poll is complete and can be picked up any time.'

I put the phone down and sat back at my desk. It was done. I looked at the case in front of me, which I had started as male and would now finish as female, in a way! The official certificate needed a signature, I had been practising it for some time, as so many women do in advance of marriage should they decide to take their husband's name. I took the pen, flawlessly signed my new name and photocopied the document for my personal files, grinning broadly, possibly breaking every data protection law in existence but not caring.

'Hey Frank,' I called to my boss, 'I'm official now, I'm Philippa as of today!'

My colleagues congratulated me and I smiled for the entire afternoon, desperate to pick up the form but also enjoying the anticipation. I rang the HR manager and asked for an appointment to finalise everything, and the next morning walked over to the High Court, got the form, made ten copies and dropped one into the HR manager who embraced me. It was the Thursday before Easter and the manager said it would just take a day or two to process the change. 'I'll let you know what your new login details for the computer system will be next week, but I imagine everything will be done when you come in on Tuesday.'

I walked in the following week in a knee length skirt, blouse and 3" heels. The first person to see me, another woman, wolf-whistled at me.

'Wow, *Philippa*, you look great!'

I walked into my section, conscious of the eyes of the entire office on me. I felt amazing. My colleagues all smiled at me, no obvious awkwardness or embarrassment. It all seemed so right, and as they got back to work I just wanted someone to come up to me and use my name again. I didn't have to wait long. The messenger dropped a letter on my desk from HR with details as to my new login. Every official communication would now be in my new name, the telephone switch operators had all been informed and would now refer any enquiries to my male name to myself. I wondered what the solicitors would think and why they could no longer speak to my 'brother'? And a few minutes later, a call came through.

'Philippa? I have a call for you' the operator said. I grinned all through the simple enquiry, putting down the phone a minute later.

'So,' I thought, 'that's another hurdle overcome, what's next?'

Next of course was the bathroom. So quietly I put my new handbag over my shoulder and walked casually by the facilities I had used for so many years to the next door, which had a simple outline of a person in a skirt. Was it going to be full of glitter balls, make-up assistants, nail technicians …? I was smiling broadly as I entered, thinking of all the trouble this had caused, and of course how unremarkable it was. When I had mentioned how I would be expecting to use the female facilities once my Deed Poll and transition had been completed (though I would be pre-surgery) I was told that I would have to wait for the outcome of a discussion between the female members of staff.

Walking up to chat to my friend Louise on another part of the floor later she insisted I use the opportunity to practise my 'catwalk' and it became a running joke between us. Yet I certainly started swinging my hips and tossing my hair a lot more, smiling as I did so. I haven't stopped since.

Ten days after the Deed Poll I had my new passport, new name and gender clearly stated – my first proper piece of official identification in my true name. I did wonder about the identification number and whether there was a hidden marker referring to my previous identity concealed within. But in some ways I didn't really care. I wouldn't deny my past, was indeed quite proud of it, and felt privileged to be able to live the rest of my life in the gender identity that I should have been assigned at birth.

Shortly after I received my Deed Poll, I made an appointment to see the manageress of my gym. I had been a member for many years, under my old name of course, but just as it was in work there were issues before I had surgery if I used the female changing rooms.

'I can hardly continue using the male facilities!' I said to the manageress who nodded. I told her how difficult it had been in the past few years hiding and not wanting to hide myself in the changing room, how it was difficult to keep painted toenails and make-up from the guys if it was busy.

'And of course there were the two different occasions when I walked in on a Sunday morning to find the entire Irish rugby team in the changing rooms! I was very femme with a handbag and heels, intending to just drop my bag before I went to church. I walked in to find them just after a session, mostly naked and sweaty. God what an amazing sight! I didn't enjoy it at all!' So we came to an arrangement where I would basically be discreet until surgery, using the female changing rooms at quiet times.

Jenny received some very important support at this difficult time for her when she told her best friend, Izzy, of my situation. They both attended Our Lady's Secondary School in Terenure, forming many friendships and becoming involved in sports and theatrical productions. Yet I was concerned that perhaps her school friends had been talking about me behind Jenny's back. For the previous two years or more Jenny had internalised her feelings about me, as I tried to stay as much in the background of her life as I could. Izzy gave her an outlet to discuss her fears and worries and both Helen and I were immensely grateful to her. Izzy became somewhat like a second daughter to us and we later all went on a very enjoyable holiday together to Disney World in Florida to celebrate their sixteenth birthdays.

***

An issue of GCN, the LGBTQ+ community newspaper, had an ad for a new Bed & Breakfast venue, Serenity, just outside Wexford. It was Ireland's first fully inclusive LGBTQ+ B&B and I suggested to Helen that we drop down for an overnight that summer.

I was walking through the city centre a few days later, passing a quirky jewellery shop, when something drew me in. The jewellery was attractive and reasonably priced, all unique to the shop. As I looked around I saw a selection of rings and a thought struck me. I grinned and chose a ring, an idea gestating in my mind.

The trip down to Serenity was a short two-hour bus ride. We chatted, read and dozed but at the back of my mind was the thought of what was to come, the question I would ask later that night. We had arranged to be picked up by one of the guys from the B&B when the bus arrived.

We found ourselves shortly afterwards in a lovely room with a nice view over a babbling brook and some woods. Unpacking quickly, we made our way downstairs to find coffee and biscuits waiting and Glenn introduced us to Shaun, his husband, explaining they had been married in South Africa recently. Dogs and cats were also (occasionally) in evidence and we felt very comfortable and relaxed.

Helen had been tempted by the offer of a luxurious bath on arrival and when she saw the ornate, free-standing tub in the beautifully decorated bathroom she was delighted. A few minutes later and she was happily soaking her aches and pains away. It gave me the opportunity to chat further with Glenn and I decided to come out to him as trans.

We arranged to have dinner around 7.30 p.m. I felt very comfortable and at ease with Glenn and confided in him that I was going to ask Helen something important at the end of the meal. Glenn grinned and said: 'Well there are no other guests tonight and we'll make ourselves scarce when you want us to, we try to be as unobtrusive as possible anyway!'

We changed for our meal having relaxed in the lovely bedroom for an hour. I was on edge but tried to hide it. We had come so far as a couple over the past few years, but I wasn't entirely sure of Helen's answer to the question I was about to ask. I thought of that rainy evening in Leeds city centre some twenty years ago when I asked Helen to marry me – at least I didn't need to kneel on a wet pavement this time!

The meal was wonderful – Shaun was an award-winning chef and it showed. The attention to detail, comfort and surroundings delighted Helen and the guys were hardly visible at all, only turning up when needed. Dessert and coffee over, the last of the wine sipped and Helen looked relaxed and happy. I smiled at her.

'Hey hon, you ok?' Helen nodded sleepily so I realised I had to ask the question quickly before she suggested bed.

I produced the small, decorative bag containing the ring and placed it on the table.

'What's that?' asked Helen.

'Well,' I said, taking a deep breath. 'I've been thinking of this for a little time now. This is a little token of my love, but it comes with a question. We've moved on so far in my transition and now that I have a rough idea of when I am going to go for surgery I wanted to ask you … will you renew our vows, this time as Helen and Philippa?' There was a tremor in my voice as I got the words out and I looked at Helen.

'Of course I will. Did you ever expect me to say no?' and she grinned. On cue, Shaun and Glenn appeared with glasses of champagne and we toasted a momentous night.

We woke the next morning to start planning the ceremony which we agreed would be a perfect fit for the Unitarian church and later that week I arranged a meeting with a lay minister from the Unitarian church who performed weddings and other ceremonies, for her input as to what type of event it could be.

A week before our wedding anniversary we had thirty-five friends assemble in the church. The only link with our wedding was Declan, Helen and I. None of our family were asked, none of the friends who had attended the wedding apart from Declan came. And that spoke volumes as to acceptance. I wanted people who meant something in my transition to speak so I asked Declan and also our good friend Margaret who, at short notice, produced an intelligent and witty testimonial to us that had everyone in the pews laughing.

The church looked lovely, with rainbow roses and a decorative candle. Jenny was stunning, confident and supportive, sweet and charming to the guests as they arrived. I had asked Sara to be one of the ring bearers and was honoured when she accepted. Declan was to be the other, of course.

Some of the science fiction community arrived, the majority of the *Albedo One* magazine gang and our long-term friends Noreen, Dave and Nicola also attended. Helen was delighted too that her boss arrived to wish us well.

Of course, the trans community was there in force. Such a public expression of support between a couple was a rare event. We were both aware that most of relationships ended due to the trans status of one of the couple. It made the day all the more special to have people who cared, who understood, present for our little celebration.

Pamela, the minister, began as usual by welcoming the group to the church, talking of the broad and open-minded ethos of the Unitarian faith and how delighted she was to welcome everyone, at the first trans service she had performed. She spoke with wit but also with sincerity; she and I had been for a few glasses of wine over the previous few months as I had become more interested and involved in the church activities and I knew just how humorous she could be.

Helen and I sat at the front of the church, on two large and ornate chairs, with Jenny in the first pew behind us. Following a hymn Pamela said: 'Now some friends of Helen and Philippa would like to say a few words, then we will hear from Philippa followed by Helen.'

Declan talked of the friendship we had developed over the years since first meeting in secondary school, our common interests in science fiction and *Star Trek* and how the friendship had grown and changed as our lives progressed. And the tectonic shift that had occurred when I told him of my trans situation and how that had allowed us to grown even closer.

Margaret spoke with wit and intelligence, and I thought, again, as she entertained the congregation with her words of how lucky I was to have such amazing and accepting friends and how I hoped the ceremony could possibly help others.

A few minutes later, I walked up to the lectern. I wore a purple and black dress, with a bow around the neck. A consultation with a personal stylist had been useful for both Helen and I, but I wasn't entirely happy with the result. This wasn't intended to be a wedding, yet neither was it a party and it was hard to get the right look. My make-up was courtesy of Brown Thomas, my nails also, both done a little time while before the ceremony. I felt I looked as well as I could.

My speech was heartfelt but not exactly inspiring. But it was the best I could do. I knew from past experience (our wedding in particular) that I could not talk without notes so I spent quite some time writing, editing, redrafting and rewriting a short piece in which I praised Helen for her commitment and loyalty, her love, humour and wit. For giving me Jenny, for many years of excitement, joy and surprises. I talked of Helen's commitment to her work and her obsessions, which at that point included needlework and gay literature. It wasn't worthy of the woman of course, there was so much more, but it was the best I could do. Laughter and applause filled the church as I made way for Helen.

Helen talked of how my trans identity had developed

over the years, how it had started as an occasional incidence of dressing and turned into something much more important. How she had struggled with the issue, with seeing her husband turn into her wife, how difficult it had been for her. It was emotional listening to her, and once again I marvelled at her way with words. The overriding message from both testaments was one of absolute love, of a respect and appreciation of each other that transcended gender or social norms and expectations.

The audience settled down as Pamela called for the ring bearers.

'We are here to acknowledge the love and friendship that Helen and Philippa have for each other.' Our friends were smiling as Declan gave Helen one of the rings and Sara handed me the other. As I slipped the ring on Helen's finger and received hers we kissed with applause and laughter filling the church as Josh, the organist, played the theme tune from *Star Trek*. Jenny joined us and we all hugged to the sounds of the music that had brought us together in the first place so many years previously.

After a few photos in and outside the church, we made the short walk up to the hotel on Harcourt Street that we had organised for some light refreshments. Sara and our friend Deanna had planned a surprise and performed a few songs while Helen and I mingled among the guests, chatting and having photos taken. It was inevitable that our trans and science fiction friends more or less stayed apart but some did cross over – Margaret and Declan particularly. Jenny was the star of the occasion though, getting many compliments and glowing as she went between the groups. It was an emotional afternoon but very enjoyable.

As we chatted to the guests, we were touched to discover

that many had been in tears with the words spoken by us of each other, and how wonderful and appropriate they had found both the ceremony and the venue. To me this was just a natural progression of the relationship we had but others viewed it as something quite monumental. When it came to my relationship with Helen I didn't do things for show, I did it because it seemed right and out of love. Jenny was also confident in her discussions with people, at one point saying: 'When I found out about Pippa I could have freaked out but instead I just got on with it.' How I wished everyone else in my life could have done the same and that they could have shared this lovely moment with us.

After the savouries had been served the hotel staff brought out the cake. I had brought the knife used to cut our wedding cake over twenty years previously, a symbolic link between two momentous occasions in our life together.

Then, all too soon, we realised it was getting late and people started to leave. It had been a truly special day, hugely important to our relationship and I had enjoyed every minute of it. Outwardly and legally nothing had changed between us, it was back to work the following day for us, and to school for Jenny. Yet within me something had. I had always known of the support Helen had for me but to have it expressed so publicly was all I had ever hoped for, and more. She had come a long way from the afternoon when she expressed her doubt about ever going out in public with me. We had both endured pain and sorrow to arrive at this point. There were still a few hurdles to cross of course but the momentum was building. I was almost there.

The time had also come to tell Helen's family in the UK. Her parents had died fifteen years previous and she had two sisters and two brothers, with one of her brothers married to a Polish Catholic. The family was spread between Leeds and London and I wondered how they would take the news. With perfect timing, the pope had recently described trans people as more of a threat than global warming, so any deeply held religious leanings could be influenced by 'El Papa'! But following the commitment ceremony we agreed that it was time and we sat down to write a letter together which we sent off by email a few days later.

I had always liked Angela and Bernie, feeling I was respected and understood by both and sharing a common passion for music with Bernie. Helen's other siblings, Tessa and her husband Ian and her other brother Peter were all older than us and I wondered would that have an effect on their reactions.

We didn't have to wait too long for a response. Tessa rang first, spoke to Helen and then me. She was worried about Helen, didn't seem to understand that this situation was something that had been in existence for many years, but as long as Helen was happy then she was willing to accept me for who I was. It was a lovely call, everything I could have hoped for.

No sooner was the phone put down than it rang again, this time it was Bernie. Supportive, delighted and accepting, I was thrilled with the reaction. Both he and his lovely wife Grazyna were again, understandably, concerned about Helen but their obvious support for me too touched us.

A long email from Angela followed a day or two later and then I was surprised to see a Facebook friend request from her. I hadn't mentioned that I had a trans name, Philippa James, used within the community and in any media interviews, and I was a bit surprised to get the request. Then there were a couple of emails from Bernie and Angela about my LiveJournal diary, saying how much they had enjoyed reading it – again, that was something I had intended to remain within friends only and was a bit disturbed to find it being found so quickly.

We were thrilled with the reaction of Helen's family and I looked forward to being with them as my true self.

***

It was common knowledge that the team in St Colmcille's Hospital were very conservative with their prescribing for trans patients. I had been informed when I started Zoladex that the preferred maximum was two years. However, I also knew that some people had been left on the treatment for longer and with my transition going smoothly and my operation in the near future I was hopeful of being allowed stay on it. I was disappointed when I was told that I could continue with the oestrogen patches but Zoladex, once the current prescription ran out, was to be stopped. I tried to argue, saying that international research had shown no ill effects of being on the blocker for longer but in the end the decision was the teams' and conservatism ruled. The trans community were generally frustrated and angry at the reluctance to prescribe similar levels to the UK and this led some to obtain higher doses through their GPs or, in extreme situations, by going abroad or online.

Not surprisingly, a few weeks later I found my libido rapidly increasing. So at my next appointment in Loughlinstown I explained, 'I was taken off Zoladex a few months ago and I have been suffering since. My sex drive has gone through the roof, it's as if I'm a teenager again.' The consultant looked at me, surprised. 'That's disappointing. This is an unusual reaction, once you've been on Zoladex for a few years the body begins to regulate testosterone production and the oestrogen regime suffices by blocking its production after Zoladex is withdrawn.'

'Well I know my own body, Doctor. It's very upsetting and stressful, it's not something I'm imagining!'

The consultant seemed about to try to persuade me that I must be imagining the physical changes to my body when I said, 'well I know what I'm feeling and more particularly the way my body is reacting! What was my previous testosterone level compared to this time?'

'Your level last time was normal female, less than 3. There was no test done this time.' I demanded a test which a few weeks later showed I had much higher levels of testosterone than I should have had and I was given a new prescription. It had been months of me feeling confused, frustrated and depressed. My very positive view of the Loughlinstown medical team changed for the worse.

***

I met Declan at the Central Bank on a beautiful sunny May evening for one of our usual trips out for a meal at Juice, a vegetarian restaurant and one of my favourites. If time allowed we would follow it with a film. Sitting at the table we were immediately engaged in conversation, arguing, in as much as we ever did, about what to go to in the cinema or indeed if we would even make it there. Declan interrupted me in mid flow when he saw a friend of his just about to leave who chatted to us for a while and told me about the Orwell Wheelers women's cycling group.

So a few days later, I cleaned and oiled my hybrid bike, a Giant Rapid. I had a lycra top and shorts and was very concerned that the bulge in the front of my shorts might give my secret away. When I arrived I found three women outside the shop, all with very expensive bikes, all wearing Orwell Wheelers lycra and looking very intimidating.

'Oh hell,' I thought, 'these look like serious cyclists!' A small woman spotted me and called out.

'Hi, are you Philippa? Nice to meet you.' Just then Declan's friend pulled into the car park on her bike, followed closely by two other women. A brief rundown of the rules and we were off, for a quick, gentle spin up to Enniskerry and a coffee stop. Nothing I hadn't managed before. The leader of the spin was very professional, pointing out minor safety and comfort points for me to consider. She also commented on my bike: 'it'll be fine for these short spins. If you decide to join the club you'll have to get a proper road bike and get insurance through becoming a member of Cycling Ireland.'

I found the beginner's outings of fifty kilometres a bit of a challenge initially and I ached the following day. Gradually my body acclimatised to the pain and I found myself pushing more and more, eventually being able to complete the Wicklow 200 with two of the other women in the club who had become friends, Nicole and Orathai. The 200 kilometre event took in some of the amazing sights and steep mountain climbs of that county, we were eleven hours in the saddle, at times in heavy rain and freezing cold despite it being held during the summer, but it was the highlight of our cycling to that point and the pain was worth it.

The sometimes-challenging cycles of course had a personal and practical reason behind them: strengthening my body and improving my general health in preparation for my upcoming surgery. So a 45 minute spin to the hospital wasn't a problem. This one however was the beginning of the end of a journey for me, to drop off my application for

Overseas Treatment for gender affirmation surgery. After four years on hormones I felt ready to progress to surgery and the operation would be taking place in London.

However, despite many calls and a couple of visits by the end of the year, the form hadn't been signed. I was angry and wrote a letter to my local TD, who happened to be a government minister, about the situation. Three days later, I received a letter from the Loughlinstown hospital administrator. My application would be completed in the coming days, and then I received confirmation that my forms had been sent to the HSE Overseas section for approval. I was thrilled and called Sara to discuss the next steps but during the conversation I realised that the letter I had received was different to Sara's. Mine said 'assessment for surgery' whereas hers said 'surgery'.

I was furious. I needed a new form filled out, signed by the consultant and then approved again. How many others, in considerably worse situations than me, were going through this? I was so lucky to have a supportive partner, a secure job and a good network of friends to help me. I was privileged and I knew it. How could others cope? Was it any wonder that trans people had the highest incidence of attempted suicide?

'We have to jump through so many hoops, satisfy so many other people that we are who we know we are. Bureaucracy and basic lack of humanity is putting people's lives at risk,' I thought.

I was determined that TENI should initiate a patient support group and develop ways to put pressure on those who made the decisions. But it was only one aspect of the wider trans situation and I knew that to concentrate solely on the medical side would upset many in the community.

MY NAME IS PHILIPPA

Of course, once money was mentioned the right-wing press became very excited, highlighting the resources that trans people were diverting from whatever other marginalised group they decided to focus on that week. The more I thought about the issues the closer it brought me to tears. We just wanted to be ourselves!

However, a few weeks later my revised approval form arrived and this time it said: 'referred for surgery'. The consultant had already referred me to James Bellringer, the lead surgeon in Charing Cross Hospital, and someone I had actually met previously at a TENI organised event when I jokingly commented, more in hope than true belief, that I would be seeing him shortly. He had shaken my hand and at the time, with some amusement, I had thought of where I hoped that hand would be, and soon!

Up until this point, I had only dealt with the Irish health service and it was a remove to Charing Cross, London, a different system. 'Out of sight, out of mind' and I simply hadn't allowed myself to really consider what happened once I entered the UK NHS. But now it had happened. I had a patient number! Here I was, close to surgery and I still hadn't seen 'the op' on television or online. I knew it wouldn't put me off or make me reconsider so I didn't feel there was any point in potentially upsetting myself or worrying Helen. Some trans people felt the need to know everything about the hormone treatment and surgery but I had faith in the system. I did what I needed to do. So far, it had worked out.

After much back and forth between the fax machines of London and Dublin I eventually received the letter I was waiting for. I had my first appointment, with the NHS psychiatrist, for early 2011. But before I went, I received an unexpected call from Sara, inviting me to accompany her on her second trip to the assessment clinic in London. It would be a great opportunity to see what I could expect on my trip early the following year and I thoroughly enjoyed the journey with my good friend.

Normally Charing Cross allowed Irish patients to skip many of their requirements as by the time they were seen they had been living the 'real-life test' for some time. Though I felt that two years was too long, I did agree with the principle for those progressing to surgery. It was an irreversible decision, and not one to be taken lightly. By the time I was seen the following January it would be twenty months since my Deed Poll, the acknowledged beginning of the 'Real Life Test'.

A few days later I had another difficult conversation with my mother, sitting in the car as she again complained about how I looked arriving at her house. She said, not for the first time, that I was always happy as a teenager and how could I have been feeling this way? She would have known. I explained to her, pleaded with her to understand and accept me, that it wasn't her fault. I couldn't tell her that her femininity had always inspired me and really wished I could show my love and appreciation for her in some way. But again and again, this week as every week, the argument continued along the same lines.

I thought of my father, who had died ten years previously, and how he might have viewed my changes. Could he have accepted me? Would he have cared if I was male or female or was I simply a child to be loved? Would he have been embarrassed or concerned about what the neighbours would think? I didn't believe so and wanted to believe he would have accepted me for who I was. But had he also been a product of his generation, with all the limitations and reservations regarding acceptance of difference and diversity?

I knew that, as a teenager, if I had ever challenged my parents' view of the world – with music, dress sense, hairstyles or my attitude towards those that portrayed a lifestyle that didn't fit in with their way of looking at the world, then I would have been quickly told off, by both of them. I remembered with some amusement an incident with my friend Colum who met my father and I one Saturday. Colum had arrived with newly coloured hair – blue. Years later my father still used the incident to remind me how strange my friends – and I – were.

Yet I believed that my father had a somewhat hidden streak of rebellion within his personality, and it was something he couldn't share around my mother. There always seemed to be a little glint of amusement in his eye. So maybe, just maybe, he would have understood. I wished I could have shared my true self with him.

**

My work with TENI gave me a lot of exposure to journalists and some were anxious to delve into the personal and would sometimes look for the sensationalist aspects of the story. I remembered the horrible 'exposés' that had been visited upon some of my friends, one of whom had appeared on the front page of the *Irish Sun*. So I was very anxious, for the sake of my immediate family particularly, to minimise my visibility. Yet I also knew that my story, being mostly positive, was something that should be brought into the public domain, to let other trans people see that there was the possibility that it could all work out. So when the opportunity arose to be interviewed with Helen for a large and overall sympathetic piece in the *Sunday Times* I decided to use the name that I was best known in the community by, Philippa James, and we asked that no photos be taken. It gave me the confidence to engage more though I chose the media outlets with care, refusing quite a lot.

***

I was looking forward to my trip to Charing Cross for my initial consultation. I booked the flight and hotel a few weeks earlier, was packed and well organised, just checking my emails before going to bed. I noticed an email from the hotel, assuming it was just a confirmation and glanced through it. Then read it more carefully in horror. My room had been cancelled as my credit card was invalid! We had changed our cards a few weeks earlier but after I had booked the hotel. The hotel had emailed me a few times – the emails were in the Spam folder – and, receiving no response had cancelled the room.

'Hon, I have a problem!' I called out to Helen and we discussed the options.

'Why don't you ring Bernie and ask if you can stay with him overnight? I'm sure they wouldn't mind.'

'But don't you think it's too soon after telling them about me? I wouldn't want to put pressure on them, especially with the kids.'

But I was in a difficult situation and decided to phone. Grazyna answered the phone and I explained the situation.

'So basically Grazyna, I've nowhere to stay and was wondering if I could sleep on your couch for just one night?'

Grazyna was enthusiastic and genuine in her response, seemed thrilled at the opportunity to see me and we agreed a time and place for me to be picked up.

I put the phone down, delighted. It was lovely to know I had support from Bernie and the wider family in the UK.

I thought of one of my good friend's and the wonderful acceptance shown by her sister who, when confronted with the news that she was losing a brother answered immediately: 'Yes, but I'm gaining a sister! Shopping, nights out, fun!'

My flight was in the early afternoon and I arrived in a wet London just as dusk descended on the late January day. I had a single change to make to get on the tube line that would take me towards Wimbledon and where I met Grazyna.

'I'm really grateful to you both for doing this at short notice. Normally I wouldn't put someone under such pressure, and with the kids I'm particularly anxious to make sure that you're comfortable with the situation Grazyna.'

Grazyna shook her head.

'Everything is fine, Philippa. The children understand, we have told them about you and they are comfortable with it.'

The evening was very enjoyable, only referring to the reason for my trip a little and ending with Bernie and I listening to music. The following morning the kids were heading to school as I left and Bernie, knowing of my nervousness about the appointment, told me to 'just be yourself, you'll be fine.' I was, I felt 200% me!

I hopped off the tube at Hammersmith and, after a little confusion, found Fulham Palace Road. The Gender Identity Clinic was just past Charing Cross hospital where, possibly the following year, I would be undergoing life-changing and life-affirming surgery and I smiled as I looked up at the large building, emotionally thinking of those within who were at that moment having, or recovering from, gender-affirmation surgery.

A few hundred metres further and I saw the clinic. A woman emerged and, smiling, held the door for me. After a short wait at reception my name was called and my heart quickened. I entered the consultation room confidently, dressed in my favourite suit, a grey tunic dress and jacket. I felt amazing as I held out my hand to the man behind the desk who rose as I approached.

'Hi, you're Philippa?' I confirmed my name and date of birth and sat down, easing back into the chair.

'Now, this is an initial consultation to assess you for surgery, to make sure you're happy with proceeding along that route and to ensure that you can cope with living full-time in your chosen gender role. Now, have you started a real-life test yet, do you know what that is?'

With a start I realised that he didn't know much about me and so I quickly filled him in, producing the documentation showing my successful transition and assuring him that I had been through two psychiatric and a number of psychological assessments in Dublin.

'Ah, I see. You're a lot further along than I thought. I should have known, you seem very confident in yourself.'

'Thanks,' I said with a smile. 'I am happier now than I ever have been. I just want to get to surgery so that I can then move ahead with all the other things I want to do with my life.'

'And what do you think surgery will do for you? Why do you want it?'

'Because I realise that I can't stay on testosterone blocker forever, my body seems wrong to both me and my wife, and I'm anxious to complete this amazing journey. It will, as I said, allow me to move ahead with my life knowing I have the body that I feel I always should have had.'

He made some notes and then looked up. 'You mention your wife. How is your relationship with her since you transitioned? Are you still together?'

I nodded. 'Yes, I wouldn't be where I am today without her, she's been wonderful. I won't say it's been easy, our relationship has had some very tough patches, but the underlying love is still there, both for and from her and our daughter.'

He smiled and said, 'That's good to hear. What about your sex life? Are you still attracted to her?'

'I am, but my interests have changed a lot and I would say I'm more interested in men now, I suppose I'd describe myself as bisexual. In a way, it's easier. For me though it's simply not about sex, it's about who I am in myself.'

He was nodding as I continued. 'It's my gender identity, not my sexual preferences, and that's something that a lot of people get confused about.'

'You're very well-informed Philippa, you obviously have thought this through.' He made a few notes and looked at me. 'Well I'm happy with you. You've been through the system in Ireland, you obviously know what's ahead, you have support around you and appear to have made a very successful transition. I don't think there's any need to see you again, so I'll be writing a letter to the surgical team recommending that you progress to surgery. Is that ok?' From the smile on my face, he saw it was and we shook hands again.

Letter from NHS psychiatrist to HSE psychiatrist:

At interview Ms Ryder was an individual who had been natally assigned male but whose presentation was straightforwardly feminine in terms of clothing, mannerisms and general appearance. There was no evidence of psychopathology, whether affective, psychotic or cognitive. She voiced no thoughts of harming herself or others. We spent a while discussing her thoughts around genital reconstruction surgery, the benefits of which she saw as completion ('the final cog in the process') and being able to fully be herself as a woman …

Opinion:

On the basis of this assessment, and the previous correspondence available to me, I would concur with the diagnosis of Ms Ryder as a male-to-female transsexual with a long history of gender dysphoria. She has established a stable female societal role over the last two years or so, has been fairly thoroughly assessed by the Irish gender service, and I would readily support her as a candidate for genital reconstruction surgery. She is both eligible and ready for this in my opinion ...

I went back to reception to get my appointment letter stamped to say that I had attended (to ensure I had no problems being refunded for my travel expenses by the HSE), thanked the staff then made my way down the steps to the street. I gave a little jump of joy, just as Sara had, but I was a little disappointed that none of my friends were there to see me.

I didn't have too long before my 8 p.m. flight but I was keen to share my news with my friends and family. Helen, Sara and Declan all got texts and I was delighted with the responses, especially from Helen. I was now firmly on course for surgery, I had skipped a second psychiatric appointment and thus saved about three or more months on the journey. Surgery could be this year. The thought that it was so close had me grinning broadly and I looked up on the tube to find an attractive guy sitting opposite smiling at me. 'The day just gets better and better,' I thought.

Following my appointment in January I was expecting a letter a few weeks later detailing the next steps in the process, and a new appointment. When it hadn't arrived by mid-March, I decided to ring but was told that I would get it shortly. More time passed and I became worried, wondering if it had gotten lost in the post. I arrived home on a Thursday evening in early April to find a letter from the Mental Health Centre in London. I grinned as I opened it, then turned white:

> 'Dear Ms Ryder,' it said. 'As you did not arrive for your appointment on Monday, 28th March 2011 we wish to advise you that you must ring the number below to arrange another.'

It went on to explain how it was understood that Irish patients had problems receiving post from the UK, which I knew. And the reason was, as they had been told on numerous occasions, that insufficient postage was being used on the letters! Sara and others had missed letters as a result.

Early the following day I rang the appointment centre and was given a choice of either mid-May or the following Monday. Could I manage to organise flights and hotel that quickly? I agreed to attend on Monday, talked to my boss about taking the afternoon off, rang the HSE Overseas section to organise the E112 form which I picked up later that afternoon, and cycled home as fast as I could! I managed to get a flight flying out Monday morning and returning Tuesday evening, got a hotel room at a reasonable price (ensuring the credit card was valid this time) and then fell back in the chair, exhausted.

I was more confident this time getting to the centre and despite having a very early start found myself sitting in the waiting area in plenty of time. I had dropped my overnight bag back at the hotel earlier and was quite relaxed, despite the last-minute rush to get here. I chatted to the receptionist, discovering she was of Irish extraction, but I ended up being delayed for quite some time before the surgical nurse called my name. Entering the room, I realised there was a man sitting just inside the door and he made me start when he glanced up from his desk to greet me.

'Hi, you are … Philippa Ryder?'

I smiled as I took the outstretched hand and sat in the chair he indicated. Glancing through my file he said, 'now, you have been referred to me for Gender Reassignment Surgery and I have a few basic questions to ask you. You are aware that this is an irreversible surgery, the outcome is not guaranteed. From your stats here you seem to be in good health, everything seems fine for progression to surgery. I'd like to do a small examination, so if you could remove your skirt and underwear.'

The nurse indicated a sectioned off area and helped me undress. The surgeon came in and, putting rubber gloves on, poked and prodded my male anatomy.

'Yes, that's fine. Apart from the minor blood pressure issue is there anything else I need to know about? Are you happy proceeding to surgery and fully understand the implications?'

I nodded and he produced a form for me to sign. Without hesitation, I signed my name and handed it back.

'So that seems to be it Philippa. Just look after yourself between now and your surgery, don't do anything crazy! Do you have any questions for me?'

'Just one. I'm a very keen cyclist and I was wondering when I'd be able to get back on the bike after the operation?'

He shook his head and said, 'of all the sports, you had to choose cycling! You know the lead surgeon is a keen cyclist? Well, we'll assess you at your post-op check-up, about eight weeks after the operation. We'll see how you're doing then, but you should be able to get back on the bike quite quickly. Now when you leave here go to the hospital and say you've been referred by me, hand them this letter and they will be able to give you a date there and then.'

I smiled and thanked him, waving to the nurse as I left

the room. I made my way to the hospital a short distance away, a building that I had passed a few times before and one that I had looked at longingly each time, wondering just when I was going to have my life-changing event.

I was given a number of options for surgery all shortly before our twenty-fifth wedding anniversary in August! But when I went back the following day I had another date. 12 September would be the day my body would finally change to match my brain.

Letter from surgeon to my GP:

> … Firstly she is aware that it is irreversible. The testes and penis will be removed and this will of course remove any chance of her fathering children. She is aware that the vagina is created using skin from the penis, and we are able to create a clitoris from a bit of the tissue of the glans of the penis. She will spend eight days in hospital, and she will need to be dilating regularly prior to discharge, and will have to continue indefinitely into the future. We cannot guarantee the results of surgery, in that the depth or width of the vagina may be variable and sensation isn't always perfect. Some patients will not be able to reach orgasm.
>
> Some patients can experience complications with poor healing of the skin or loss of the clitoris, and the vagina may be narrow and tight. Occasionally there are rare complications such as rectal injury or deep vein thrombosis, or unexpected reactions to drugs. This means that while the operation usually goes without problems very rarely there can be very serious complications.

Helen was delighted for me once she heard about the surgery.

'So hon, how are we going to handle Mum? What will we tell her?' she asked. I had a vague plan, thinking about some injury that I could 'suffer' that would explain my being off work and yet not worry my mother too much.

'How about if I get a slipped disc, a back problem like you had a few years ago? I would be limited in my movement and I could explain that I have to skip work for a few weeks. It's so vague that Mum might not suspect. And as for the ten days for surgery, I'll just say it's a very long conference. But I think it's time to tell the family that I'm going to have surgery, just so they know and can be a support for Mum. What do you think?' Helen nodded agreement.

Unfortunately the conversations with the family didn't go well, disappointing and upsetting me. But of course the bedrock that allowed me to move forward, Helen and Jenny, were there for me and Helen commented: 'You have us, Jenny and I support you. You don't need anyone else.'

I knew that of course, but the rejection still hurt. Deeply.

11

Rebirth

Age: 50

Helen and Jenny had a few plans to celebrate one of my big days of 2011, my fiftieth birthday. 'How are people supposed to feel when they're fifty?' I asked Helen at one point. 'I feel full of life, fitter than ever, I certainly don't consider that my life is more than half over!'

The girls had given me lovely cards and presents which made a wonderful start to the day. From my mother came a lovely large globe which I had spotted in Brown Thomas a few months previously; with my work in cartography, it was the perfect present.

Helen surprised me with a lovely meal in One Pico, one of the top restaurants in Dublin. I had decided that the wine at the meal that night was going to be the last before my operation. It was, in a way, another small personal sacrifice that I wanted to make, a pledge that I intended to break only once, at our anniversary in August, just before my operation. I was determined that nothing that I could control was going to affect my progression to surgery.

I knew that Helen still wasn't comfortable being seen as lesbian – reluctant to hold hands or kiss in public – but I hoped that eventually she would come around. Whenever we kissed in public Helen always complained that I was doing it for show, an accusation that hurt me but one that was also a little true, but not for the reason Helen had in mind. I was so happy with my progression, the acceptance most people showed towards me, and didn't want to feel that I should hide the love I felt for Helen. If there was an element of 'showing off' then so what?

I took unpaid leave – 'term time' – from my civil service job again, as I had the previous year, this time to be with Jenny as she started her first major state exams, the Junior Certificate. I had stayed in the background a lot during the time she was in secondary school, sad to be missing out on that part of my parenting, but glad that Helen could almost always go in my stead. It simply wasn't worth the potential teasing or worse Jenny might have had to endure in school. She was being forced to sacrifice her father and she was coping with a smile and with love for me apparent in everything she did.

She came home after most of the exams with a smile, having studied thoroughly and comprehensively – or at least so it seemed to us. We didn't push her, she appeared to have a good system and a strong work ethic. She certainly didn't get that from me!

I took a short trip to see Sara and a couple of other girls after their operations in London in early July. Sitting on the plane I thought: 'Just one more trip, for a check-up in August, then it will be my trip to surgery.'

As I sat beside Sara's bed in the ward, I thought how well she looked and hoped I would be able to come through as she had. Of course, there would be pain, occasional minor issues and dangers with any operation, but I felt quite emotional being in the very place I would be in a few short weeks' time. I simply couldn't wait, taking in all the details, watching the staff humorously and efficiently deal with their patients. Even the surgical smell of the wards and corridors excited me. My September date with destiny seemed too far away!

I had suggested that we make a family holiday out of my pre-operation check-up in Charing Cross with a long weekend in London. It would serve a few purposes: it would show Helen and Jenny where the hospital was, where they would be visiting me, and allow Jenny to understand fully what was happening. It was a subject that we had only referred to in passing, and I was not sure that Jenny realised what was happening. Did she need to know? Perhaps it was better that she didn't know the full details, but it was important she knew it was a major operation and more importantly what I had been building up to for most of my life.

Unfortunately Helen had to work on Monday, so she was only spending the weekend with us. As a treat for Jenny I had arranged for a trip to the ballet at the Royal Opera House, and just hoped that my check-ups would be finished to allow us time to get back to the hotel, change, get something to eat and make our way to Covent Garden.

The following day we had a leisurely breakfast then, not surprisingly, Jenny wanted to go clothes shopping. I treasured my time with her, she and I were on the same wavelength, same silly sense of humour and take on life. I'm not sure who influenced whom more.

'Don't forget the whole purpose of this trip is for me to get my medical checks hon, so I can't be late!' I reminded her on a number of occasions as we walked quickly around the busy streets, but there was never any possibility of me being late for this appointment!

The initial appointment was for 1.30 p.m. at the Mental Health clinic, followed by an appointment in Charing Cross hospital itself.

We arrived shortly after 1 and, having checked in I dropped Jenny to a Starbucks near the clinic. The appointment was with my surgeon and the surgical nurse specialist again. Once again, the procedure was explained, ensuring that I understood all aspects and particularly that it was irreversible. Signing a form saying I had been informed of all the risks and that success was not guaranteed ended the appointment and I thought, as I signed it, 'the results will be much better than what I have now!'

Having picked up Jenny, we walked slowly to the hospital. Time hadn't allowed us to visit it as a family, but I was confident Jenny would remember the location. Not that it was hard to find anyway!

I found the reception area, on the twelfth floor of the large building. Jenny was happily ensconced in the Costa Coffee in the foyer of the hospital, 'Thank God she can entertain herself!' I thought but also remembered that one of the things Jenny said about how she coped with stress was to read to distract herself.

More forms, more waiting and I was watching the time carefully, thinking of the ballet. Then a staff nurse came in, took me to a separate room, took my blood pressure, weight and height, then asked me to go to a different floor for an ECG.

I sat chatting to another patient outside the cardiac room before being taken in and asked to remove my top and bra. Six electrodes were placed on various parts of my body and the machine switched on for two minutes. I felt a little stressed, knowing that any issues discovered here might possibly result in my being unsuitable for surgery. How would I feel if that was the case? Devastated, to come this far, to suffer so much, and to fail at perhaps the very last hurdle. My only worry was my family history of cardiac problems and this was one of the reasons that I had tried to minimise the risk through a reasonably healthy lifestyle.

All these thoughts whirled around in my head, then the examination was over. I was given an envelope with the print-out and sent to see the cardiology registrar who was going to examine the results.

I sat in the waiting area nervously. 'Ms Ryder?' An Asian doctor appeared at the door and motioned me to come into the room.

'Ok I have your ECG and everything seems fine. I see no problems with sending you forward.'

And that was it, I thanked the doctor and receptionist, nurse, cleaner and anyone else I could find, smiling broadly and making my way down to find Jenny on the ground floor. It was 4 p.m. earlier than expected and we could go and enjoy ourselves!

We made our way back to the hotel and changed. Jenny wore an amazing dress which showed off her lovely figure beautifully. I had bought a short black and white polka dot dress a few weeks earlier that I wore with black tights. Jenny complimented me, and I complimented Jenny, a mutual appreciation society!

The ballet was fabulous, and Jenny sat entranced for the entire performance. Staged by one of the leading Russian companies, the Marinsky, previously the Kirov, Jenny knew the history and leading stars, reciting their names and commenting on some of the pieces as if she was a prima ballerina herself. Having started late in ballet when she was thirteen, she became enthralled with the graceful art of dance and progressed as far as she could before teenage life got in the way. It was a lovely way to spend the evening, made even nicer at the end when another audience member, an older man, engaged us in a long conversation and encouraged Jenny to continue with her ballet studies.

Having bought the obligatory t-shirt and leggings, we wandered happily into Covent Garden. 'Fancy dessert? Let's see if we can find an ice-cream!' I suggested and Jenny nodded.

'Hey darling, do you fancy going clubbing?' a guy called out to Jenny as she passed him, and I laughed and said: 'Oh for heaven's sake she's only sixteen!'

'Well the two of you go then, you can make sure she doesn't get into any trouble', but we had moved on. A few minutes later we were eating large ice creams and watching the crowds move past us, enjoying the late evening warmth. There was a happy buzz about Covent Garden at this time as we discussed the fashions of the well-dressed people wandering around, delighting in each other's company. A true *wow* moment with my beautiful daughter.

As my date drew ever closer, I found myself suffering hot flushes. Six weeks before the surgery I had been required to stop the oestrogen patches I had been applying twice weekly. I hated the marks the patches left on my skin anyway, but the flushes, the increase in the coarseness, the density of the hair on my body and feeling more emotional made the period quite difficult.

***

I got out of bed to get ready for a cycle, leaving Helen to doze a little. She looked at me and said: 'Will you miss it?' indicating my penis. I stood beside the bed, somewhat taken aback by the question.

'Well, without it we wouldn't have Jenny! So I'm happy

that it's given me her – and you! But I feel it's time to move on, see how I get on without it ruining my shape!

'I do think I'm privileged to have been able to explore my male side and now to go forward for the rest of my life as female, as I always should have been. So, will I miss it? No. Not now. But if you'd asked me ten or more years ago, maybe I would have answered differently.'

Helen smiled and said 'Good answer!' and went back to sleep.

On my way home I was pushing myself on the bike, enjoying the feeling of my body being fit. I turned a corner, slightly too fast, and saw the group of teenagers standing right across the cycle lane! I skidded and came off the bike, sliding on the ground a little before coming to a halt in front of them.

'Are you all right love?' asked one or two of them looking down at me. I assured them I was, dusted myself off and tried to ignore the pain in my hip. When I got home I looked at my side, seeing the bruise beginning to develop and laughed. A fraction of a second later in my reactions and I might have caused some serious injury to the teenagers or myself. But I had survived and took it as an omen, and a good one at that!

**

I left my bicycle locked to the railing outside the doctor's surgery. It was 2 September and this would be my very last Zoladex injection. Some people self-injected, saving a monthly doctor's visit, but I would not have been that confident, afraid of puncturing my stomach lining with the massive needle. So I had been going to see Edel, the doctor who had treated me throughout the process of transition.

I enjoyed the chat and support given and was happy to educate her somewhat in trans issues.

Edel was confident that I would easily come through the surgery. She had given a lot of support over the years, listening with interest and mild concern as I explained the lack of support from some but the wonderful encouragement from others, the difficulties and the joys of transitioning.

The needle entered me, I felt the small capsule settle in my stomach lining and then it was over. The end of one process. At least there was no chance of having too much testosterone again after surgery! I got down from the examination couch and Edel embraced me.

A few days later Declan rang me in work, suggesting a night out. 'What do you want to see tomorrow night? Is there anything on in the IFI?'

I had been so busy with preparations for the upcoming trip to Charing Cross I hadn't even looked at the cinema listing. My mind was elsewhere, not surprisingly ... I glanced at the brochure sent monthly as part of my membership package. One film stood out as perhaps having a common interest to both of us.

'How about "The Skin I Live In" by Almodovar? Sounds good, about plastic surgery and some science speculation. And Almodovar is supposed to be an interesting director too.'

A few moments passed as Declan checked the blurb on the IFI website.

"Em, if you're sure you'd be ok with it?' he said, with a strange note in his voice.

'Oh yes, it'll be a night out, see you tomorrow usual place and time?'

I put the phone down and surveyed my desk. Not quite

as tidy as I had wanted to leave it, but I knew that the work would still be there when I got back. I had only told my immediate boss and some close friends about the upcoming surgery, certain that the momentous news would be common knowledge shortly. Nonetheless, I did mention to another woman who worked close to me at lunch hour that I was going to be out for a few weeks 'for a little operation'. It was clear from the woman's face that she knew what operation it was, and just before I left I was presented with a small 'Good Luck' card signed by some of the staff.

'If we'd known you were going, we would have organised something!' said a good work colleague and friend, Louise, perhaps worried that I had felt no one cared. I assured her that I had wanted a low-key departure and was genuinely touched that I had received the card. I left the office smiling, waving to the doormen who had also been understanding and supportive during my transition.

The following day Declan and I settled down to have a quick meal before the film, laughing and chatting as we always had. He asked if I was nervous, but he knew the answer was going to be no. He 'got' me, in a similar way to Helen, Jenny and Emer, and loved the fact that I had challenged him and his view of the world, loved the fact that here was something new, at least to him.

As the film started, I realised what the subject matter was. I glanced at Declan as the story became clearer. He was grinning, looking at me. It was a story about enforced gender reassignment, full of detail and some graphic images. I couldn't believe my eyes. I simply had not realised, had not read the description in the brochure fully.

The film ended. The audience were talking excitedly about it. 'Stupid idea,' some said. 'Too graphic,' others were saying. I was grinning broadly thinking 'In four days' time I'll be going through that!!!!' We got outside the cinema and broke up in laughter.

'You knew what that was about!' Declan accused me.

'Dec, I swear I didn't! I saw the line in the programme about plastic surgery and new techniques and that's as far as I read!' but Declan looked at me with amusement, not quite believing me. We went for a drink, even though I was still on my self-imposed break from alcohol and talked about the surgery further. One of the scenes in the film had showed three dilators, small, medium and large, penis shaped devices which were used daily to keep the new vagina open. I knew I would be using them two or three times a day initially eventually reducing to once or twice a week. Declan looked uncomfortable when I mentioned them, and I let him know that I was getting no small amount of pleasure from his pain.

'Hey, it'll be me that has to insert them!'

'So you really weren't put off by seeing the op? I really can't believe you didn't know about the story!'

'No, I really didn't know and no, I wasn't put off at all. I want this, more than anything else at the moment!' We chatted a little longer and parted. The next time I would see him would be eight days from now, post-op. How would I feel? What wonders or terrors awaited? I would have my vagina, be using those dilators, have some approximation of the woman's body I had always wanted to have. My external would match the internal. *Wow.* It was happening!!!!

***

I woke at 3.45 a.m., listening to Helen gently breathing and loving her even more in that moment. She had enabled me to get to this point and I would be forever grateful. As I lay in the bed, I heard Jenny say something in her sleep, the bed creaked and then silence again

'Ok girl,' I said to myself, 'time to get up for the next stage of your incredible journey.'

I showered quickly, dressed in jeans and a blouse and did my make-up. It was a little chilly, so I slipped on a jacket, checking the time. Sara was due shortly. My suitcase was packed, heels, three or four changes, some make-up and lots of cheap underwear for afterwards. I knew there would be a lot of discharge for weeks, maybe months, afterwards and had been told to buy larger size underwear than normal, and plenty of it. Finishing my make-up quietly in the bathroom, I looked in again at both Helen and Jenny, silently saying 'I love you' to them both before going downstairs.

I waited by the window, watching for the car lights. Plenty of cars went by ('where was everyone going at 5 a.m. on a Sunday morning?') and then I saw Sara's car pass by, turn and pull up beside the house. I hopped in the car, putting the small suitcase in the back and squeezing Sara's hand. 'Hi hon, I'm ready!' I said grinning broadly. Sara smiled at me and squeezed my hand back as she accelerated away towards the motorway.

The airport was quiet, we checked in quickly and went for breakfast, chatting amiably. Sara had organised with the hospital to have her post-op check-up at the same time and it was wonderful having her accompany me, a great friend and also of course someone who could tell me what to expect. She had given lots of advice regarding what supplies to bring and emphasised especially the entertainment I should pack.

'You'll have a lot of time on your hands and the Wi-Fi in the hospital is intermittent at best. So bring dvds, books, music …' I had toyed with the idea of bringing a book on computer programming. I was feeling so fit, so full of energy, that I felt I could do anything and even a major operation like this was not going to affect me much, was it? I was determined that it would only be a minor inconvenience. We chatted about how I felt, how Sara had recovered and more, much more.

As we boarded the plane I realised with delight that a track from Sigur Rós was playing. It had to be a good omen!

A few hours later, I walked onto the ward with more than a few butterflies in my stomach. The sanitised smell, the busy staff moving around the narrow corridors, the atmosphere of the wards – it was wonderful and I was grinning broadly when one of the male nurses who had looked after Sara approached us: 'Hi Eric, remember me? It's my turn now, Sara's here to support *me* this time.' Eric smiled and looked at a wall-chart behind the desk where I saw my name. Philippa Ryder. I almost cried with delight.

'Ooohhh, darling you *must* be special. You have a private room!' He indicated the room to me and I walked in to what would essentially be my home for the next few days.

'Does this meet with your approval, princess?' asked Eric, laughing and I nodded.

I was about to unpack when Eric came in with the charge nurse, some forms and a machine to take my various observations, the first time of many over the next week. Sara started to grin when, looking around the large room she saw the private bathroom, a sliding sign prominent and set to 'Male'. I walked over and pretended to walk in as Sara took a photo. Then I changed the sign to 'Female' and walked out. Another photograph and we broke out laughing.

'Classic,' I said, thinking of how much Emer would have approved.

Visiting hours were almost over anyway and it had been a very long day. We hugged and Sara promised she would see me both before and after the op. She walked out of the room leaving me alone. Not for long though as another nurse was soon back to do more obs and this time a band was attached to each arm, Philippa Ryder CC****94. Just in case I had second thoughts and ran away, I suppose. No chance.

'Nothing else to eat or drink now, not even water, before your operation, ok?' said the nurse, then I was left alone for some time, time to think and contemplate and smile. This was it, this time tomorrow it would be all over, and I would be in recovery. I felt my heart begin to race and I grinned, enjoying the frisson of nervousness, of anticipation and even the fear of the unknown.

Texts from Helen and many friends followed. I settled into the bed with my IPOD playing loudly, watching as nurses and some patients passed the doorway. The lights were dimmed, and a male nurse came in.

'Good evening gorgeous. Now you have a big day tomorrow and the first thing that will happen is me giving you an enema at about 6.30! So, make sure you get some sleep and I'll see you bright and early tomorrow morning.

***

The night passed quickly and I was woken by Nurse Eric. We chatted as the nurse put on a pair of gloves. 'Now darling, I want you to turn over and open your legs ...'

I grinned and said: 'It's not the first time I've been asked to do that!'

I felt fine after he left the room, lying on the bed and watching the doorway, thinking. Will I be taken for surgery in the morning or afternoon? I wanted it to be as soon as possible – in the back of my mind I thought about what could still go wrong – would they re-examine the paperwork, the obs, my psychiatric evaluation. Would there be a hugely important phone call from home, a natural disaster, HSE refusing to pay at the last minute – as all the things that could go wrong and prevent me from achieving my life-long dream raced through my head I started to laugh at myself and remembered some of the meditation techniques I had learned. 'Breathe deeply girl, clear your mind, still the pond.'

A few hours later, the surgical nurse and surgeon disturbed my reverie and musings.

'So, Philippa, all set? Everything seems fine and we'll have you on the table this afternoon, all over by this evening. Now you do understand the operation? This is gender reassignment surgery. You understand what that is? And are you aware that it is irreversible?'

I nodded and smiled and said, 'well at this point I should, shouldn't I? No, I'm fine and I understand fully the operation and the consequences.' He nodded and gave me some forms to sign.

'You will see this form again just before the operation and you will just have to confirm that it is your signature. Do you have any questions for me?'

I signed the form with a flourish and shook my head. 'No, thank you. I'm looking forward to the future, maybe not so much the pain though!'

'You needn't worry, there will be plenty of pain relief,' he said as he and his team left the room.

Suddenly I was on my own again, the hustle and bustle of the busy wards passing by my door but, apart from a nurse dropping in every few hours to take my obs, I was left alone. The waiting was ... boring! I wanted to either to be doing things or else in recovery, but this was frustrating. The time passed very slowly, I couldn't get the television to work properly, got up to look out at the nurses and other patients as they passed my room, joking with the male nurse who had done my enema.

I lay on the bed. It was 12.30. Suddenly the enormity of what I was about to undergo hit me. I missed Helen and Jenny. I felt tears in my eyes, a lump in my throat. I needed someone. What if the operation went wrong? What if I had a bad reaction to the anaesthetic? What if I never saw the two girls again? I began to panic, feeling my heart race, sweat forming on my brow. 'Not good, girl, stupid. This is what you want, this is what you need. You're silly to worry, they're specialists and they've done this so many times it's second nature, they've seen and dealt with everything.'

I began to laugh and relax. 'Ok if that was my panic attack then I can handle anything!' I thought.

As I lay there, calm, I thought about the future. A line from 'Heart of the Sunrise' by one of my favourite groups, Yes, came to mind: 'Dreamer easy in the chair that really fits you.' For many years the line had resonated with me and finally I was going to be sitting in that chair! How would I feel? How would I look? Would I hate or love my new body? Would Helen and I be intimate? Would I ever have sex with a guy? Sex was far from everything to me, but I looked forward to some sort of intimacy in my new female form. In the middle of my day-dreaming, I saw someone enter the room.

At 12.50 p.m. Sara had managed to get in, avoiding the restriction on visiting hours,

'You only have a few minutes now,' called Eric from the corridor. For all too brief a time we chatted then Sara was ushered out. They had come for me!

1 p.m. More obs. Then a good-looking attendant in a surgical gown came to my bed, putting it flat and moving it towards the door.

'You ok?' he asked, casually.

'Yes, very much so.'

My heart was racing, I smiled all the way down the corridor, to the lift, to the twelfth floor and down another corridor and into pre-op. The nurses and attendants barely acknowledged me. To them I was just another patient and I was happy that they were taking this casually. It might be a huge moment for me, but to them it was their everyday job.

'Hi,' said someone. 'Can you confirm your name and date of birth for me please?' I complied.

'Thank you. Now can you confirm what surgery you are here for?'

'Gender Reassignment Surgery – male to female I hope,' I said, getting a laugh.

'And can I ask you to confirm that this is your signature and that you signed this form this morning?'

'I confirm it is, and I did.'

'And that you are aware that the surgery is irreversible and that you are happy to proceed.'

'I am and I am,' I said, smiling, then, unable to resist, I added, 'but … then again … No, only joking!'

The assistant stopped, looked carefully at me and said

with some seriousness, 'it's ok to back out at any time, until you go under anaesthetic. Are you sure it's what you want?'

I started to laugh, 'don't worry, I've been waiting all my life for this! It's just my sense of humour.' He smiled at me.

'Ok I'll now get the nurse to put in a line so we can anaesthetise you.' I quipped: 'well you shouldn't have a problem getting a vein, my wife who works in a hospital says they're great!'

'Oh dear,' said the assistant, 'you're putting her under pressure to perform now'.

The clock opposite read 1:45:32 p.m.

'So do I count back from ten or something?' I asked. 'If you like,' someone said and …

I woke up as I was being wheeled along the corridor. 'So,' I said, hardly recognising my own voice, 'can I have babies now?' The attendant smiled down at me, then I heard a voice: 'so here she comes! What took you so long?' It was Sara.

'Where's my champagne then, honey?' Sara laughed and took my hand briefly.

'It's on the way, I promise!' I hadn't realised how close I was to the ward and within a few seconds I was being wheeled into my own room and could begin to take stock of how I felt.

'So it's over,' I thought. Then thought again – 'well I assume it's over!' There was numbness around my stomach and groin, I had two tubes coming from my hand, and others from between my legs. Eric, the nurse, came in and asked, 'so how are you darling?'

'I feel ok thanks Eric. Have I had the op? Hate to think I've got all these tubes and numbness if I haven't.'

'Oh, you have, all done now and you're fine.' I felt groggy, hearing my speech as quite slurred but I felt hungry. Surely a good sign. As if by magic, the caterer arrived and put pizza and chips down in front of me.

'Just eat what you can, important to get your strength back. Drink lots of water.' I nibbled on the pizza cautiously. I felt good, so started eating normally. Sara was in the background watching me and asked: 'So how do you feel then?'

'Great actually. No pain. What time is it?'

'Almost 6.30, you were in recovery for quite a time.'

'Yes, I usually am. Last time I had an operation, to have my wisdom teeth out, it took all night for the bleeding to stop! Thanks for waiting though.'

'No problem ...' and I felt myself begin to doze.

I woke later with a pain in my stomach. Sara was still there.

'Sara, could you get me a bowl or something, tummy's upset!' and Sara quickly got a container from a passing nurse. As soon as I threw up, I felt much better, though very tired and I found it difficult to keep talking to Sara, drifting off regularly. My pain relief had been two shots of morphine and the drug hadn't agreed with me. I heard Sara distantly saying goodbye and saying she would be in the following morning. I began to feel stronger now, and started to send texts to people, Helen and Jenny first of course, followed by Declan and Emer, then others. Helen rang and I was thrilled to hear her voice, taking care to assure her that I felt fine. Indeed, I did feel fine. I had some aches and felt very tired but otherwise was wondering what all the fuss was about. When the night nurse came in, a lovely South African woman, I chatted amiably to her and though I didn't really need it, was grateful for the reassurance that yes, my vital signs were fine.

'And you've done very well on the pain management, it looks like you've only used the morphine once or twice. But don't be afraid to use it when you need to, that's what it's for. And drink as much water as you possibly can. Just looking at your urine it's very concentrated and dark, so we need to get that clear. Just press the call button if you need anything.'

All through the conversation I realised the nurse had been holding my hand and when she let go I suddenly felt lonely. I lay back in the bed, tears rolling down my face, smiling and almost enjoying the emotions coursing through my body. Almost. I missed Helen and Jenny so much.

The sun came up over the skyline of London and my world was glowing. I woke knowing my body was finally how I wanted, needed it to be. It would be some time before I would be able to feel the new sensations associated with it as the drips, tubes and bandages were still present, and the pressure was intense. But I was bearing it with a smile. I was ecstatic. I looked forward to seeing the results, to trying out my new anatomy, even as far as the simple process of urinating! How would it feel, how different would it be? And sex, orgasm – all lay ahead, a wonderful cornucopia of so many different sensations to be explored as Philippa, truly Philippa.

The night had passed so slowly though. While I wasn't in pain, I did feel some increasing discomfort, but it was bearable. The contrast between the previous night and this was immense. I had felt so full of energy the previous day, despite the really early start and travel, I felt I could do anything. Today all I could think about was how tired I was. The nurses dropped in regularly to do my obs and I drank copious amounts of water, sick of the taste of it, but my urine was still not clear enough for them.

'Keep going hon,' Eric would say, 'drink more, got to keep the surgeon happy!'

As the morning drew on I was happy at the thought of eating again and devoured the cereal and toast brought in by the smiling caterer. More water and tea. I felt much better but now there was definite pain in my groin, and I wondered when I would get some relief. I noticed that the line for the morphine had been taken out – 'Oh well,' I thought, 'no chance of me becoming dependent then!'

I knew I should be getting my medications at 8 a.m. and that visits from the surgical team were due, so I had a lot to look forward to today! And of course, Sara would be around as soon as she was allowed.

By 9 a.m. I was in some serious pain and with some relief saw a nurse pass the doorway, glancing in and indicating she would be back.

A few minutes later and she walked in, smiling. 'So, Philippa, how are you? The surgeon says he's pleased with how the operation went, no issues. How do you feel?'

I looked up at her, 'I feel wonderful! I haven't had any meds yet so I have a few aches and pains, but I feel fine and hungry! I'm anxious to get up and moving, do I have to wait until tomorrow or can I try it today?'

'Well we are anxious to get you mobile as soon as possible so just listen to your body. Normally we just want the patient up and moving by Wednesday but if you can manage it today, all the better. Just take it very slowly … Now, I'll be back shortly with the rest of the team and we will be removing some of the tubes. That should make you a lot more comfortable. And I'll organise your meds now, you should not be feeling any pain at all, there's no need.'

She left the room and I put my IPOD on, wanting to

listen to something fast and loud, to match my positive mood. But any movement was hurting me, so I ended up lying in the bed and thinking about Helen and Jenny going through their normal daily routine, and wishing they were here with me. And Jenny would be getting her Junior Cert results tomorrow. And it was Mum's birthday today! I laughed to myself at all the thoughts running through my head as I felt giddy.

'I've had it! It's over!' Tears of joy ran down my cheeks again. Then the pain again. But soon afterwards, a nurse came in with my meds, an endless supply of tablets to take. Minutes later the surgical team came in.

'So Philippa, all ok? I'm very happy with how the operation went, you should be fine and pleased with the results. I'll be back later to check on you once some of the tubes have been removed.'

And with that he was gone, leaving two nurses at my bedside.

'Now Philippa, we just need to take some of the drips out and redo your bandages after.' She indicated to the other nurse to pull the bedclothes back, raised the bed slightly and then I saw just how large the bandaging was. I looked like an adult baby! They started to remove the padding and plasters, causing me to grimace.

'Sorry, it needs to be very sticky to ensure the wound stays clean.'

She started instructing the nurse to prepare some implements and then said, 'we have to remove two tubes from you. It will be painful but will only take a few seconds. Once we've done that you'll be able to move a lot easier.'

'Ok,' I thought, 'I can handle pain.'

But almost before I realised it I felt excruciating agony in my groin. Then it was gone.

'How was that?' asked one of the nurses. 'You did very well. Just one more. Are you ready?' I indicated to her to wait a moment while I regained my composure. 'Ok, go for it …'

Even worse than before, and longer, then it was over. I lay on the bed, sweating and weak.

The caterer came in, what did I want for lunch and dinner? Then more obs and checks. So much for getting lots of reading done or anything else for that matter. It was 11 a.m. and I thought about what to do. Mum. Her birthday. A quick phone call would mean a lot to her.

'Hi Mum,' I said, 'Happy Birthday!'

'Oh, hi B … hi. Thanks'. My mother had not called me Philippa, but at least tried not to use my old male name either. We chatted for a little, I mentioned I was just on a break from the 'conference' I was attending. When the call ended, I waited for a text from any of the family but nothing arrived. I lay on the bed crying, astounded that I could feel this way.

Time passed slowly and I drifted in and out of sleep. I was feeling tired but otherwise fine, and the painkillers had worked. The surgeon appeared at the door.

'So, let's have a look, see how you are.' Suddenly the room was full of people again and my bandages were removed.

'Yes,' he said, 'a lot of swelling there. Let's keep an eye on it, nothing to worry about yet, no need for any intervention. Otherwise all ok.'

And he was gone again, the room cleared, and lunch arrived. I had been delighted to see a variety of Indian food on the menu and had ordered it for lunch and dinner. If I wanted I could have three courses for both meals and the way I felt now I could eat them all! The slight nausea I had felt immediately after the op yesterday was totally gone and I was hungry. I devoured the meal, drank lots of water and felt great.

When the nurse came in again, I asked if I could walk to my bedside locker. Once again, I heard the words 'Listen to your body. If you feel you can, then do it. Just be careful.'

I smiled and said I would. A few minutes later, I pushed back the bedclothes. Ouch, that hurt a little. Then swung my legs out to hang over the bed. Yes! A sense of achievement already. I remembered the urine bag attached to the side of the bed and took it in one hand. Yuck. How did I feel? Fine. 'Go for it, girl!' Smiling, I stood up. No bright lights or dizziness.

'Oh this is easy' I thought and started to walk around the bed. Whoa! Bright lights, sweating, exhaustion – but I made it to the chair by the bed. And sat there, weak, so weak. A nurse looked in.

'All ok?' she asked. I nodded. 'Ok, just call if you need anything.'

Half an hour later, the nurse looked in again.

'Are you sure you're ok? You look a bit pale …'

I laughed and said, 'No I'm fine. I was determined to get out of bed today. Now how do I get back into it?'

But I stood up and completed the huge three-metre trip easily and lay back, happy at my achievement. Recovery comes in little steps I knew. And that was one small step for a woman, one huge leap for womankind. First target achieved.

Sara arrived shortly afterwards, with champagne, a balloon, chocolates, fruit, a card and a teddy bear (who I immediately christened CC after the hospital) and I told her of my excursion to the bedside locker. We chatted amiably for quite some time before she left for her check-up and I felt alone again. Initially I had felt pleased to be given the private room but now realised that although I had privacy I also became quite lonely, looking forward to the brief interactions with the staff when they came in to check on me. I spent the evening attempting to watch films on my laptop but couldn't connect to the hospital Wi-Fi. So, listening to music, reading, and texting occupied my time but the boredom was beginning to set in already. And I so missed Helen and Jenny. I fell into a deep sleep, interrupted only by the inevitable obs (they had been fine apart from my temperature which had risen a little, approaching the level where I might need to have blood work done to check for possible infection). Ruth, the lovely South African nurse, had been on again and we chatted for some time before an emergency occurred in a nearby ward and Ruth went running off. As morning came I enjoyed the sight of the sun rising, the light beginning to stream into the room. There would be more activity now and I would be less likely to be bored. And today was huge for us as a family. Jenny's Junior Certificate results. She had worked so hard, she seemed so confident and capable that I knew she would do well.

I felt much stronger, excited and positive after the few lows of the previous day. Breakfast was gorgeous – but then with my mood at that moment anything would have been nice! I felt exhilarated, indeed I felt so high I wondered if my meds were wrong! As the morning went on I realised once again the meds were late and a nurse, checking on me around 9 a.m., seemed quite annoyed that there was a delay and went off to get them. When she returned, I asked if the window in the room could be opened as it had become very stuffy and warm. The nurse, having attempted to open it said she would get someone from maintenance to sort it out. As the morning passed, I began to feel stir-crazy and decided to gently move out of bed to the chair again. I was surprised and delighted to find that it was much easier than the previous day and I decided to go to the door after a brief rest in the chair. It was as if a whole new world was open to me. I waved to the nurses I recognised, seeing them smile back.

'Hey Philippa, great to see you on your feet. Don't over-do it though!'

I was thrilled, feeling like I could run a marathon – then the tiredness hit, and I wobbled back to the bed, collapsing into it, heart pounding, but smiling.

My dressings were changed and the nurse asked if I would like to see the result of the operation. I was nervous. What if I hated it? What if it was so horrible I just couldn't identify with it? This was my new body and I was going to live with this for the rest of my life. I had anticipated the moment for so long. This was a huge event and one that had actually taken me somewhat by surprise. The nurse saw my hesitation.

'You don't have to look. Your vagina is very bruised and swollen but it will settle down.'

'I'd love to see, it's just an emotional time for me, that's the only reason for my hesitation,' I said and suddenly the nurse produced a small mirror and placed it at the end of the bed, between my legs. I saw my new anatomy. God but it was a mess! Swollen, bruised, actually even a little disgusting. Yet it was me! I thanked the nurse and smiled. Yes, it was ME! And hopefully it would look better in a few weeks' time. At the moment, it was anything but attractive. But it was an amazing moment as I realised that finally my dreams had come true, after forty years wondering and questioning myself about who I truly was, I could come to terms with the reality of my new, true, anatomy. I was ecstatic – but I really hoped the swelling would reduce quickly!

I lay in the bed, dozing for a while, listening to music and wondering when I was going to hear from Jenny with her Junior Certificate results. In my half-conscious daze, I saw someone walk quickly into the room and, just as I thought 'Ah, maintenance guy for the window,' he said: 'Ok, let's see what we have here ...' and he was standing at the end of the bed about to pull the bedclothes down. It was the lead surgeon in his cycling lycra! I let out a very girly giggle and lay back while he examined the work of his colleague.

'Yes, that's fine, nothing to worry about. The swelling should subside soon. I'll drop in again tomorrow.'

And he was gone, a whirlwind, I couldn't help but laugh at the situation and my reaction. I didn't even have a chance to thank him or ask any questions.

It was approaching 12 midday. Jenny should be getting her results. I was so upset at not being there for her, it had just been bad timing but then I had every confidence in my wonderful daughter and knew that the support of Helen and Mum would be more than enough. And anyway, it was a moment for Jenny, her friends and the presence of her 'dad' might detract from it. No, it was actually fine that I wasn't there.

Soon though Helen confirmed that Jenny had the results and was happy. But how happy? A minute later and Jenny rang.

'Hi!!!! Guess what???? 9 As and a B!!!!' I could hardly

speak due to the emotion coursing through my body. I managed to force out 'Oh darling I'm soooooo proud of you! Well done!!! You're with your friends honey, well done again and I'll talk to you later.'

I rang Helen immediately: 'Oh hon, she is amazing! Oh, I'm so proud! Is Mum there? Is she delighted?'

Helen replied that yes, they were all together and she and Mum were watching the girls jumping up and down and laughing with relief. We chatted a little, Helen managing to ask how I was without giving the secret away to my mother sitting nearby and then we said goodbye. As I laid the phone down on the small table, I was overcome with emotion. I was so proud of Jenny, she had coped with the situation of my transition so well and, despite the pressure associated with it had managed to finish in the top few percentile in the country. I was wiping the tears away when Eric came in and asked if I was ok.

'Oh Eric, my little girl just did her, well you'd call them GCSEs and got all As except for one B. I'm so proud!'

'Well she's obviously clever like her Mum!' he said and squeezed my hand.

Lunch – more Indian, still gorgeous – and more texting and a quick call to Helen and then I dozed. I was receiving painkillers regularly and only had some slight discomfort, I felt my energy returning and wanted to go on a longer walk. When I had my obs done, and a new urine leg bag fitted, I asked the nurse if I could walk to the end of the corridor.

'Of course, Philippa, if you feel up to it.'

I was conscious of how Sara had been on the third day and wanted to see if I was as well as she was. I felt the room was becoming a prison cell so I got out of bed, getting used to the awkwardness of the urine bag (still a bit cloudy according to the nurse – drink more water, the usual mantra), walked easily to the door – and out! It was the first time I had seen the corridor properly since the trip to surgery and it was as if it was the beginning of a new life! I felt a little weak but managed to walk as far as the day room, sitting down in a chair awkwardly. There was discomfort but no pain. A few minutes rest and I was up again, feeling better, and I got as far as the end of the corridor as the door opened and 'Freedom' by George Michael started on a loop in my head! As tempted as I was to go through and towards the coffee shop I didn't want to risk fainting so satisfied myself with a careful walk back to the day room. Then back to bed and a rest, more texts, lots of music and dinner. I felt great. So great that for the first time since the op I washed and put on a little make-up. My mood went from great to amazing! *Wow.*

Sara had reached Manchester, had her meeting and was in her hotel room with a bottle of wine. Silly texts between us had me giggling hysterically 'you'll make my stitches come out!' I said and indeed made a mental note to ask just how much I could move without risk. One of the nurses came in and said there was a phone call at the main desk for me – it was Cat and could be put through to the phone in my room. I hadn't even noticed the phone beside me on the table and found the number which I sent by text to Helen with a RING ME! message. I chatted to Cat and Leslie, delighted at the chance to tell them of my condition, then to Helen – tears as I heard her lovely voice! – and then sent a text to Emer, asking if she would like a call. A minute later and Emer rang the room phone, sounding so delighted for me. I was so happy to hear from my amazing friend and confidante and yet so sorry that it was unlikely she would ever experience the joy of physically being the true woman she was inside.

A beautiful Indian nurse made my night special. I had found the day exhausting and emotional, and I was feeling a little low when I was woken up just before midnight to have my obs done yet again. I saw the nurse smiling as she stood beside me and I asked her name.

'Manju,' she said, 'and I will be looking after you tonight. Now I have some questions for you. Is your name ...' and she took my hand, looking at the wristband, 'Philippa Ryder as it says on this chart?'

I smiled, loving the feel of her hand holding my wrist. She was so gentle, so sweet.

'Yes indeed. That's me.'

'All right then. I can give you your meds for tonight. Are you feeling any pain? Is there anything else you want? Make sure you drink lots of water ...' she looked at the chart, 'you need to get your urine completely clear and water will do that.'

I assured her I felt fine, feeling totally at ease with her. And Manju was still holding my hand.

'Now Philippa, your obs are fine, you're doing very well. And don't worry about anything, no matter what the problem is we can fix it here.'

It was said so matter-of-factly that I felt Manju believed they could cure death itself. We chatted quietly for a few more minutes and then Manju told me to get more rest.

I woke after a good night's sleep, delighted at my progress and thinking about what I could do today. Definitely a trip to the coffee shop and outside to the small courtyard just to get some air. The window was still stuck and I mentioned it to a nurse again as she popped in to check on me. She also told me it was best if I had a bowel movement today, one of the big events of the week! Before this, I had only been passing urine through a catheter and at this point the stitches in the 'wound' as the nurses called it should have healed enough.

'So sit on the toilet and wait. It'll happen. If it doesn't then we can give you a laxative, but you'll probably be ok. Don't push though!'

I asked her about movement, bending and stretching.

'Limited movement is fine, you're not going to dislodge or disrupt anything unless you bend over and touch your toes! So just be careful but don't worry unnecessarily.' She was very matter-of-fact and sometimes seemed dismissive of my concerns but I certainly had confidence in her expertise.

The surgeon came around later, checking on my progress. I asked about the swelling, and would a follow-up operation be required, but he assured me it would reduce rapidly, and draining the lips of the vagina would only result in them filling up again. No, he said, I would be fine in time.

I became more and more annoyed at the window and decided to attempt to open it slightly myself, which I managed after a strain. 'Careful girl, don't dislodge the stitches!' But the air was wonderful, energising me and lifting my mood. More music, more reading, and a little sleep. As I dozed, the lycra-clad shape of the lead surgeon checked me again and he assured me that everything was progressing nicely.

After lunch, it was time for a visit to the coffee shop. It would be a long walk of about 200 metres but I was very keen to attempt it. I had been up and down the corridor endless times by now, out in the courtyard once or twice too. Time to see the real world again.

I walked casually past the nurses' station half-way along

the corridor: 'I'm off to the coffee shop,' I said. 'If I'm not back in an hour send the search party out!' Eric laughed and agreed that he would personally go looking for me.

'Promise, Eric? Maybe I will stay until you come to find me …'

I walked. To the door, I pressed the release button. It opened. I went through – George Michael serenaded me again in my mind as I walked, grinning broadly. The walk to the foyer of the hospital was, in my current state, about five minutes. I felt a little discomfort towards the end but reached my goal and ordered a latte, sitting on a hard seat but feeling ecstatic. The coffee was poor, but the freedom was wondrous. I realised though that I probably didn't look my best, despite putting a little make-up on, so I went back to the ward after half an hour. Eric greeted me with a grin.

'Darling I was coming to look for you!' I stuck my tongue out at him and went back to bed for a short time, texting Helen to tell her of my achievement and waited for dinner.

I was delighted with my progress, and in two days Helen, Jenny, Declan and Nicole would all be coming to visit me.

I noticed a spot of blood on the floor. Then a few more. I looked inside my pants. Oh, a few spots there. I pressed the call bell and waited for the nurse to come.

'Yes Philippa, how can I help?' It was a nurse who I had seen before but never had to deal with. I explained the problem and the nurse examined me carefully. She called in a doctor and, after a few attempts at stopping the bleeding and a conversation with the surgical nurse, he said: 'Ok Philippa. This is nothing to worry about. I'm going to put a serious pressure dressing on you and that will stop the bleeding.'

As I lay in the bed I panicked slightly and my mind

turned to Helen and Jenny, 'what if I never see them again?'

After two minutes or more, the doctor called for tape and started to apply it, much tighter than before. He smiled down at me and said, 'Ok, that's it. That will not move and you won't bleed again. I know how to apply a pressure dressing!'

'Will this loss of blood affect my recovery?' I asked, weakly.

'Not at all, you'll be fine.'

'But what if I need a transfusion?' I asked. The doctor and nurse smiled and said: 'it may have seemed like a lot of blood but really it wasn't, you'll be fine.'

I was exhausted and traumatised. Everything had been going so well and now was everything going to be ruined? Had I brought on this bleed by doing too much, by straining too much with the window yesterday? I felt sick but managed to fall into a fitful sleep, desperately wanting reassurance from anybody …

Friday morning dawned, bright and sunny. The birds were singing, the sound of aircraft or cars on the nearby main road just audible. Why was it London seemed to get great weather? And would I be able to enjoy it today or would I be stuck in bed again?

'Good morning Philippa, how are you today? I believe you had a bit of a bleed last night, that's great. That will be the swelling going down and will help your recovery. Now let's just take a look …' The nurse began removing the sticky bandages causing me to wince.

'Hmmmm,' she said, 'that's not quite what I thought. But don't worry, it's perfectly normal to have bleeds at this stage.'

'Will it delay my release on Monday?' I asked nervously, worried about the flight home with Helen and Jenny on Tuesday.

'Not at all. As I said these sorts of bleeds are quite common, it was a urethral incident and they tend to be quite voluminous. We'll be in to see you later but you're fine.'

I asked about walking and moving around and she was keen for me to do so, with care.

I was left alone with my breakfast, to contemplate and relax as best I could. Emotions flooded over me, I had been so worried that my release would be delayed now I was reassured and was getting my confidence back.

A little while later (so much for the privacy of a private room!) a nurse came in and described the next few days: 'You will have a boring day today but then an exciting one tomorrow. Your pack comes out and you will start to dilate.' The nurse produced two long cardboard containers.

'These are your two dilators. Have a look at them and make sure they're not damaged.'

I took them out – two clear glass smooth implements, 7 inches in length. I had seen dilators before and the thoughts of using them didn't worry me. There was no massive ten-inch version as in the film I saw (only a week ago!) with Declan.

'Thank you, I feel reassured now. I was very worried for a while.'

My mood was much improved and I felt energetic again. I wandered down into the larger ward where Sara had been but didn't feel in the mood to start any conversations. I was getting quite lonely now, texting Helen and Jenny regularly and telling them how much I missed them. I felt strong enough again to walk to the coffee shop, hating the urine bag strapped to my leg and trying to hide it. I was comfortable walking normally by this stage but sitting down was different, and I was feeling a little discomfort after a few minutes of squirming and shifting position. Sara and Declan both sent a few texts and I occupied myself by rearranging all the photographs on my computer hard drive, smiling at the many memories they evoked.

I was lying on the bed, dozing, when the charge nurse came in carrying a huge box.

'Philippa, this is for you and we're all very curious as to what it is!'

She placed the box on a table and left, still smiling. I looked at it carefully. Where or who was it from? The labels didn't give any return address. I walked to the nurses' station: 'well I can't get it open without a scissors so if you want to know what's in there, you'd better find me a pair!'

A scissors was produced and I went back to the room to attack the box. Eventually the lid was open revealing a big hamper with chocolates, a balloon, a teddy bear and other goodies. And a card. It was from Helen and Jenny. I started to cry, loving them both so much at that moment as always. The enormity of the past few days hit me all at once. The sobs wracked me, and I lay on the bed trying to regain my composure. I lined the cards, balloon and teddy bear up on the windowsill and went out to see the nurses to tell them about the lovely present.

Then boredom. I had done everything I could. I was over the trauma of the previous night and looking forward to the following day which promised to be another momentous one. Most of the UK trans patients were being released today but the Irish patients, because of the extra distance to be travelled and the fact that there wasn't a straightforward referral centre in the case of any problems were kept in until Monday, then asked to stay in London overnight. So,

I listened to music, walked, wrote my diary and sent texts until late in the evening, then fell into a deep sleep, my best so far.

Saturday: I was woken by the caterer for breakfast – had they even taken my obs? I didn't remember and hungrily ate the cereal and toast. A nurse I recognised came in and said that they would be back soon to remove the packing from my vagina, but that it was a straightforward, simple procedure. I imagined a huge ball of cotton wool being removed with forceps, as if I was giving birth to something alien (how appropriate!) and was almost disappointed when the nurse came back, arranged my legs and pulled a narrow strip of wadding out. I felt a sensation deep within me and smiled, thinking: 'That's a sensation I've never had before, from my vagina!'

The nurse then explained the procedure of using the dilators, recognising that it was an emotional moment for me and over the next hour I practised under her instruction. Basically the intention of the long slim glass devices was to keep the vagina open and although very painful, especially with the larger one, the procedure would have to be done regularly into the future.

'That was super for your first time. Now, I'm sure you'd love a shower, just be very careful ...' and she left the room.

I walked to the bathroom, took off my nightdress and turned the shower on, testing the water. I was going to enjoy this! I put my head under the shower – and almost passed out. Bright lights and dizziness, total lack of power in my legs. I barely managed to fall into the chair in the shower provided for just such an occurrence. I sat there for what seemed like half an hour, sick, weak and light-headed. I eventually felt my strength return and managed to quickly place my head and most of my body under the still running water, managing to enjoy the sensation of getting clean after six days without a shower.

I was back in bed, heart pounding and Eric came in to take my obs.

'Hey hon,' I said, 'bet my BP is pretty low, if not non-existent!' and told him of the incident.

'Do you feel ok now then?' he asked, concerned.

'Getting better.'

He finished his obs of me. 'Wow, you weren't joking Philippa. Your BP is 80/40 now, and that's … what, forty-five minutes after your incident?'

I nodded and said, 'so I'm staying here for a while!'

He laughed and said he'd be back for more obs in a few hours.

Helen and Jenny were due to arrive at the beginning of visiting hours and I had already received texts to say they were at the hotel, going shopping briefly and then coming out. I was desperate to see them.

'Come out now!' I pleaded in a text and got the reply 'soooooon' from Jenny. Lunch, then another dilation and I realised just how messy this was going to be.

I washed again, put on the large hospital underwear with some pads, did my make-up and dressed in my nightgown and dressing gown. The urine bag was still attached to my leg and I really wanted to hide it from Jenny particularly, so tied it as tight and as far up my leg as possible. Then Jenny walked in, closely followed by Helen and my heart leapt.

'Pippa!!!' We hugged and laughed, and everything was well with the world again.

'Baby! My clever baby!!! Well done on the Junior Cert results!!!'

'Thank you,' said Jenny with a smile, looking around the room. Helen stood back a little, also looking around and grinning when she saw the hamper, balloon and other presents. We kissed and hugged more, Jenny hopped on the bed and we chatted. I felt so happy, all I wanted to do was hug and kiss both of them forever.

'Would you like tea or coffee? I can get it for you' I asked Helen.

'No, we're fine, we had lunch.'

'Well, let's go up to the coffee shop in the lobby anyway, I need to get some air.'

Helen's concern for me was apparent and I wanted to show her that I was as well as I had said in the texts and phone calls. We walked up slowly, hugging and kissing and chatting all the way. I explained the incident in the shower to Helen quietly saying it was nothing to worry about and, apart from that, everything had been great today.

It was as if I had only been away from home an hour, the conversation quickly turned to mundane matters and I stared at Jenny, deep in a book, nibbling on a cookie. They both looked wonderful and I hoped I wasn't worrying them, as I must have looked awful. But I felt so happy because the arrival of my visitors today meant that it was less than forty-eight hours until I could leave!

Soon afterwards, I received a text from Nicole, my cycling friend: she was just outside with her boyfriend. It was a delight to see her – I had felt the need to come out to her just a few weeks previously, explaining the reason why I would be missing from the club spins until probably around Christmas. Nicole had reacted well, as I was confident she would, and indeed it turned out that she was quite familiar with trans issues as a former workmate had also transitioned.

I assured her that one of my more immediate goals was to feel the wind in my hair as I flew down from Sally Gap on my road bike again, sharing the experience with her and the rest of the Orwell Wheelers women's group.

It was approaching dinnertime and Helen and Jenny had been with me for a wonderful four hours. I hugged them both as they left to get some dinner of their own, and maybe do a little late-night shopping. Now I was waiting for Declan, who would be my last visitor of the day.

Almost an hour later after I had finished dinner and freshened up I was still waiting, slightly impatiently. He sent a text from within the hospital. He was lost. I walked down the corridor towards the lobby and saw him.

'Declan!' I called and almost ran to greet him. He turned and we embraced, his getting lost was just oh-so-Declan! He probably did it just to make me laugh.

We walked back to my room where he gave me a cuddly talking R2D2 and Chewbacca, both from the *Star Wars* films, and other presents. The nurses looked in occasionally at the laughter and the sounds from the cuddly toys, I suggesting that perhaps obs should be taken for them too. Declan was as usual interested in the scientific side of everything and the nurse Eric was especially interested in how long we had known each other. Amazingly Eric had never seen *Star Wars* and I promised to give him a copy on DVD when I came across for my check-up in November.

Then suddenly Declan was gone, visiting hours were over and I settled in for a good night's sleep after the momentous and exciting day. More tomorrow!

Sunday was a day of waiting. Waiting for Helen and Jenny to arrive then followed shortly afterwards by Helen's brother Bernie and his wife Grazyna. I was touched by their genuine concern. All through the conversation I tried to hide the horrible urine bag, feeling so exposed, as though my most intimate parts were on display. I felt energetic, enthusiastic and positive. All the issues and problems of Thursday and my bleed seemed so long ago that I could almost forget them. Dilation was fine, still very sore but it was a day of looking forward to the next stage in my recovery, removing the catheter and being discharged. It was wonderful seeing everyone, but I hoped that the shock for Jenny of seeing me in discomfort and some pain in such a location as this huge hospital would not affect her too much.

I wanted to ensure that the girls got to see a little of London, not wanting them to feel that they had to stay with me all the time. After all, what more can be said after the first hour, it wasn't as if I was really sick and needed constant care and attention. So once Bernie and Grazyna left I suggested that the girls go too, to allow me to have dinner and rest. Texts from Sara and Declan brightened my evening, then the next stage of my recovery began.

The charge nurse came in and told me that they would be taking the catheter out at midnight. I was then to drink lots of water and, if I passed urine in the morning, I would be discharged. Big day to come then!

And just as I was about to fall asleep, the nurse came in. She gently removed the tube from my groin. It was a strange sensation, I could feel movement from within my core, but it wasn't painful. Then it was out.

'So Philippa, drink lots of water as usual and don't worry. Most people have no trouble with this stage. I'll see you bright and early in the morning.'

Monday: I slept well again, getting ready for my big day. The nurse woke me at 8 a.m. for obs, then it was breakfast time.

'Should I go and pee if I feel like it?' I asked and the nurse said 'of course'. So I sat on the toilet and waited. Nothing. Oh well, too soon I thought and went back to bed. Sometime later, the surgical nurse arrived.

'Hi Philippa, how have you been over the weekend? Everything seems to be fine and you're on course for discharge around lunchtime. Have you passed urine yet?'

As I shook my head she said, 'Ok don't worry. It'll happen. Drink lots of water and keep trying. And if it doesn't then we'll reinsert the catheter and you can have it removed at home later in the week.'

'So if I can't urinate it won't delay my release?'

'Not at all, just a bit inconvenient for you,' she replied.

That put my mind at rest, and I settled down to listen to music.

The morning passed but unfortunately I didn't, and I became more uncomfortable. The nurse returned and said she would have to reinsert the catheter. I was upset but resigned to it. She was very good and I hardly felt the tube being reinserted. I decided to dilate, and had just finished when I noticed the nurse had returned.

'Ok Philippa, how are you getting on with dilation? Let me see you use the larger one.'

I just wasn't in the mood and found it difficult to insert the dilator, only getting it about half-way.

'Now you can do better than that Philippa. Do you want me to help you?'

'Oh if you want,' I said, annoyed and upset, frustrated at the catheter.

'I'm sorry Philippa, you have been so good over the past week and I know you're very confident. If you want me to help I will, or would you prefer to try it yourself?'

I apologised and said I'd do it myself, indeed managing much more depth the second time, more relaxed now.

'When you've finished drop into me and I'll show you some pictures of post-op girls similar to you,' she said as she walked past the room, glancing in at me getting ready to leave.

She showed me before and after photos which did put my mind at ease. I could expect a normal labia in about six weeks according to her. What I was certain of was that I did not want Helen to see me in my swollen state. Whatever possibility there was for intimacy later, the sight of my vagina looking as it did now would be a real turn-off.

Helen and Jenny arrived soon after, taking my bags and offering to help me walk. But I felt great and was just a little disappointed that there were not many of the nurses I recognised as I left.

Then I was out. The girls had organised a taxi to the hotel which I found a little awkward, every movement caused me to wince a bit. It was a very warm day and I became increasingly uncomfortable, but then we checked in (after a slight mix-up over the bookings) and I lay on the bed, tired. A little while later, following a nice lunch and dinner Helen and Jenny went off to a show leaving me to relax in the room, missing them terribly but knowing the following day was our trip home.

Tuesday: Helen had thought of everything for the trip home and, although our flight was in the early evening, suggested we make our way to the airport very early in the afternoon, to allow for any delays.

The tube was quiet and thankfully I got a seat. Helen had organised a wheelchair for me from check-in to the gate but as we had planned on eating dinner at one of the restaurants

I ended up being wheeled there by an assistant, getting priority access through security and just a few quizzical looks from the staff as I explained about the urine bag. We sat eating as a family, laughing and joking as usual. I was going home!

The flight was comfortable, the staff at Dublin airport were waiting with another wheelchair and a little while later I walked in the door of our house to begin the next stage of my recovery, of my life.

Helen had arranged to be off the following day and helped a lot, but showering was difficult and even climbing the stairs was an adventure, having to ascend and descend sidewise, crablike. But I was thrilled with being home.

My days were dictated by the television schedule. I had become very fond of *The Gilmore Girls* (thanks to Sara) and as it started at 10.20 that was the time I aimed to get up. Breakfast, then dilation, then lunch, sleep, more dilation and then the girls got home from work and school. In the evening, I would dilate late and have a salty bath. As the days progressed, I wanted to do more, to push myself, but when I did I found I was exhausted the following day. I had emailed a few questions to Charing Cross hospital, receiving immediate and detailed responses, I chatted on the phone to Sara and she dropped in once or twice. I was happy with the progress I was making. And I even started thinking about the bicycles in the garden shed.

I had asked Helen to drop into the local GP, to ask about medical certs and to organise an appointment to get the catheter removed. I had a letter giving a date of ten days after release for the removal.

'Plenty of time,' I thought, 'just hope they don't have to put it back in.'

Helen came back from talking to the GP, Edel. She was happy removing it but was unused to reinserting catheters so suggested a local area nurse, who initially agreed but then once she discovered the reason for the request – possibly my trans status? – refused.

Helen had managed to get me an appointment with a GU (Genito-Urinary) specialist nurse in St James's and I decided to go there first.

I turned up in my wide light blue trousers at St James's, registering at reception before waiting to be seen. I was nervous at what would happen if I still couldn't urinate after the removal.

The nurse was very sympathetic and understanding. I explained what had happened; the nurse was not at all fazed and she quickly removed the catheter.

'So all I want you to do is walk and drink lots of water, coffee – liquids! It's not a problem to reinsert it if necessary but I doubt if we'll need to.'

A few hours of drinking water and walking did indeed produce the desired result. I sat on the toilet happily, enjoying the new sensation of urinating for the first time physically as a woman, and sent a text to Helen. 'Niagara Falls!!!' The sensation had been intense, starting from much deeper within my body and was very pleasurable.

Finally, I could really begin my recovery properly, to regain my strength, my energy, my passion for life. As I left the hospital, I skipped towards the future.

Walking into the bedroom naked after my shower the following day Helen glanced towards me, smiled and said: 'You look right now.' Yes, I was finally, physically now as I always had been mentally, the woman known as Philippa.

12

AFTERMATH AND THE FUTURE

Age: 51 –

To those who are gay, lesbian, bisexual or transgender – let me say – you are not alone. Your struggle, for the end to violence and discrimination, is a shared struggle. Today, I stand with you. And I call upon all countries and people, to stand with you too. A historic shift is underway. We must tackle the violence, decriminalise consensual same sex relationships and end discrimination. We must educate the public. I call on this council and people of conscience to make this happen. The time has come.

Ban Ki-Moon, Secretary-General, United Nations

I felt like I was missing a purpose. Had the end of the journey to surgery been the highlight of my life and was I now just going to decline into old age and decrepitude? I needed more challenges. The whole world was open to me, yet I was so unfocused. But I knew I also needed a rest and to be able to enjoy myself for a while. So, when Declan suggested (nay, forced!) me into writing this book it seemed the obvious way to put my thoughts in order about the whole process, to act as catharsis after such an experience. I also wanted to keep cycling, read a lot more and had the idea of writing something around the early history of Irish Science Fiction, a subject I was suited to. And, of course, work, family and friends would keep me occupied. As it turned out the ten years since surgery have been some of my most productive, exciting and sad years of my life.

One year after my surgery – 12 September 2012 – I

walked along the familiar corridors of Charing Cross Hospital with three boxes of chocolates and three cards. There was a lump in my throat as I approached the desk. The nurse looked up, slightly concerned. 'Yes, can I help you?' I could hardly get the words out, emotion was coursing through me. 'Hi,' I managed. Gulped. 'I was here this time last year ...' The nurse now looked worried. 'And is everything ok?'

'Oh yes! I just wanted to drop these in for you all to say thank you for all you did.'

As the nurse said: 'Thank you so much', I turned and left, unable to say anything else. I gulped in air and began to smile.

Some, on hearing of my trip, called it a closure of sorts. Yet the experience, the journey, was never closed for me. I always thought back with gratitude to the eight days in the hospital, always remembering on a Monday morning how I waited on the bed for the surgical team to arrive and looking forward to my life afterwards. I didn't want closure as I never wanted this experience of being the true me to end.

***

While I didn't manage to make it back every year, I ensured that most years I dropped in to Charing Cross Hospital and 12 September became one of my annual birthdays, to go with my actual birthday and also the day I chose my name, 9 October. Childish it may seem but each date meant a lot to me in different ways and I encouraged Helen to mark them all (which she usually didn't, saying, rather unfairly I thought, that one birthday was enough!)

Of course, if you've read this far in my memoir you will realise how much music means to me. If I'm on my own in our house, there is music in every room, Usually, it's Lyric FM, the classical music station, when I'm doing housework – we have four radios permanently tuned to the station. But if I want to listen to music properly, I'll put on headphones so as not to disturb Helen (or the neighbours) and 'pump up the volume'. And one of the likely cds or vinyl albums that will be played is from the Icelandic group Sigur Rós. So, when I discovered they were playing a gig in 3Arena I was probably the first in Dublin to get two tickets.

I invited Declan to accompany me, hoping he would appreciate the music, certainly more than Helen who simply couldn't take the falsetto singing style of Jonsí, the lead singer. Declan knew what music and more specifically what the group meant to me. I wasn't wrong. From the moment we entered the venue I was in another world. I felt I was with one of my tribes.

The concert was without doubt the highlight of my musical life. The music and stage show, the atmosphere and the emotion each track brought out in me left me spellbound. I had discovered the group at a momentous time of my life, in 2006 as I was starting hormone treatment. All through the previous seven years, I had felt they were with me on the journey. Now here I was, the journey complete, with my best friend, seeing them for the first time. Of course the soaring melodies and vocals were going to affect me as I thought back to significant moments – catching the flight to Charing Cross for my operation and hearing one of their tracks being played on-board being surely the most incredible – and I wasn't hiding the tears rolling down my cheeks for pretty much the entire concert. There simply are no words to describe how I felt.

Jenny started a degree in History and Political Science in

Ireland's prestigious university, Trinity, in 2014, having just missed out on a place at Oxford University. But it was one of our proudest moments seeing her making her mark within the walls of the university through student societies such as 'The Phil', working on 'Repeal the 8th' with the Students Union, then a year abroad in University of California in San Diego (of course we had to go and see her a few times, meeting her new American boyfriend Tom who is still part of our family) and eventually graduating with First Class Honours in 2018. When the subject of her parents came up, she would simply say she had two mums. Each time I walked through the main square of the campus on my way to work, I thought back to the little bundle of joy that I took out for a walk a few weeks after she was born, and what she had become. And she was only getting started.

***

Our favourite jeweller, in the Royal Hibernian Mall in Dawson Street, Carol Clarke, had been looking out for a special pair of earrings for Helen and we got a call to come in to look at some suggestions. We arrived on a beautiful summer's morning just as Carol was opening and she showed us in to the small but well stocked shop where a couple of years previously I had bought Helen her REGARD ring (comprising a Ruby and Emerald, Garnet, Amethyst, Ruby, Diamond). It was something she had wanted for years, the original of these rings having originated in the Victorian era though hers was a modern take on the concept. We chose a beautiful pair of pearl drops with square cut pale blue gemstones. Perfect for her ears. Then Helen mentioned that my left hand had been missing something since I transitioned. My finger held my wedding ring but no engagement ring. Carol produced a tray for us to examine and chatted, explaining the history behind some of them and their composition. I always hated spending money on myself but Helen was insistent and we chose a beautiful delicate two stone ring which just needed a little sizing to fit. And a few days later we picked it up, Helen humorously placing it on my finger. 'Now you're truly a married woman!' I was surprised how much it meant to me and we embraced in the shop, with Carol, a big supporter of the LGBTQ+ community, looking on smiling.

There was a slight autumnal breeze coming through the trees as we settled into the wooden chairs in the RTÉ gardens in Montrose. The reporter and cameraman discussed angles and lighting in the challenging conditions as the sun dipped towards the horizon in the early evening. I chatted quietly to Helen and Jenny sitting beside me, all of us shivering slightly. We were preparing for an interview on the prime-time news programme that evening on the day that the legislation for the Gender Recognition Act (GRA) had been signed into law. I felt incredible.

It had been a long journey to get to this point. I was fifty-four and finally about to be recognised legally, fully, in my own country. I felt emotional thinking of it, this monumental change in the law and its effect on the lives of so many. TENI and Sara in particular had done so much for trans rights in Ireland, they had brought it to this point.

The RTÉ reporter, joined us at the table and began with a simple question: 'So Philippa, how do you feel about finally getting your true birth certificate, of being accepted for who you truly are?'

I had answered similar questions so many times before. The media always wanted the personal, not wanting to confuse their audience with technical questions about legislation or medical facts. So this question was an easy one for me.

'Happy. And with my family here around me, so proud. Of them, of my country and even of myself.'

The fight for Gender Recognition legislation in Ireland had begun with Lydia Foy in 1990. It had continued all the way through the 1990s, 2000s and up to the establishment of Transgender Equality Network Ireland in 2005. Then the real push started as the organisation campaigned and helped Lydia by highlighting the issues, raising public awareness and educating the media, steering clear of the sensational and trying to focus on the facts, the simple fact that all transgender people wanted was to be themselves and live their lives free of discrimination, prejudice and violence.

The reporter continued with the questions, some directed at me, some at Helen and Jenny. Jenny was confident and smiling as she emphasised the point she so often made, and one that always got to me: 'Philippa has to be true to herself, she has to be who she is.'

The cameraman indicated he wanted to change the position of the camera. 'You're all very relaxed, it's a great interview so far. You're obviously a very close family.' We were just being ourselves we told him, showing the solidarity of our family to the world and how supportive we were to each other. A few more questions and the interview was over. RTÉ paid for the taxi home and we set the video recorder wondering how the finished piece would play. The reporter had seemed positive and supportive, but an editor can twist and manipulate the recording, putting a different spin.

We needn't have worried. It was wonderful.

Yet, it was almost a choice between my marriage and my birth certificate. When the proposed legislation to allow transgender people to get their true birth certificates was introduced, Ireland did not have same sex marriage. If the Gender Recognition Act had passed without Marriage Equality the loving relationship that Helen and I had, the twenty-nine years we had spent together, would have been seen as a same sex marriage and I might have had to choose. Our fight had been two-fold: to win Marriage Equality and to help ensure the GRA was enacted – for our own selfish reasons as well as the good of our community and indeed society.

The fight started in earnest for us months earlier in February 2015. The snow had been falling thickly as Helen and the others trudged their way on the first canvass for the Marriage Equality campaign. I had dropped in to see my mother who hadn't been well for the preceding few months, so I missed the first session. I knew there would be a lot of other opportunities to convince people in the south-west Dublin electoral area to support a basic human right, the right to marry the person of their choice. Helen sent a photo of the team, snow sprinkled through their hair, Senator Katherine Zappone amongst them. Despite the conditions, they seemed to be having fun. I expected that some difficult and challenging days and nights lay ahead, and I hoped we would all be smiling at the end.

A few days later though and I got the opportunity to join them. The weather had improved a little and the crisp late winter air cleared our heads and minds for the sometimes painful, sometimes aggressive conversations we were about to have.

Tonight's canvass was a short introduction and I was nervous as I went up to the first door with my colleague. We were in pairs for safety! Our instructions were clear: be polite, don't be drawn into arguments if they're obviously voting No and be positive to everyone.

I rang the doorbell and an elderly man came to the door. My voice quivered as I started:

'Hi, sorry for disturbing you. We're from YesEquality and we're campaigning for a Yes vote in the Marriage Equality referendum.'

A puzzled look crossed the man's face. 'The *what* referendum?'

'The Marriage Equality one in May, to allow same sex couples to marry,' I answered, smiling. It was very early in the campaign and it was to be expected that the vast majority of people didn't know about the issues, busy with their own lives, probably only interested in getting dinner before settling down to watch soaps on television. The elderly man shook his head and said, 'No, that's not right', and closed the door. My colleague and I looked at each other and smiled. 'I hope it gets better,' I said and Darragh, a seasoned political campaigner, replied confidently, 'it will.'

It did.

A few weeks later, I got an invitation from Sara to join her and the team from TENI at the Dáil for an important debate. The Gender Recognition Bill was progressing through the early stages of its passage through to enactment. The campaign was being very well managed by TENI, with Sara at the helm, and support from organisations such as BeLonGTo, GLEN and others were ensuring the negativity being expressed from the usual conservative quarters was being mitigated and silenced. At least to some degree. This morning's debate was likely to be a pretty sedate affair and we took our seats, chatting amiably. 'Please turn your phones off now' the ushers had said as we climbed the steps to enter the gallery which overlooked the Dáil chamber. A large group of schoolchildren made their way past us, bringing back memories to me of being brought on a tour of the Dáil as a teenager with my father.

The debate ended and I was feeling confident as we broke for lunch. The Dáil chamber had few TDs present, an unfortunately typical situation. This was a debate that most of them had little or no interest in, but at least the comments made had been very positive and boded well for the future.

'I wonder what happened to the usual suspects?' I asked Sara and she just shook her head. 'It's too early in the process, they won't waste their time appearing until later. I'm sure they'll have plenty to say in due course.'

As we made our way through the heavily carpeted halls leading from the chamber I was struck by the paintings and adornments that told the history of the Irish state. Mostly men of course, but our two female presidents and some notable TDs and Senators also hung proudly. Ireland wasn't perfect, like all countries we had our problems. But in many ways we were quite progressive.

The restaurant was little more than a fancy canteen, busy and noisy, full of politicians and their guests. The politicians made their way to and from tables, discussing matters of state no doubt, though from the laughs and general atmosphere I wondered how much work would actually be done.

I glanced at my phone and saw a missed call from my sister. A little surprised I called her back, hearing a worried voice answer.

'It's Ma, she's been taken to hospital. You need to get down here. I found her on the floor when I went out this morning.' My heart skipped a beat and I quickly made my way to St James's Hospital, wondering what I would find. I remembered receiving a similar call fifteen years earlier from a neighbour and discovering that my father had died. Mum hadn't been well for six months or more, despite her regular visits to the doctor and I had been visiting more and more, very worried for her. My sister had been wonderful, dropping out even more, doing some housework on occasion but my mother, independent in the extreme, found it difficult to let go of the house, her pride and joy. We had sensed her body was failing her, following a fall on a golf course a few years earlier.

I nervously walked down the busy corridors, following the colour coded lines on the hospital floor. Turning a corner, I found a scene of organised chaos, trolleys everywhere, small cubicles separated by thin curtains, staff walking quickly and purposefully around, managing a smile to anxious and sometimes angry visitors and patients. Then I saw her, the woman who had inspired me so much over the years, who had taught me so much, and who had embodied the femininity that I strived for. She lay on a trolley in the busy and noisy corridor, asleep, with my sister sitting in a chair nearby.

Talking to the doctors over the next few days it appeared that she probably had stage four cervical cancer, but she refused to allow them to do any but the most basic tests. They really didn't expect her to last more than a couple of weeks but couldn't give a more accurate assessment. Even Helen, who worked at the hospital, couldn't persuade her to relent. We were really just waiting for the end.

But it was clear that she was in denial. At first, she dismissed a male doctor, then a female consultant came to discuss her situation. Mum simply refused to accept it, saying that she felt fine, just a little tired and she would be leaving the ward to go home soon. It was devastating to us to see her refusing any possible treatment apart from pain relief. She knew.

For the next twelve weeks, I juggled my life between daily visits to Mum, canvassing perhaps twice a day and trying to concentrate on my civil service job. It was the most difficult and stressful time of my life. Canvassing, actually doing something positive, being with friends and having something to focus on, allowed me to cope. The thrill of the campaign, the fury when the No posters appeared, the regular polls which seemed to show our large lead beginning to slide, all of this helped. In the background, the legislation for Gender Recognition made its slow but steady way through the Dáil. It all helped.

On each visit to the hospital it hurt me deeply to see a once proud, strong and independent woman lie in a hospital bed totally helpless, hardly even recognising us at times.

Shortly after she was settled on the ward Helen and I realised that there was something that we needed to do. For the wider family, despite my having transitioned a few years previously, didn't know about me. Unbelievably a conversation held in the kitchen some six years before came to my mind. She had demanded that my transition was to remain secret, kept between us. She had been so disappointed and upset, worried about what the neighbours would think. 'I wish you were only gay' she had repeated at times. So as a result, my aunts, uncles and cousins didn't know anything about me as Philippa. This certainly wasn't the ideal time to tell them but there was simply no other way. It had to be done now.

Helen and I had just been to visit her, and we knew that my aunts and cousins were due to visit around the same time. I made my excuses and left her bedside a little earlier than usual, feeling slightly sick at the smell from the disinfectant used to clean the wards. As I looked back at the frail body in the bed, I felt sad. Sad that society had forced us to be this way, forced us to look on difference and *the other* as wrong. For six years I had kept this from the wider family, thinking of the many times we would have dinner with her and she would say how proud she had been of me and how, now, she was embarrassed by me and worried in case she met me while out with her sisters. For years the secret that was me had been eating away inside her. Like her cancer. As I made my way down in the lift, my heart aching, to wait for my aunts in the hospital restaurant I knew that I had to continue in my work to help change that very culture, that I had to redouble my efforts to ensure that no one else would have to do what I had to now do. No excuses. No apologies for intolerance. I had to be who I was meant to be as Jenny had said. The proud woman lying in the hospital bed was not at fault for the prejudices society had given her.

Some time, later Helen came down from the ward with my aunts. She had told them a little on the way, so it wouldn't be too much of a shock to them. They were very supportive and understanding, everything that I could have hoped for. The telling was emotional, sad, funny. I reminded one of my aunts of how we had been on a picnic when I was about nine and how she had accused me jokingly of wearing eye shadow. 'I'm now really wearing eye shadow, Pat', and we embraced. Shirley joined us and we all chatted briefly, sadly, aware that the end was near. Mum had seemed ageless and the reality, to have to accept that soon we would lose this amazing woman, was difficult for us all to accept.

Hospital, work, canvassing, leafleting, attending Marriage Equality Referendum (MarRef) events. I found a store of energy within me that I never expected to find. I found areas of Dublin south-west that I didn't know existed, traditionally seen as the 'rough', underprivileged areas and the people I found there were amongst the nicest I have ever met. And hugely supportive of our campaign. It was the more affluent areas where the businessmen in their suits, within gated communities at times, would argue and belittle, seeking in some cases it seemed to provoke and upset us. Did they feel their masculinity threatened? It certainly seemed so to us and sometimes my male friends would arrive back to debrief in tears following particularly tough sessions.

I felt for Mum's friends and the wider family. Her popularity was undeniable, a steady stream of golf buddies, relations and friends. To many of them I was undoubtedly a surprise, even a shock, but nobody said anything, at least to my face, simply expressing their condolences and sorrow. As Mum lay in the busy hospital, just how much of the conversations did she hear and what was she thinking?

Yet, even at this sad and difficult time there was humour. As the evenings became brighter approaching the Referendum date of late May, we began to stay out canvassing longer, later. There were many wonderful highlights of that time: being invited in by elderly women for a cup of tea, a glass of wine and even, amusingly, for dinner by an Eastern European guy. The challenge was to be pleasant and grateful for the support and offers and to politely leave the doorstep without engaging with the obvious No voters, of whom there were too many. Yet it was also sad and worrying to hear, again and again from women on the doorsteps, that 'My husband doesn't want that here in Ireland and so we'll all be voting No.' We were frustrated at the thoughts that these women were being denied the right to choose, the right to think for themselves. Talk of a referendum to overturn the constitutional ban on abortion was mentioned regularly. 'The next step' in the fight for women's rights. That was going to be much harder than MarRef.

YesEquality was the national organisation set up to run the campaign, led by Grainne Healy and Brian Sheehan. Funding the campaign was always an issue especially as it appeared that the No campaign had money from American anti-LGBTQ+ groups pouring into the country, using various loopholes to avoid the law prohibiting campaign donations from outside the state. So, bake sales, rallies, table quizzes, and many other events all raised funds for the ever more active and visible campaign. I organised events in my office and, nearer the voting day, a well-supported Spin for Equality around the streets of Dublin on bicycles.

It was a bright, breezy March morning when I saw the first of them. A typical family: man, woman and a cute baby girl with the slogan: 'Every child deserves a mother and a father.' I looked again and saw that almost every lamppost along the road had at least one, sometimes two of the posters, some with different slogans. I was sickened, they were as bad or worse than I had feared. How could we compete with that intolerance, that funding? T-shirt sales surely couldn't raise that much money. And where were our posters?

My Facebook stream was exploding with fury. How could we combat them? Should we tear down their posters? Report them for incitement to hatred? An online fundraiser was started. As the day progressed, the total began to rise. We donated. And then donated again as it continued to rise, ever faster. By the end of the day it had raised €100,000, a massive amount and a great beginning to the fundraising. The posters energised our campaign and we began to get volunteers on our canvasses that had been provoked by the No side, open-minded people who wouldn't allow the prejudiced to win.

Between Shirley, Helen, Jenny and I we visited Mum on the ward at least once a day. Initially she was lucid but in denial of the seriousness of her condition. We tried to persuade her to accept a few tests, to listen to the doctors and follow their advice. When one of the consultants took Shirley and I aside and told us that, in her opinion, Mum had a week to live it wasn't a surprise. It wasn't my mother lying in the bed, shrivelled and sick. It was just little more than a vessel for a once proud and independent lady whose time had run out. Each visit she seemed weaker, less aware of her surroundings and the morphine was obviously affecting her mind. Yet still she hung on and, though I wished her peace, knowing there was no hope, I was immensely proud of her determination not to give in.

The YesEquality badges started to appear. Initially one or two people had them, mainly the volunteers, then more and more strangers came up to us asking for them and they began to go on sale, along with other merchandise such as t-shirts, sweatshirts and lots of stickers. Then our posters began to adorn the lampposts, vying for valuable space with those of the No side. We heard through the grapevine that teenagers were taking down No posters and dumping them. Not that we condoned it but it did raise a smile or two.

One of the very contentious issues dominating the

nightly news at the time of MarRef was that of water charges. It was amusing to hear the teenagers of south-west Dublin yelling 'Hope you're not here about f*cking water charges' and cheering when we said who we were. 'Go on ye gays' reverberated around many of the estates in south-west Dublin in the late evening April sun.

Thankfully I didn't have any problem getting time off work to visit my mother, either cycling or taking the direct tram to the hospital. Yet sitting there beside her, seeing her get weaker and weaker made me feel helpless, frustrated and angry and I found it difficult to stay long. My aunts and uncles, cousins who I hadn't seen for years, friends of my mother and colleagues all came to the ward and it was rare that I would be with her on my own. Jenny too, in the midst of studying for exams, came up every day.

The YesEquality campaign was reaching the final few weeks and becoming intense. Darragh, our Dublin South West campaign manager, wanted us to cover all 70,000 houses in the electoral district before the vote and we were out every night in large groups. Television debates and newspaper articles, carefully giving both sides of the issue to avoid the perception of bias, were appearing daily. How that frustrated us, giving an equal voice to hate and ignorance. We heard stories of verbal harassment of Yes canvassers, occasional threats of violence but thankfully nothing worse. After each canvass, we compiled statistics, how many houses visited, how many yes, no and any unusual or potentially valuable responses or arguments. We heard back that the margins were shrinking, our once seemingly unassailable lead was now single digits. It seemed impossible as on Dublin South West doorsteps we were seeing Yes votes in the 70% range. Were we being lied to, to our faces?

Mum's breathing began to become strained. Her morphine dose was increased, leading to delirium but usually she just slept. It was close to the end and we began to prepare.

I received a call from one of the organisers of the LGBTQ+ Noise group, inviting Helen and I to appear in the audience of an RTÉ prime time show which would feature a debate on the referendum. 'The transgender angle is simply not being covered Philippa,' he said, 'and I really feel you should be there to give that valuable viewpoint.' Helen and I were a ready-made example of a same sex marriage that was positive and one that could potentially be split by the wrong result.

Mum hung on. Again and again, the doctors told us that it was 'only a matter of time' and if she would allow a few tests, a more accurate estimate could be given. But my mother's stubbornness continued, though by now she was barely lucid for the vast majority of the time. The pressure was telling on us all, the frustration of our inability to do anything, a feeling of utter and total uselessness. All we were capable of was gently holding her frail hand, moving her slightly to a more comfortable position in the bed. But the important fact was – we were there.

Other patients came and went on the ward, most of them just in recovery following operations. At one point, as Helen and I said goodbye to each other and kissed a 'tut-tut' came from some of the visitors to another patient and I could have sworn I saw a bible being brandished in our direction. The YesEquality badges that I had kept off my coat for the hospital visits went straight back on from that point on.

22 May was Referendum day. As I woke that morning,

curling into my wife with a cat meowing loudly for food downstairs I thought of the day ahead. Polling booths opened at 7 a.m. and it would probably still be bright when they closed at 10 p.m. How would we feel after twelve weeks of baring our hearts and souls to the people of south-west Dublin and beyond?

I had aimed to be first at the polling station, situated in the local school (how I had wished for more elections as a kid as my school was always used for the votes). When I walked through the car park however and saw the queue, an actual queue, waiting to vote my spirits rose. Surely, they all had to be Yes voters this early?

I cast my ballot and quickly got a photo outside, explaining to the young businesswoman that today's decision was very important to my family and me. She wished me well and whispered, 'well I'm voting Yes!'

The rest of the day was a blur, handing out leaflets, 'I voted' badges and making a last sweep of the areas we knew had to come out for Yes, some of the more deprived areas but equally some of the most vocally in favour. Helen joined us for the last, final painful push as we stood on the road beside a major bypass madly waving Vote Yes placards and cheering with what was left of our voices as the car horns sounded. One or two homophobic comments failed to deter us, only making us shout and cheer louder. And at 9.30 p.m. we stopped, exhausted, and made our way to a local hotel for food and debrief. The die was cast, we had done our utmost and more. What an experience and, no matter the result, one I would never forget.

Dublin Castle was where the official results would be announced. It was likely to be packed from early so Helen and I decided to spend the day at the YesEquality party for canvassers. We had it all planned: early breakfast in town then out for a nervous few hours until the results were in. Darragh, the YesEquality lead for our area had told us there would be no point in arriving before midday.

We left the house at 9 a.m. as the first ballot boxes were being opened. On the bus into town I was checking Twitter and Helen was on Facebook. After fifteen minutes it was all over, 'bar the shouting' as the No side conceded. It became apparent that some areas were 100% Yes and they realised there was no point in pretending. Ireland was voting in favour of love, in favour of equality, in favour of marriage for all. We were ecstatic, smiling and talking excitedly, tears in our eyes, as the bus made its slow way into the city centre. We just wanted to be with our friends for this incredible moment. It wasn't supposed to be this 'easy' we said, laughing. We were supposed to be nervously chewing fingernails as results came in, moaning and groaning at the No side winning areas (in the end there was only one area they triumphed in, Roscommon. The rest of the country was Yes). Indeed, that was the reason we weren't at any of the count centres as I had said that seeing every No vote would be like a knife in my heart. Well it looked like the knives were staying in the cutlery drawer today.

We arrived at the party hotel with a few of our friends already there and already on the Prosecco. It was a good day! People came and went, politicians and celebrities, media and many, many of our friends. The whole world seemed to want to share our joy, feel the positivity that Ireland was sending to the world.

But of course we had sadness to contend with also and we paid a visit to Mum in St James's Hospital across the city, sitting quietly with her, accepting the congratulations for the result of the referendum from the relatives who came, while also looking at her, wondering how she felt about the changes that had occurred in her country in her long life. Since 1934, she had seen a World War, the birth of a republic, many economic crashes and so much social change. This latest change was one she wouldn't, couldn't, really accept, nor the changes in me. Yet, looking in her eyes, I could see the love within the pain she was feeling. She may not have been able to accept but I knew she was happy for us.

Arriving back in the hotel, we discovered we had missed the Taoiseach Enda Kenny and ex-President Mary McAleese, but the ballroom was full and hopping with music and excited and slightly drunk canvassers and friends. The theme tune of the campaign, Snow Patrol's 'Just say Yes' seemed to be on a continuous loop and each time we shouted and screamed Y E S!

The official announcement came from Dublin Castle at about 7 p.m.: 62.07% Yes. More roars and screams, tears, dancing and celebrating. Food appeared and was devoured along with endless bottles of Prosecco. We did our best to last but after twelve hours of celebrations interspersed with the visit to Mum, we were exhausted. Home to one happy daughter and two not-so-happy cats.

The day after the day before. I left home early to experience Dublin in the early summer sunshine, walking slowly around the now quiet streets. Yesterday fire engines and ambulances had sounded their sirens in celebration as they struggled through the streets filled with people on their way back from calls. Today I suspected any sirens would be met with groans from the sore heads. But everyone was smiling. Everyone was holding hands. Ireland was equal. At last.

A few days later, the end finally came for my mother.

As I sat at my desk in my office, I received a call from one of my aunts. 'Philippa, you'd better come up to the hospital. She's almost gone.'

For about a week we had known the call was coming. Her breathing had become very laboured, she had been asleep continuously and we knew we had already said our last words to her. How could it end this way? How could a body, so active, so fit and so energetic simply just stop? It didn't seem fair.

I arrived at the bedside a little while later. My mother had passed, replaced by a cold motionless body. I felt sad but relieved. The previous months had been traumatic for her and indeed for us. Having her kept alive just for the sake of it seemed pointless. The mother I knew had left that body many weeks ago.

The funeral was simple, no fuss. I gave the eulogy, collaborating with Shirley and the wider family. I told the funny stories, how much she had meant to us all, of her grace and her selfless love. And I almost got through it without getting emotional, just failing when I heard the children in the local school playground and went off script, mentioning how much our mother had loved children. But of course, you're supposed to get emotional at times like that. After the funeral one of my aunts mentioned how the husband of a friend of hers had also transitioned and if only Mum had told her, she could have been a support.

That evening as I lay in bed, I thought of the sobering fact that I now was the oldest in our family.

***

All through my life, I have been drawn to committees and wanting to help others and be involved in interesting projects and initiatives. Sometimes I find myself leading but I'm also happy enough to be in the background. I enjoy passionate, enthusiastic and energetic people around me, suggesting new ideas but I also expect commitment from those I work with, soething that is hard to find on voluntary committees. So in recent years I have chosen with care the projects and groups I have become involved with, trying to do more than I physically can and becoming frustrated with myself when I take on too much and can't deliver. Just some of the highlights are given below, all of which were both different and wonderful and gave me the chance to show a positive view of beings trans and being true to oneself.

One lovely request came in towards the end of 2015. Helen, Jenny and I were delighted to be asked to be interviewed for the ex-RTÉ reporter Charlie Bird's lovely book, *A Day in May*, about the Marriage Referendum. Our interview filled four pages of the book, with a stunning full-page black and white family portrait. An extravagant launch in the National Gallery in 2016 with the Taoiseach Enda Kenny, Senator Katherine Zappone and many friends and allies from the community attended. And it was lovely to have my sister and her husband present at one of the highlights of our lives. Their presence was important to us that evening and I hoped it indicated a positive future for our relationship.

A series of trainings to line managers on Unconscious Bias were due to be held in 2016 in my civil service organisation and I was asked to give a brief ten-minute talk on my experiences in transitioning, the challenges I had faced and any lessons that could be shared. These talks were very emotional for me as they were the first time I had spoken so publicly about my personal journey to my colleagues. In the end, I talked to the entire staff as the programme was broadened out and from it came a Diversity and Inclusion initiative, with a specific LGBTQ+ strand of which I am chair. Before my transition, I was relatively quiet in work, just coming in, doing my job and going home, living a seemingly typical life in the eyes of those who didn't know the internal turmoil I was going through. But after the talks that all changed and the LGBTQ+ strand of the D&I programme moved forward with energy and enthusiasm with some wonderful friends and allies. It was quite a change from the office I had joined thirty-seven years before and it was an honour to play a part. And as we progressed our programme within the PRA we were asked to advise other departments on setting up their own D&I initiatives, giving me the opportunity to briefly tell my story and the great support I received from my colleagues and management.

Some of the many other memorable events include the lovely film 'Under the Clock' featuring people who had stories about Clery's Clock in Dublin. When the producers heard of my story of waiting in vain some sixteen years earlier for my friend before going to the Gemini club to meet other trans people for the first time they were delighted and a wonderful film was produced which was shown on RTÉ and in cinemas around the world. Another opportunity for me to show the positive side of being trans and the importance of listening to trans voices. The premiere was held in Dundrum Cinemas in south Dublin and it was a wonderful experience to be accompanied by Helen and Jenny, both of whom appeared in the film, along the red carpet. We had a wonderful party afterwards, and Jenny looked stunning, even more of a focus than me. We were asked for mother and daughter photos by the rest of the wonderful cast and crew, who still to this day stay in touch. What a strange and fortuitous sequence of events had led me to appear on the big screen, something that most people can only dream of. I was full of gratitude for the opportunity.

In 2018, Gay Community News, the publication for the LGBTQ+ community, had a little notice which ended up giving me another opportunity I never imagined I could possibly have. It mentioned that a team was being organised to travel to the World Gay Games (essentially the Gay Olympics), which were being held in Paris later that year. I was delighted to become involved with the Team and as the Paris Games featured cycling as one of the sports I knew I'd have an opportunity to compete and represent my country – for the first time in sport. I was determined to be serious about my participation and quickly found a coach who developed a programme for me around training and nutrition which I hoped would allow me to compete with some sort of competence – well, I didn't want to finish last! We held a press launch at Government Buildings with An Taoiseach Leo Varadkar, Minister Katherine Zappone and Junior Minister Brendan Griffin. Photos of the Team appeared in a few publications and websites, including the *Irish Times*. Then, shortly before the Games we had an amazing reception in Áras an Uachtaráin where I had the privilege of addressing the President, Helen and my teammates in an impromptu and emotional speech. I'm constantly reminded how my transition has given me so many opportunities that I couldn't have dreamed of, so many incredible and memorable moments.

The Games took place from 4–12 August and the Irish

team of 140 came home with over forty medals in a host of different sports. I was delighted to win two silver and a bronze in three different cycling events and travelled throughout the beautiful city trying to support as many of my teammates as possible in their various disciplines. Standing on the podium with a medal and an Irish flag around me ranks as one of the proudest moments of my life. Dermot McCarthy and Roland Hempel, and many others on the team remain good friends and great sportsmen and sportswomen.

Following the Games, the organising committee set up Sporting Pride, a national LGBTQ+ sports organisation which is encouraging our LGBTQ+ community to get out and get active, with quite some success. I'm honoured to have played a part in such a great initiative as it gave me the opportunity to indulge many facets of my life in one experience.

Due to my profile, I get many requests to give talks, advice and interviews. So one morning in February 2019, I was invited to a breakfast meeting with Gillian Fagan and Dermot McCarthy 'for a chat'. Dermot and I had first encountered each other at a Diversity summit in Eir a few years previously and I had worked with him on Team Ireland at the Paris Gay Games the previous year. He is a good friend. Both Gillian and Dermot are qualified psychotherapists and counsellors and I thought they just wanted my input on a few ideas they had.

But two hours later 'Under the Rainbow', a social enterprise agency delivering talks, trainings, counselling and online support was born and I was a director. A few weeks later we had a city centre office, shortly after that a website and many requests from government and the corporate sector to deliver Diversity, Inclusion and Belonging sessions to their staff. It has been a pleasure to work with such passionate, knowledgeable and enthusiastic people like Gillian and Dermot and our Team continues to expand. The requests keep flooding in as we adapt to the changed environment brought about by the recent pandemic. Never has it been more important to make society aware of the importance of Equality, Diversity, Inclusion and Belonging training and we have found that the online environment allows us to present to a worldwide audience.

And finally…

Helen and I were contacted by the Ryan Tubridy radio show in 2019, asking if we wanted to appear on his programme. Rearranging our work schedules a little, we made our way to the RTÉ studios, not for the first time. But this interview was one of our favourites as Ryan delved into how we met (and our mutual passion for *Star Trek*), what it was like for Helen when her 'husband' turned into her 'wife' and a few other topics. People listening to the show later commented about the obvious chemistry between us all.

Ryan had recognised that chemistry and so, at the end of the show he asked us, on air, if we would consider appearing on *The Late Late Show*, Ireland's long-running television chat show, an institution in Ireland and one which he also hosts. A quick glance at Helen who nodded, and I said 'Yes, we'd love to'. Leaving the studio on a bright summer morning, Helen and I laughed and said 'surely he was only being nice, he doesn't *really* want us on *The Late Late* …'

But a few months later, following a lot of phone calls and meetings with the researchers from the show we had the date of our show: 7 February. Cue panic, to some degree at least! It was mid-January and we had actually been asked on for the following week but Helen had a bad cold and we put it back for a few weeks.

So much to do in such a short time. What would we wear? Should we do a little media training? Of course we were well used to interviews in the newspapers, radio and even the occasional brief television appearance but *The Late Late Show*, the most popular show in Ireland and watched by millions – different story altogether! And who should we invite as our guests? There were so many we wanted with us. We had only two guests (but I pleaded and we got two more). And most importantly – could Jenny get home for the show from New York as the show really wanted her too.

We had a brief media training session with a contact made through Under the Rainbow, two hours of tips and tricks but just basic reassurance and the importance of enjoying the experience – that would come across in the interview and would engage the audience.

Our outfits were from Pamela Scott in Grafton Street. Helen wore black dress trousers and a satin red blouse. I was delighted with my final choice having tried on about ten different dresses, being well looked after by the staff who were really keen to help especially when they heard what it was for. A dark rich forest green dress, ankle-length and sleeveless with a lovely flared skirt which I wore with gold accessories and black heels. My only concern was tripping as I walked onto the set. Talk about a dramatic entrance!

We were assured by RTÉ that our make-up and hair would be done in their studios so that was one worry off our minds leaving us to concentrate on what we were going to say. We spent a few minutes talking about it and then looked at each other and laughed. We knew we just needed to be ourselves, that's what Ryan wanted and what we could give him.

Friday the 7th was a beautiful sunny day and Helen and I had arranged to take the afternoon off from work to prepare. RTÉ had organised a taxi for 8.30 that evening so we had plenty of time for all the pre-show nerves. Following a quick lunch together where we tried not to think about the show we went home, pottered about, played with the cats and ended up resting in bed because we had too much time and were getting nervous!

We changed into our show outfits and did basic make-up knowing that the artists in RTÉ would know what best to use for a screen appearance. The taxi arrived a little late – more anxiety – but we made it to the studios almost on time to be met by our researcher. As we were shown around the green room and then to our changing rooms we were met by an exuberant Ryan who laughed when I said that I hadn't really believed we'd be on his show. We began to relax and we were introduced to the other guests on the show in the green room – Irish Olympians, Brian Dowling of Big Brother fame, comedian Andrew Maxwell and others. We chatted and had a few photos taken with them before going to our private room to relax. Some chance.

We were taken to hair and make-up where the beauticians spent about thirty minutes making us presentable, all the while consulting with us over colours and coverage and ensuring we felt comfortable with the results which of course we were.

In the green room, our researcher ensured we were well looked after though with soft drinks – the alcohol came later! We were texting our friends who had all arrived and were busy having fun taking photos before being brought into the studio. In the end it was such a difficult choice but we decided on a guest from both of our workplaces: Angela Montgomery, a colleague of Helen's in St James' Hospital, Collette McNulty, a colleague of mine and a wonderful ally on the PRA Diversity committee. Of course Declan was a given and I was delighted when my friend and colleague from 'Under the Rainbow' Dermot agreed to come along too. I had asked my sister a few weeks previously if she would like to come with us. It would have been wonderful to have her in the audience but she declined.

The show started. The countdown to the biggest appearance of our lives was on.

And the time dragged! We could see the show on the various screens in the green room but hardly anyone was paying attention, either chatting to the other guests or to the RTÉ staff who were flitting around. One of the researchers seemed to have been tasked with simply looking after us and we talked to her quite a bit. We were relaxed and looking forward to our twenty minutes of fame. I had told RTÉ about the importance of Declan in my story and was assured that the director would cut to him once I mentioned him. I put a mental note in to do just that, hopefully my nerves wouldn't make me forget him, my oldest friend.

Then it was finally time. The stage manager came in to escort us on the short walk to the back of the set, a mass of plywood and cables. 'You'll be on in about two minutes ladies', she said and I quipped: 'Is it too late to back out now?'

'That's been tried before so we lock the doors now!'

she replied and we laughed quietly. Fisherman's Friends lozenges were given to us to ensure we didn't cough or have a clogged throat.

We stood at the top of the stairs knowing we had a few steps to go down on the other side and out onto the set. 'I hope I don't trip' I thought and 'Remember to mention Declan.' I felt relaxed. This was our time. We had been through so much together and this would be fun.

The music began, the audience applauded, and we two women walked out, hand in hand and into the arms of Ryan Tubridy to share our story of almost forty years of love.

Ryan was wonderful, his questions were excellent and didn't probe beyond the subjects we had talked about. Indeed one of the topics he wanted to mention was our previous appearance on *The Late Late Show* when the legendary Gay Byrne was hosting and William Shatner of *Star Trek* fame was a guest, in the early 1990s. But of course that was me in my previous gender and I agonised over whether I wanted it shown. It was such a difficult decision but ultimately I felt I should allow it be shown. I didn't deny my past, I had moved on.

We were comfortable, relaxed and didn't want the interview to end. Then Ryan said, 'we have a message from someone special for you both.' Jenny appeared on a screen above us and I squeezed Helen's hand harder. Having graduated with a First from Trinity, she had moved to the US to be with her boyfriend Tom and they were living at that time in Brooklyn. We had hoped so fervently that just maybe she could have found some way to come home. It turned out RTÉ had tried everything to get her home as a surprise! But because of the status of her US visa, she wasn't allowed to travel so she had recorded a beautiful message to us. Our emotion was evident on screen, we missed her so much and to have her walk out on the set into our arms would have made all the difference.

When Jenny finished her short message the audience applauded loudly and we smiled. Our family, united in love in front of the nation. I looked towards our friends, hard to see with the studio lights in our eyes but I didn't need to see them to feel their love and support. We were floating on air.

The interview finished with me announcing the acceptance of this memoir by Mercier Press, just agreed that day. Then Ryan brought the show to an end and suddenly our incredible experience was over. We stepped down from the set as the audience filed past, smiling and nodding to us. Our friends came down from their seats and embraced us, we brought them back to the green room for drinks, snacks, chat and endless photos with some of the other guests and, later, Ryan who complimented us on the interview. I had forgotten to mention Declan though and I apologised to Ryan and Declan who both laughed. I'm sure the director had been calling me names as I knew the camera team knew exactly where Declan had been sitting! And on social media we were certainly getting plenty of plaudits, some of the media websites saying we had the audience in tears. Of course, there was negativity but overwhelmingly RTÉ's Twitter was hugely positive.

We stayed in the Green Room until after 2 a.m. before being poured into a taxi. As I saw Helen dozing beside me, so trusting and loving in her sleep, I remembered her words during the interview that had been picked up by everyone: 'I realised I wanted a living wife, not a dead husband'. All we had been through was expressed in that simple line. Acceptance and understanding is all I sought, it's all any trans person seeks. How lucky I am to have her as my wife. And this book is for her and the wonderful daughter she gave us.